Cape Cod
BED & BREAKFAST
Guide & Innkeepers'
RECIPES
Including Martha's Vineyard & Nantucket

By Bobbi Cox and Beth Flanagan

CAPE COD LIFE
Including Martha's Vineyard & Nantucket

…sharing the Cape Cod experience.

Osterville, Massachusetts

Editor and Publisher
Brian F. Shortsleeve

Assistant Publisher
Donna J. Murphy

Project Editor
Colleen M. McEwen

Consulting Editor
Rebecca Morris

Cover Design
Donna J. Murphy and Martha Flaherty

Interior Design
Martha Flaherty

Cover Art
Lou Barnicle
Margo Tabb Graphic Design

1989-1990 Edition

Library of Congress Catalog Card No. 89-61220
ISBN 0-9622782-0-3

Table of Contents

Continued next page

Table of Contents *Continued*

Foreword

The authors of this guide live and work on Cape Cod. One of us, Beth Flanagan, is an innkeeper and the other, Bobbi Cox is a real estate broker. Both occupations provide us with inside information for the traveler to Cape Cod, Martha's Vineyard, and Nantucket that we would like to pass on to you.

We are especially excited about the recipes in the book. Each innkeeper gave us his or her favorite and we have taste-tested each one.

All the information provided here has been verified personally to the best of our ability. It is our intention to present a comprehensive guide to bed and breakfast inns, not rating them but describing them as accurately as possible so that their differences will become apparent and our readers may make informed choices. If our readers are aware of omissions, we ask them to inform us so that we may include them in future editions of the guide book. We sincerely welcome letters from readers on changes, or from those whose opinions differ from ours. Please send your letters to Bed & Breakfast Inns, Cape Cod Life, P.O. Box 222, Osterville, MA 02655.

Acknowledgments

Our thanks to our husbands and families for their encouragement and patience and the following friends who have helped in various ways to bring this book together ... from our first mailing to the innkeepers, to the recipe testers!

Jim Craddock, Doug Watmough, Bob Norton, Joyce O'Connor, John Curley, Karen Etsell, Carol Whitney, Betsy Good, Judy Keim, Katie Spinzola, Peggy Curry, Shelly Chase, Elaine Vyse, Dottie McGillen, Carol MacKay, Marylee Meehan, Myrna Luazon, Sandy Chevrie, Louise Silva, Debbie Blakely, Margaret Lynch, Arlene Thibbetts, Sally Fleming, Judy Wright, Elizabeth Alexander, Nancy O'Neil, Kay Quelle, Helena Roemer, Kathy Smith-Brown, Maureen Cronin, Regina Gulliver, Dottie Averna, Virginia Curley, Helene Karle, Eileen Kandianis, Linda Knightly, Carol Powell, Patricia Bartlewski, Nancy O'Brien, Sheila Crowell, Anne Sparks, Elaine Panachello, Jackie Woods, Mary Goldstein, Kathy Brown, Shirley Lafler, Betty Perone, Lolly Campbell, Nita Myers, Maggie Tyson, Nancy Brodhead, Sue Sears, Nancy Nash, Alice Ryan, Lucy Messer, Phyllis McCracken, Sharon Leary, Ruth Wynkoop, and Richard P. McCarthy.

Some Important Notes

The story of the settling of New England is the story of Cape Cod, Martha's Vineyard, and Nantucket.

Soon after the Pilgrims landed at Provincetown and then sailed on to Plymouth in 1620, Cape Cod became a refuge for some who sought independence from that rigid community. Farming and fishing occupied the people, and whaling later became a booming industry and brought great wealth to the area. Sea captains built beautiful mansions on the Cape as well as on Martha's Vineyard and Nantucket. Simpler taverns provided lodging and food to weary travelers along the present Routes 6A and 28.

Part of this history has been dusted off with the rise in popularity of bed and breakfast inns. Many of these quaint, historic old mansions and colonial taverns have been restored to their original beauty, and welcome visitors today much as they did more than two centuries ago.

The Cape is 70 miles long and bent like an arm with its fist upraised: Buzzards Bay and the Cape Cod Canal are the shoulder; Chatham and Nauset Beach are the elbow; and Provincetown is the fist. Cape Cod is surrounded with miles of coastline, the greater part of it gleaming beach. Waters on the Bay side (the North Shore) are cooler than those on the South Shore. The ocean beaches have a strong surf as opposed to the calmer beaches on Cape Cod Bay.

As a major highway on Cape Cod, Route 6A, (the Old King's Highway), has been replaced by Route 6, also called the mid-Cape highway. All driving directions to the inns on Cape Cod assume the driver is crossing the Sagamore Bridge and traveling on Route 6. Falmouth is the exception, as directions to the inns in Falmouth assume a crossing at the Bourne Bridge. Directions to inns on Martha's Vineyard are necessarily limited to the entry points at the Vineyard Haven dock and the Oak Bluffs dock. Nantucket directions are based upon entry at Straight Wharf or Steamboat Wharf. Many inns offer "fetching service" at the major transportation sources, so check their listings. We have included this information when provided with it.

All phone numbers should be preceded by the area code 508. This number changed from 617 in July 1988.

All rates listed are for two people, per room, and are the rates during late spring through late summer (the most expensive season). Check your favorites for lower off-season rates. They all include breakfast unless otherwise stated.

Credit card abbreviations are as follows: AMEX=American Express, DIS=Discover, MC=MasterCard, VISA=VISA, DC=Diner's Club.

Enjoy!

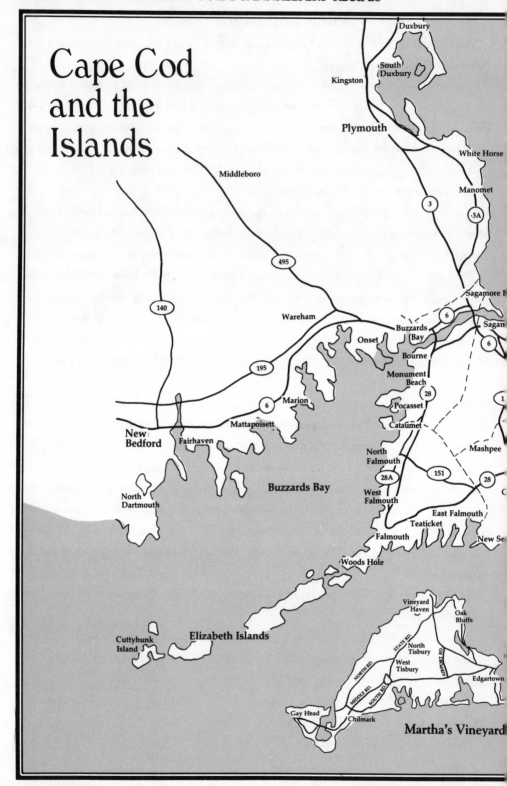

Cape Cod and the Islands

Duxbury

South Duxbury

Kingston

Plymouth

White Horse

Manomet

3

3A

Middleboro

495

140

Wareham

Sagamore I

6

Sagan

Buzzards Bay

6

Onset

Bourne

195

Monument Beach

28

6

Marion

Pocasset

New Bedford

Mattapoisett

Cataumet

Fairhaven

Mashpee

North Falmouth

28A

151

28

North Dartmouth

Buzzards Bay

West Falmouth

East Falmouth

Teaticket

Falmouth

New Se

Woods Hole

Vineyard Haven

Oak Bluffs

STATE RD.

North Tisbury

Cuttyhunk Island

Elizabeth Islands

West Tisbury

AIRPORT RD.

NORTH RD.

Edgartown

MIDDLE RD.

SOUTH RD.

Gay Head

Chilmark

Martha's Vineyard

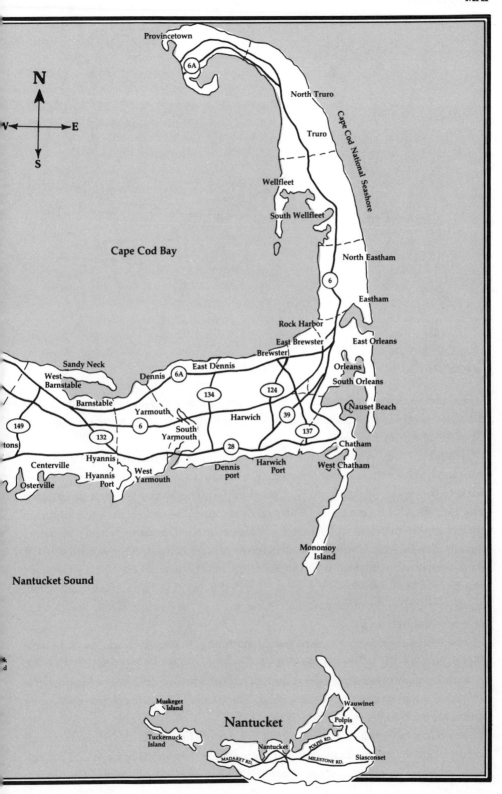

Barnstable

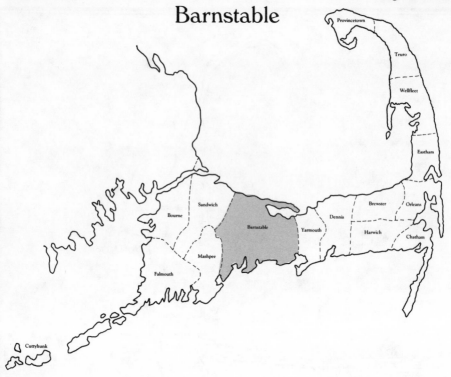

The town of Barnstable contains several villages. We have included information on bed and breakfast inns in the villages of Barnstable, Centerville, Cotuit, Hyannis, Hyannis Port, Osterville, and West Barnstable.

Barnstable village is home to the County Courthouse and therefore is a busy center year-round. Many visitors come to research their roots at the Sturgis Library, circa 1644, the oldest public library building in the United States. The library houses a genealogical collection of early Massachusetts families and a maritime history exhibit. Other historical exhibits can be found in the old Customs House in the Donald G. Trayser Memorial Museum. The Barnstable News Store, an old country store on Route 6A, is worth a visit. For beachgoers, there are Millway Beach off Route 6A and Hathaway Pond. Millway Beach is a great place to sit and watch a magnificent Cape Cod sunset. The Barnstable Comedy Club, founded in 1922, is the oldest amateur theater group in the country. Whale Watch boats leave from Barnstable Harbor.

Centerville's claim to fame is the renowned and beautiful Craigville Beach, one of the most popular on Cape Cod. Another landmark is the Four Seas Ice Cream shop where it is a tradition for many to stop after a day at the beach. The 1856 Country Store on Main Street is one of just a few country stores still around. The Centerville Historical Society Museum offers a look at how life used to be on Cape Cod.

Main Street in **Cotuit** is in the National Register of Historic Places and the Historical Society maintains a museum and restored homestead in the town. The Cape Cod Baseball League plays in Cotuit, and golf can be enjoyed at High Ground Golf Course. The Cahoon

Museum of American Art contains a well-known collection of early American art.

Hyannis is the commercial and transportation center of Cape Cod. Barnstable Municipal Airport, and the bus depot, for travel to and from New York and Boston, are located in Hyannis.

The John F. Kennedy Memorial on Ocean Street is visited by thousands every summer, as well as Kalmus Park Beach, Orrin Keyes Beach on Sea Street, and Veteran's Park. The Cape Cod Melody Tent features professional musical entertainment. Ferries to Martha's Vineyard and Nantucket arrive and depart from the Ocean Street docks.

Osterville has a quiet, small town atmosphere, but is home to some of the wealthiest and best-known names in America. The Historical Society maintains and offers tours of a sea captain's house. Two tennis courts off West Bay Road are open to the public at no charge. A charming shopping district has fine specialty shops.

West Barnstable is more rural than other nearby villages. Route 6A is dotted with the shops of many crafts people, including weavers, potters, and other artists. The area is one of the best on Cape Cod for antique-hunters. Scenic Sandy Neck Beach is off Route 6A.

Ashley Manor

3660 Old King's
Highway
Barnstable, MA 02360
(508) 362-8044

Innkeepers:
Donald & Fay Bain

Open all year.
6 rooms with private
baths.

Rates: All year, $100-
$145 (for two).
AMEX/VISA/MC

Amenities: No
children. No pets.
Working fireplaces in
guest rooms. 15-
minute walk to the
beach.

Directions: Route 6 to
Exit 6. Take Route
132 North. Turn right
at the intersection of
Route 6A to
Barnstable village.
Proceed through the
traffic light, to the inn
6/10 of a mile ahead
on the left.

Ashley Manor

Ashley Manor is an intimate yet spacious country inn. Most rooms have a working fireplace. Two double rooms on the second floor have terraces overlooking the gardens. Wide-board flooring and Nantucket spackling are historic features which date the inn from 1699.

A full breakfast is served in the summer on a brick terrace overlooking two acres of park-like grounds and a charming gazebo.

Ashley Manor's Granola

2 lbs. rolled oats   1 C. sunflower seeds
1 C. wheat germ   ½ C. honey
1 C. bran   ½ C. oil
1 C. chopped walnuts   1/3 lb. brown sugar
                 ½ C. water

Mix dry ingredients together. Mix wet ingredients into a light syrup. Mix wet and dry ingredients together. Spread out on 2 baking trays, compacting ingredients. Toast in 250° oven. Turn about two or three times to toast uniformly for 20 minutes. Cool and serve with chopped dried fruit such as apricots, peaches, plums, raisins, and apples.

Barb &
Dick's
B & B
110 Salt Rock Road
Barnstable, MA 02360
(508) 362-6556

Innkeepers:
Barb & Dick Polson

Open all year.
2 rooms/1 bath.

Rates: $45/single;
$48/double, per room
(for two). No credit
cards accepted.

Amenities: Children
welcome. No pets. 5-
minute drive to the
beach.

Directions: Route 6 to
Exit 6. Go straight for
1 ½ miles to the traffic
light. Turn left and go
1 ½ miles to the next
traffic light. Turn right
onto Route 6A. Take
the first right onto
Braggs Lane. Take the
first left onto Salt
Rock Road.

Barb & Dick's B & B

Barb & Dick's B & B is one of those little known inns which is a great find. Two very large rooms in the 1972 Cape-style house share one bath. Guests are given a key to the front door and are free to come and go at will. There are comfortable chairs in the yard and on the deck to relax in after antiquing and dining in the great restaurants nearby.

Full breakfasts feature the inn's wonderful homemade goodies, including the Egg Souffle featured below.

Barb & Dick's B & B's Egg Souffle

8 slices of white bread (Wonder style)
½ lb. grated cheddar cheese
5 eggs

1 t. salt
1 t. dry mustard
2 T. melted margarine

2 C. milk

Remove crust from bread and cube. Grease a deep 8" x 10" pan or a round pan. Add 1/3 of the cubed bread and sprinkle with 1/3 of the cheese. Repeat until you have used the entire mixture. Combine milk, eggs, salt, and dry mustard and pour over cheese and bread. Store overnight in refrigerator. Melt margarine and pour over the top of mixture. Cover with foil and bake 60 minutes at 375° in a pan set in hot water.

The Beechwood

2839 Main Street
Barnstable, MA 02360
(508) 362-6618

Innkeepers:
Ann & Bob Livermore

Open all year.
6 rooms/6 baths.

Rates: 5/1 to 10/31,
$90-$125 (for two).
AMEX/VISA/MC

Amenities: No
children. No pets. Four
working fireplaces. 15-
minute walk to the
beach.

Directions: Route 6 to
Exit 6. Take Route
132 North. Turn right
at Route 6A. The inn
is about ½ mile ahead
on the right after the
railroad overpass.

The Beechwood

The Beechwood is a beautiful example of Queen Anne Victorian restoration. It is furnished with unusual period antiques, including a carved queen-size canopy bed, a hand-painted cottage bedroom set, and a fainting couch. A new, large suite on the second floor is suitable for three people. It has its own entrance, a restored old fashioned bathroom, plus a separate shower room.

Tea is served by the fireplace in the parlor during the winter, and lemonade is served on the veranda in the summer. Croquet and badminton are favorite pastimes here—a real retreat to the graciousness of the 19th century. A full breakfast is included.

The Beechwood's Apricot Pastries

Roll slices of white bread thin. Cut off crusts on one side. Spread sweet butter rather thick (let butter get quite soft first). Spread 3 t. apricot or strawberry preserves on bread. Roll up and cut in half. Spread sweet butter on roll. Bake in 350° oven for 30 minutes. Sprinkle with mixture of cinnamon and sugar, then roll in confectioner's sugar. Tips: Use inexpensive bread as it is best for rolling. Make sure that the cut side of the bread is on the bottom when baking or it will unroll. This is a favorite sweet at tea time at The Beechwood.

Charles Hinckley House

The Charles Hinckley House is one of the most frequently photographed inns on Cape Cod, thanks to its well-known wild flower gardens. All rooms have working fireplaces and four-poster beds. One suite is accented with rich plum tones and a cushy chaise in front of the fireplace. A connecting plant-filled sitting room offers glimpses of the bay.

An English country breakfast is served in the dining room. The parlor is always open to guests.

Charles Hinckley House's Fruit Compote

In a pretty dish, put seedless grapes, pineapple chunks, or strawberries. Sprinkle top with fresh ground cinnamon, brown sugar, and sour cream. Fold everything together carefully. Refrigerate for ½ hour. There are no set measurements, just mix the amount you need.

Charles Hinckley House

Route 6A and
Scudder Lane
Barnstable, MA 02630
(508) 362-9924

Innkeepers:
Miya and Les Patrick

Open all year.
4 rooms/4 baths.

Rates: $95-$125 (for two). No credit cards accepted.

Amenities: No children. No pets. 5-minute walk to the beach.

Directions: Route 6 to Exit 6. Take Route 132 North to Route 6A. Turn right on Route 6A and proceed 1 ½ miles to the corner of Scudder Lane; the inn is on the left.

Cobbs Cove
Powder Hill Road
Barnstable, MA 02630
(508) 362-9356

Innkeeper:
Evelyn Chester

Open all year.
6 rooms/6 baths.

Rates: $129-$169 (for
two). No credit cards
accepted.

Amenities: No
children. No pets.
Fireplace in the
keeping room. Dinner
to guests only. Air
conditioning, whirlpool
tubs. 5- to 10-minute
walk to the beach.

Directions: Route 6 to
Exit 6. Turn right.
From Barnstable
village, travel east on
Route 6A through the
traffic light, then turn
left on Powder Hill
Road.

Cobbs Cove

A sweeping view of Barnstable Harbor is available from each room of Cobbs Cove, a timbered colonial country inn set on a hill. The inn, built in 1974, is fairly new by Cape Cod standards. It features large rooms, a Count Rumford fireplace in the living room, and arrangements of fresh wild flowers.

A hearty, full Yankee breakfast is served on the garden patio, weather permitting. Chef Henri-Jean is famous for his crepes and refuses to divulge the ingredients.

Cobbs Cove's
Leek & Potato Soup with Smoked Ham

3 T. butter   4 medium leeks sliced
3 C. chicken stock   (use white and tender greens)
2 large potatoes peeled and sliced   ½ lb. smoked ham cubed
                pepper and fresh chives

In a large heavy saucepan melt butter. Add leeks. Sauté over low heat and stir until softened, about 8 minutes. Stir in the stock and cook over moderate heat for 10 minutes. Mash some of the potato slices against the side of the pan. Stir in ham and simmer one minute. Pepper and garnish with chives. Makes 4 servings.

Crocker House Tavern Bed & Breakfast

3095 Main Street
Barnstable, MA 02630
(508) 362-3995

Innkeeper:
Linda and Chip
Gustafson

Open June-October
3 rooms/2 baths.

Rates: $100 (for two).
No credit cards
accepted.

Amenities: No
children. No pets.
Several fireplaces in
the common room and
guest bedrooms. 10-
minute walk to the
beach.

Directions: Route 6 to
Exit 6. Left (north) on
Route 132 to stop sign
at Route 6A. Right
(east) on Route 6A to
the inn on your right.

Crocker Tavern Bed & Breakfast

Innkeepers Linda and Chip Gustafson have restored the Crocker Tavern according to the guidelines of the Society for the Preservation of New England Antiquities (SPNEA). Entering the inn is like stepping back in time. Furniture is authentically antique and suitable for the period. The main bath has a luxurious tub on legs. Ask for a peek at the wonderful kitchen, modern, yet preserving a sense of the past.

The 1989 season will be the innkeepers' first. Breakfasts at Crocker Tavern include homemade breads and coffeecakes.

Crocker Tavern's Swedish Coffee Bread

1 yeast cake	½ C. margarine
1 C. milk	½ C. sugar
1 egg	4½ C. flour
½ t. cardamom seed	1 t. salt

Boil together margarine, milk, sugar, and salt. Add cardamom. Let cool until lukewarm. Dissolve yeast cake in small amount of lukewarm mixture, then add remaining portion. Add beaten egg. Knead in flour, mixing well. mixing well. Let dough rise in a warm place; knead again, and shape into rolls or bread. Let rise in a warm place again. Before baking, brush top with egg white. Shake on sugar and/or nuts. Bake at 350° until browned, about 30 minutes. Serve warm with butter. Makes 2 loaves.

Goss House

61 Pine Lane
Barnstable, MA 02630
(508) 362-8559

Innkeepers:
Bill & Genny Gedrim

Open 5/15 to 10/31.
3 rooms/3 baths.

Rates: 5/15 to 10/31,
$60 (for two). No
credit cards accepted.
Personal or traveler's
checks accepted.

Amenities: Children
over 12 welcome. No
pets. Smoking
restricted to outdoors.
10- to 15-minute walk
to the beach.

Directions: Route 6 to
Exit 6 (Route 132).
Take Route 132 North
to Route 6A. Turn
right on Route 6A to
the first right after St.
Mary's Episcopal
Church.

Goss House

Once the convent for St. Mary's Church, located around the corner, and a small school, the Goss House was built in 1850. The Victorian farmhouse is situated on a tranquil country lane, yet is close to everything in the town of Barnstable. It is fresh and clean with a whitewashed country look inside, and decorated with lots of pink gingham.

The innkeepers serve a full country breakfast with fresh fruit and homemade pastries. They are so accommodating that they will serve an earlier breakfast if you request it.

Goss House's Coffee Cake

Dissolve 1 package of yeast in ¼ C. warm water; set aside.

Combine: **½ C. milk**
½ C. sugar
½ C. butter or margarine
½ t. salt

Warm carefully until butter is melted, and pour into a large bowl. Cool slightly, add 2 beaten eggs, dissolved yeast, grated rind of 1 lemon, and 3 C. flour. Dough will be sticky. Cover and let rise until doubled in bulk. Spoon dough into two 8 x 8″ greased pans and press evenly over bottom with floured fingers. Brush tops with melted butter and sprinkle each with 1 ½ T. sugar and ¼ t. cinnamon. Let rise until doubled and bake at 350° for 20 minutes. Remove from oven, drizzle tops with 2 T. light cream, and bake 3 minutes longer.

the HENRY CROCKER HOUSE C. 1800
BARNSTABLE VILLAGE CAPE COD, MA

The Henry Crocker House

The restored Henry Crocker House is furnished with authentic country antiques and fine reproductions. The main house is almost entirely devoted to guests, an unusual amount of space and freedom for a small inn. Two rooms have canopy beds and fireplaces. All rooms are meticulously kept with great attention to detail. In one room, guests will find a set of antique spectacles on the mantel alongside an old Bible. Each room has a handmade quilt, a Windsor rocker, and such modern amenities as a good reading lamp and an alarm clock.

An informal afternoon tea is served each day. A hearty family-style breakfast served in the Keeping Room on stoneware hand-thrown for the Henry Crocker House.

The Henry Crocker House
Orange Oatmeal Muffins

Muffins: 1 1/3 C. quick cooking oats
        1¼ C. all-purpose flour
        ½ C. sugar
        1 T. baking soda
        ½ t. orange extract

Glaze: ¾ C. powdered sugar
      3-5 t. orange juice

1 t. salt
1/3 C. margarine
1 C. milk
1 large egg
½ t. dried orange peel

¼ t. orange extract
½ t. dried orange peel

Heat oven to 400°. In a large bowl, combine oats, flour, sugar, baking powder, and salt. Cut in margarine until mixture resembles small peas. Combine other ingredients and add all at once to dry mixture. Mix 10-12 strokes until moistened. Spoon into greased tins. Bake 15 minutes or until golden. Combine glaze ingredients. Glaze slightly cooled muffins and serve at once with creamery butter and spicy, dark orange marmalade. Makes 1 dozen.

The Henry Crocker House

3026 Main Street
Barnstable, MA 02630
(508) 362-8584

Innkeepers:
Bob & Alex Frazee

Open all year.
4 rooms/2 baths.

Rates: Memorial Day to Columbus Day, $45-$75 (for two).
VISA/MC

Amenities: Children over 12 welcome. No pets. Complimentary afternoon tea. Bicycles available for guests. Smoking allowed only on the porch. 15-minute walk to the beach.

Directions: Route 6 to Exit 6. Take Route 132 North to Route 6A. Right on Route 6A to the corner of Rendezvous Lane, just west of Barnstable village.

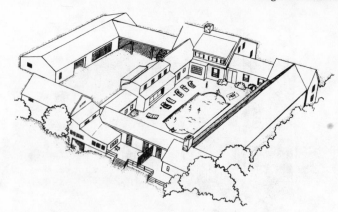

The Lamb and Lion Inn

2504 Main Street
Barnstable, MA 02360
(508) 362-6823

Innkeepers:
Joanne & Dave Rice

Open all year. 10
rooms/10 baths.

Rates: 6/15 to 9/16,
$75-$105 (for two).
VISA

Amenities: Children
and pets welcome.
Swimming pool. Color
TV in each room. Air
conditioning.

Directions: Route 6 to
Exit 6. Take Route
132 North to Route
6A. Turn right at
Route 6A and proceed
1 mile to the inn on
your left.

The Lamb and Lion Inn

Innkeeper Joanne Rice says the name of her inn comes from Jan DeHartog's book *Peaceable Kingdom.* "We chose it, The Lamb and Lion, because it denotes joy and peace. This is what we offer." The inn is on four acres of rolling land in an historic area. It offers a wide variety of accommodations ranging from motel-like rooms, to efficiency apartments and individual guest rooms.

The house containing the guest rooms is designed as an atrium around a pool, with a solarium and huge sundecks overlooking the harbor. The 18th-century barn has two efficiency apartments for families. The antique shop on the premises sells unique collectibles, furniture, and Sandwich glass.

A continental breakfast is included.

The Lamb and Lion Inn's French Coffee Cake

¼ lb. butter
1¾ C. sugar
3 eggs

3 t. almond extract
3 C. flour
1½ t. baking soda

1 pint sour cream

Cream butter, sugar, eggs, and almond extract. Alternately add flour (mixed with baking soda) and sour cream. Pour ½ batter into a 9" x 14" pan. Add ½ the topping and add remainder of batter and topping. Be sure to swirl the topping when you add it. Bake at 350° for 30 minutes or until browned.

Topping: **7 t. cocoa, ½ t. cinnamon, ½ C. sugar**

The Thomas Huckins House

Listed in the National Register of Historic Places, this 1705 colonial has been carefully and lovingly restored. Early American antiques create a comfortable, casual atmosphere. All rooms have canopy beds; two have their own working fireplaces. A two-room, one-bath suite is available for larger groups.

Breakfast is served in the Keeping Room by a walk-in fireplace or, in the summer, on the patio, surrounded by an old fashioned perennial garden. Breakfast may include muffins, fresh fruit, bacon, sausage, eggs, French toast, banana pancakes.

Thomas Huckins House's Carrot-Nut Bread

3 eggs	1½ t. cinnamon
1½ C. sugar	1½ t. nutmeg
1 C. oil	¾ t. salt
2¼ C. whole wheat flour	2¼ C. grated carrots
1¼ t. baking soda	1½ C. walnuts

1½ C. raisins

Beat eggs well, add sugar and oil. Stir in flour, baking soda, salt, and spice mixture. Add carrots, nuts, and raisins. Bake at 350° in a loaf pan for 1¼ hours.

The Thomas Huckins House
2701 Old King's Highway
Barnstable, MA 02360
(508) 362-6379

Innkeepers:
Burt & Eleanor Eddy

Open all year.
3 rooms/3 baths.

Rates: 5/20 to 10/20, $85 (for two).
VISA/MC

Amenities: No children. No pets. Working fireplaces. 5-minute walk to the beach.

Directions: Route 6 to Exit 6. North on Route 132. Right on Route 6A. The inn is 1.5 miles ahead on the right.

Adam's Terrace Gardens Inn

539 Main Street
Centerville, MA 02632
(508) 775-4707

Innkeepers: John &
Pat Veracka

Open all year. 8
rooms/5 with private
bath, 3 share bath.

Rates: $50-65, year-
round (for two). No
credit cards accepted.

Amenities: Children
welcome. No pets.
Swimming pool. 15-
minute walk to
Craigville Beach.

Directions: Route 6 to
Exit 6 towards
Hyannis. Right at first
traffic light (Phinney's
Lane). Follow
Phinney's Lane to the
stop sign at Route 28.
Cross Route 28. Follow
Phinney's Lane onto
Main Street; the inn is
approximately 400
yards ahead on the
left.

Adam's Terrace Gardens Inn

The Adam's Terrace Gardens Inn is right in the center of the village and within walking distance to all Centerville attractions. The inn was built circa 1830 as the home of Captain John Baker, skipper of the "Pride of the Port." His ghost might not care for the modern conveniences such as the televisions in each room, but the guests are pleased.

Breakfast is served in the huge family-style kitchen or on the deck overlooking the rose trellis and flower garden.

Adam Terrace Gardens Inn's Popovers

3 eggs	1¼ C. white flour
1¼ C. milk	¼ t. salt

1 T. melted butter

Put all ingredients in a large bowl and mix thoroughly, without over beating. Half fill buttered muffin tins. Put them in a pre-heated oven at 450°. Bake 25 minutes. Lower oven temperature to 350° and bake 15 minutes longer until golden brown. Makes 6 popovers. Serve immediately with Fresh Strawberry Butter:

1 C. strawberries, rinsed, well drained, and hulled
¾ C. confectioner's sugar
½ C. unsalted butter at room temperature

Place the berries in a blender or food processor until the they are pureed. Add sugar and butter and process 2-3 minutes until smooth. Store in refrigerator. Serve at room temperature. Makes 1 ¼ cups.

The Carver House
638 Main Street
Centerville, MA 02632
(508) 775-9414

Innkeepers:
Marguerite & Harold
MacNeeley

Open all year.
3 rooms/1 bath.

Rates: $40, all year
(for two). No credit
cards accepted.

Amenities: Children
welcome. No pets. 10-
minute walk to the
beach. Television.

Directions: Route 6 to
Exit 5. Follow signs to
Centerville/Craigville.
Follow Old Stage Road
to Main Street in
Centerville. Turn right
at the traffic light on
South Main toward
Osterville.

The Carver House

Flowers decorate a picket fence in front of The Carver House. Set in the middle of the village. The inn is a mere half mile to Craigville Beach and within a quarter mile of the Four Seas Ice Cream store, both famous landmarks. All three rooms have twin beds and televisions, and two of them have sinks in the room. The shady yard with its comfortable outdoor furniture is inviting.

Continental breakfast is served in the cozy dining room.

The Carver House's
Cape Cod Cranberry Bread

2 C. sifted flour
1 ½ t. baking powder
1 orange
boiling water
1 C. chopped walnuts

1 C. raw cranberries
1 C. sugar
1 t. salt
2 T. shortening
1 well beaten egg

Sift dry ingredients together. Combine juice and grated rind of orange with shortening and enough boiling water to make a total of ¾ C., and add egg. Blend into dry ingredients, stirring until flour mixture is dampened. Add nuts and cranberries. Pour into a greased 8 ½" x 14 ½" pan. Bake at 350° for 60-70 minutes.

Copper Beech Inn
497 Main Street
Centerville, MA 02632
(508) 771-5488

Innkeepers:
Joyce & Clark Diehl

Open all year. 3 rooms
with private baths.

Rates: $75 (for two).
VISA/MC/AMEX

Amenities: Children
over 12 years welcome.
No pets. 5-minute
walk to the beach.

Directions: Route 6 to
Exit 5. Signs at the
exit ramp direct you to
Centerville and
Craigville. Follow Old
Stage Road directly to
Main Street. The inn
is on your left.

Copper Beech Inn

Guests are drawn to the kitchen of the Copper Beach Inn, but can also relax in the parlor or outside on the well cared for grounds. Two of the guest rooms are on the first floor. The third is on the second floor, decorated in mauve and pink, with a king-sized bed. All rooms are nicely decorated.

Breakfast is truly a sumptuous feast and the French toast is spectacular.

Copper Beech Inn's Favorite French Toast

3 slices French bread, sliced ¾" thick

1 T. sugar	4 eggs
½ t. vanilla	1 C. milk
¼ t. salt	2 T. orange juice or
2 T. butter or margarine	1 T. Grand Marnier

Arrange bread in single layer in 9" x 13" baking dish. In bowl, beat eggs, milk, orange juice or Grand Marnier, sugar, vanilla, and salt. Pour over bread. Turn slices to coat evenly. Refrigerate, covered, several hours or overnight. Heat butter or margarine in large skillet. Sauté bread until golden, about 4 minutes on each side. If desired, sprinkle with confectioner's sugar. Makes 4 servings.

The Inn at Fernbrook

The Inn at
Fernbrook
481 Main Street
Centerville, MA 02632
(508) 775-4334

Innkeepers: Brian
Gallo and Sal DiFlorio

Open all year.
7 rooms/6 baths.

Rates: 5/1 to 10/31,
$95-$175 (for two).
MC/VISA/AMEX

Amenities: Children
over 14 years welcome.
No pets. Fireplaces.
10-minute walk to the
beach.

Directions: Route 6 to
Exit 5. At stop sign
cross Route 149. Take
first right onto Old
Stage Road. At the
next stop sign, turn
left. After the stop
LIGHT, take a right at
the next stop SIGN.
The inn is on your left.

Elegance is everywhere at The Inn at Fernbrook, a magnificent estate. The spirits of the previous owners and their famous guests are celebrated in the names of the rooms, the decor, and the gardens. The Spellman room on the first floor has its own private entrance, a working tile-faced fireplace, and a canopy bed. Another spectacular suite is the Olmstead, on the third floor. It boasts a vaulted ceiling bedroom, a living room with a working fireplace, a balcony, and a roof deck. Hardwood floors are accented with Oriental carpets and select antiques. Sheer curtains and softly printed wallpapers give the rooms a feeling of light, space, and cheeriness.

The garden cottage is a lovely hideaway for two. A stroll through the rose garden, past the pond and gargoyle fountain, will bring you to the lovely park and a large pond with ducks.

A full breakfast is included.

Fernbrook's Apple Dutch Babies

3 eggs	½ C. flour
2 dashes of nutmeg	4 T. melted butter
½ C. milk	four 4" to 5" ramekins

Preheat oven to 400°. Beat eggs well, add milk and flour alternately. Add nutmeg. Put 1 T. butter in each ramekin. Pour equal parts of batter in each ramekin. Bake 15-20 minutes.

2 small or 1 large apple, peeled and sliced	2 T. butter
2 T. brown sugar	nutmeg to taste
4 T. apple cider	2 T. rum

In a separate pan, melt butter, add sugar, nutmeg, and cider. Sauté apple(s) until tender. Add rum and cook for 1 minute. Remove Dutch Babies from the oven when sides are high and lightly browned. Immediately sprinkle with lemon juice and powdered sugar. Slide Dutch Babies from ramekin onto serving plates. Spoon sautéed apple mixture into center of each Dutch Baby and serve with sausage patties.

Old Hundred House

1211 Craigville Beach
Road
Centerville, MA 02632
(508) 775-6166

Innkeepers:
Marina & Jack Downes

Open May to October.
7 rooms/shared baths.

Rates: $35 (for two).
No credit cards
accepted.

Amenities: Children
welcome. No pets. 2-
minute walk to the
famous Craigville
Beach.

Directions: Route 6 to
Exit 5, toward
Centerville. At stop
sign cross Route 149.
Take first right onto
Old Stage Road. At
the next stop sign turn
left. After stop light,
take a right at the next
stop sign. Follow
through town, through
traffic light toward
Craigville Beach. The
house is on your right.

Old Hundred House

Built by Captain Andrus Bearse over one hundred and sixty years ago, the Old Hundred House overlooks a marsh and is a quick walk from the beach. Innkeepers Marina and Jack Downes run a family style inn. They invite you to relax on the screened-in porch with its secluded setting on the marsh.

Old Hundred House's Golden Raisin Buns

1 C. water	1 C. flour
½ C. butter or margarine	4 eggs
1 t. sugar	½ C. raisins (plump by soaking in
¼ t. salt	hot water for 10 minutes; drain well)

Combine water, butter, sugar, and salt in a saucepan. Bring to a boil. Add flour all at once, then over low heat, beat with a wooden spoon for about 1 minute, or until mixture leaves the sides of the pan and forms a smooth thick dough. Remove from heat. Continue beating 2 minutes to cool slightly. Add eggs, one at a time, beating until the mixture has a smooth satiny sheen. Stir in raisins. Drop heaping tablespoons about 2″ apart on a greased baking sheet. Bake in preheated 375° oven for 30-35 minutes. Remove to wire rack to cool slightly. While still warm, gently spread on the following frosting.

Lemon Frosting

Melt 1 T. of butter in 1 ½ T. heavy cream. Remove from the heat and stir in 1 C. confectioner's sugar until smooth. Stir in 1 t. lemon juice. Add more cream or sugar if necessary to make the mixture spreading consistency.

Sandman Inn

The Sandmans have spent some 30 years in the U.S. Foreign Service, serving at U.S. Embassies in eight countries. They speak Hebrew and French, a little Spanish, and some Korean. Guests soon feel at home in this international atmosphere, as the hosts take pleasure in doing whatever is possible to assure a great vacation on Cape Cod.

The inn is in a quiet and secluded rural setting on a hill overlooking Lake Wequaquet. The house is spacious and furnished with a collection of Asian furniture and art. Wine and cheese are served in the afternoon.

Sandman Inn's
Chicken with Walnuts in Plum Sauce

Pour boiling water over 1 C. walnut halves and let stand 5 minutes. Drain and pat dry.

1 T. beaten egg	1 t. cornstarch
1 T. oil	6 thinly sliced chicken breasts, boned and skinned, cut into ½" pieces

Combine egg with oil and cornstarch in small bowl. Add chicken pieces, toss gently to coat evenly.

½ C. oil	1 t. sugar
2 T. plum or hoisin sauce	1 t. soy sauce
1 1" piece of ginger, peeled and finely chopped	¼ t. sesame oil
2 green onions, finely chopped (for garnish)	

Heat ½ C. oil in wok over medium high heat until haze forms. Add walnuts, fry until golden (45 seconds). Remove with slotted spoon and drain on paper towels. Add chicken to wok and cook until golden (about 3 minutes). Drain well. Pour off all but thin film of oil. Return pan to heat, add plum or hoisin sauce, ginger, sugar, soy sauce, and sesame oil, stirring until all are combined. Reduce heat and simmer, stirring constantly, until sauce glistens (1-2 minutes). Add chicken and nuts, mix thoroughly with sauce. Transfer to serving platter and garnish with green onion. Serves 4.

Sandman Inn
116 Hillside Drive
Centerville, MA 02632
(508) 362-4284

Innkeepers:
Sonya & Len Sandman

Open all year.
2 rooms/1 bath.

Rates: 7/1 to 9/10, $45 (for two). No credit cards accepted.

Amenities: Children welcome. No pets. 2-minute walk to swimming at Lake Wequaquet. Two working fireplaces in the living room and study. Cable TV available to guests. Rates include wine and cheese.

Directions: From Route 6, take Exit 6. Stay in right lane to stop sign. Turn right on Shoot Flying Hill Road. Stay left of the fork in road. After Lake Wequaquet, take first right, Hillside Drive, up the hill and around to the right to the last house on the right.

Salty Dog Guest House

451 Main Street
Cotuit, MA 02635
(508) 428-5228

Innkeepers:
Lynne & Jerry
Goldstein

Open all year.
5 rooms/3 baths.

Rates: Memorial Day
to Columbus Day, $50-
$65 (for two).
VISA/MC (at 5%
surcharge).

Amenities: Children
over 12 years welcome.
No pets. No smoking
permitted indoors. 5-
minute drive to beach.
Bicycles and picnic
benches are available
for your use.

Directions: Route 6 to
Exit 2. At the end of
exit ramp, turn right,
proceeding south on
Route 130 to the end.
Turn left on Route 28
and then a quick right
onto Main Street.

Salty Dog Guest House

The smell of pine from the trees is all around as you approach the entrance to this 1850 cranberry farmer's house. Built in 1850 as the home of a cranberry farmer, the Salty Dog Guest House is on Main Street, which is listed in the National Register of Historic Places. The woods are close by, as are warm water beaches, golf courses, tennis courts, and fishing areas. Rooms with queen- or king-size beds, or an antique double bed, are available.

The continental breakfast features home-baked breads.

Salty Dog Guest House's Strawberry Bread

3 C. flour	2 C. sugar
1 t. baking soda	3 well-beaten eggs
dash of salt	Two 10-oz. packages frozen strawberries,
3 t. cinnamon	thawed, but not drained
1¼ C. salad oil	1 C. chopped walnuts

Sift together flour, baking soda, salt, cinnamon, and sugar. Set aside. In a separate bowl, mix together the well-beaten eggs, frozen strawberries (thawed), salad oil, and nuts. Fold into flour mixture, stirring just enough to moisten. Grease and flour two 8" x 4" pans. Preheat over to 350°. Bake 1 hour or until they test done. Let cool in pans for 10 minutes. Remove from pans and cool on racks. Yields 2 loaves.

Acorn House

There is a homey atmosphere at the Acorn House, which is close to downtown Hyannis and also near the beach. It is across the street from the Sea Street Market, a convenient spot for buying a deli lunch. The furnishings in the inn are eclectic, with both antiques and cottage decor. Birds flock to the many shade trees in the yard.

The innkeeper provides taxi service to and from the ferries, as well as to the bus station and the airport. Innkeeper Christmas Kelly offers dinner in addition to a gourmet breakfast.

Acorn House's Blueberry Corn Bread

1 pkg. corn muffin mix (or your own)   **1 to 1 ½ C. blueberries**
3 T. butter   **4-6 T. light brown sugar**
                  granulated brown sugar for topping

Prepare muffin mix. Melt butter in pan in preheated 375° oven. Spread blueberries on butter. Spread light brown sugar on the blueberries. Pour on the prepared muffin mix and sprinkle liberally with granulated brown sugar. Bake for 20-25 minutes. Invert to remove from pan.

Acorn
House
240 Sea Street
Hyannis, MA 02601
(508) 771-4071

Innkeeper:
Christmas Kelly

Open all year. 3 rooms/2 shared baths.

Rates: 6/1 to 10/1, $65 (for two). No credit cards accepted.

Amenities: Children welcome. No pets. Working fireplace in the living room. 5-minute walk to the beach. Innkeeper speaks fluent Spanish.

Directions: Route 6 to Route 132 exit. Take the Barnstable Road exit at the Airport Rotary (4 miles). Turn right at Main Street (2 miles). Left on Sea Street.

Captain Sylvester Baxter House

156 Main Street
Hyannis, MA 02601
(508) 775-5611

Innkeeper:
Nancy Krajewski

Open all year.
10 rooms/10 baths.

Rates: 5/26 to 9/4,
$70-$75 (for two).
VISA/MC

Amenities: Children
welcome. No pets.
Outdoor swimming
pool. Color television
in each room. Air
conditioning. 5-minute
walk to the beach.
Barbeques. Laundry
room.

Directions: Route 6 to
Exit 7. Turn left on
Yarmouth Road.
Proceed through next
traffic light to the end
of Main Street. Turn
left to the inn on your
right.

Captain Sylvester Baxter House

The setting of the Captain Sylvester Baxter House is that of a small village with granite curbs, flagstone walks, and colonial-style lanterns. Historically the oldest settlement in Hyannis, the east end of Main Street retains the charm of the era when sailors built near the harbor. Shade trees, shrubs, and flowers surround the inn, making guests almost forget how close they are to bustling Hyannis.

Each guest room has recently been redecorated in Victorian style. Behind the two historic buildings are comfortable cottages, including one-room efficiency units with compact kitchenettes, and larger vacation apartments. The continental breakfast is not included with the rental of cottage or apartments.

Captain Sylvester Baxter House's Puffy Pancakes

½ C. flour   2 eggs
½ C. milk   1/3 stick butter

Melt butter in pie plate until it froths. In a separate bowl, mix flour, milk, and eggs. Pour the batter into the middle of the pie plate. Bake in 350° oven for 15 minutes. Sprinkle with powdered sugar. Serves 4.

Cranberry Cove B & B

Cranberry Cove B & B is set near just what its name implies — eighty acres of cranberry bog. The inn is secluded, off a dirt road in a real Cape Cod house. The entire second floor is for guests. and is decorated with country-style furnishings. In fall and winter, a wood stove in the den glows with warmth. A full breakfast is served.

Cranberry Cove's Gourmet French Toast

2 slices white bread
whipped pineapple or strawberry
  Philadelphia cream cheese
apricot preserves
egg and milk batter
bananas and fresh fruits
  in season
fresh orange juice
walnuts (unsalted and chopped)

Spread both slices of bread with the cream cheese. Sprinkle with one tablespoon of chopped nuts. Dip sandwich in egg batter and brown in butter. Slice into four triangles, arrange with points facing out. Surround with sliced bananas and fresh strawberries, blueberries, or any fresh fruit. Heat 1 T. of apricot preserves and ½ C. fresh orange juice. Pour over bread slices and fruit placed in the center of the dish. Serve warm and add bacon or sausage to taste. This recipe makes 1 serving.

Cranberry Cove B & B

Rosetta Street
Hyannis, MA 02601
(508) 775-5049 or
800-992-0096 (outside
Massachusetts)

Innkeepers: Barbara &
John Siefken

Open all year.
2 rooms/shared bath.

Rates: $49, all year
(for two). No credit
cards accepted.

Amenities: No
children. No pets. 3-
minute walk to the
beach.

Directions: Route 6 to
Route 132. Follow
signs in Hyannis to
Cape Cod Hospital.
Go to the front of the
hospital and take the
road that leads directly
behind the hospital.
You will come out
onto Bayview Street.
Bear right; two streets
ahead on your left is
Rosetta Street. Turn
left and drive to the
end of the street. You
will see a bog in front
of you. Directly to the
right will be a dirt road
and you will come to a
small cottage. To your
right will be Cranberry
Cove B & B.

Elegance by-the-Sea

162 Sea Street
Hyannis, MA 02601
(508) 775-3595

Innkeepers: Mary &
Clark Boydston

Open all year.
6 rooms/5 baths.

Rates: 5/1 to 11/1,
$60-$85 (for two).
AMEX/VISA/MC

Amenities: No
children. No pets.
Working fireplaces. 10-
minute walk to the
beach. 10-minute walk
to the golf course.
Innkeepers speak
fluent French.

Directions: Route 6 to
Route 132 exit.
Proceed 4 miles to the
Barnstable Road exit
at the Airport Rotary.
Proceed 2 miles to
Main Street. Turn
right on Main Street,
then left on Sea Street.
Look for the inn's sign
on the left, about
three blocks down.

Elegance by-the-Sea

A resident cat welcomes you onto the porch of Elegance by-the-Sea, then innkeepers Mary and Clark Boydston take it from there. Guest rooms feature French-Victorian furniture the innkeepers are collecting to fill their Victorian style house. An example of the French influence can be seen in the massive Louis XV style beds in two of the rooms.

A charming Victorian parlor is available for guests. Next to it is the intimate dining room set with lace clothes where breakfast is served. Quiche and croissants are specialties of the inn.

Elegance by-the-Sea's Mushroom-Leek Quiche

In a skillet, sauté approximately one pound fresh mushrooms and one large bunch of leeks until soft. Set aside. Prepare pie crust for 9″ quich pan, and spread vegetable mixture on top. In a bowl, mix 3 eggs, 2 T. flour, a pint of cream, and salt and pepper to taste. Pour over mushroom mixture and bake at 375° for approximately 45 minutes.

The Inn on Sea Street

The innkeepers' artistic touch is seen everywhere in the transformation of this Victorian house into an elegant beach house. The first floor guest room is popular and unique. A magnificent quilt in the "fan" pattern which provides bright color to the mostly white sun porch. Other guest rooms are furnished with antiques, including a double bed with a lace canopy. In deference to their guests' wishes, Lois and J.B. have compromised their love for antiques and provided queen-size beds instead of the authentic doubles. A new garden room has wonderful charm and privacy with its own entrance, bathroom, and television.

Guests enjoy a gourmet breakfast on the hostess' best china, at individual tables set with sterling silver, crystal, and flowers from the garden.

The Inn on Sea Street's Granola

Combine: **3 C. rolled oats**
           ½ C. slivered almonds
           1 C. walnuts

           ¼ C. sunflower seeds
           ½ C. unsweetened coconut
           ½ C. raw wheat germ

Mix together: **1/3 C. water**
               ¼ C. oil

           ¼ C. honey
           ¼ C. maple syrup

Pour over dry mixture and stir. Bake in large (13″ x 13″) pan at 225° for 2 hours. Add ¾ cup raisins after baking.

The Inn on Sea Street
358 Sea Street
Hyannis, MA 02601
(508) 775-8030

Innkeepers:
Lois M. Nelson
& J.B. Whitehead

Open April 1 to Nov. 15.
6 rooms/3 baths.

Rates: 4/1 to 11/15, $55-$80 (for two).
AMEX/VISA/MC

Amenities: No children. No pets. A working fireplace is in the living room for guests. 3-minute walk to the beach. One-night stays are welcomed.

Directions: Route 6 to Route 132 exit. Turn right at bottom of exit ramp. At the second set of traffic lights, bear right. At next "Y" in the road at Kennedy Memorial Skating Rink, bear right. Go straight through traffic lights to the end. Turn right on Main Street to the next traffic light. Turn left onto Sea Street, and proceed ½ mile. The inn is on the left.

Sea Breeze Inn

397 Sea Street
Hyannis, MA 02601
(508) 771-7213

Innkeepers: Martin &
Patricia Battle

Open all year.
13 rooms/12 baths.

Rates: 6/21 to 9/7,
$60-$80 (for two).
AMEX/VISA/MC

Amenities: Children
over 12 welcome. No
pets. 2-minute walk to
Sea Street Beach. All
rooms have color
television and radios.

Directions: Route 6 to
Exit 6. Take Route
132 South toward
Hyannis. At the
rotary, take Barnstable
Road to Main Street in
Hyannis. Turn right on
Main Street to Sea
Street (look for
Dunkin Donuts). Turn
left on Sea Street
almost to the end, to
the inn on your right.

Sea Breeze Inn

From the shiny wood floors to the sparkling chandeliers, there is a sense of bright cleanliness at the Sea Breeze Inn. The lace curtains in the charming breakfast room are signs of the "lace curtain" Irish hosts. Their gentle brogue assures you of that. Rooms are tastefully furnished with careful thought given to comfort. Some rooms have ocean views.

An "expanded continental" breakfast is served between 7:30 and 9:30 in the breakfast room or on the outdoor ocean-view deck. The location of the inn provides privacy and convenience: it is on a quiet side street near the beach, yet only a 15-minute walk to downtown Hyannis.

Sea Breeze Inn's Blueberry Muffins

1 ¾ C. sifted flour   1 well-beaten egg
2 T. sugar   ½ C. milk
2½ t. baking powder   1/3 C. salad oil
¾ t. salt   1 C. fresh or frozen blueberries

Put all dry ingredients into a bowl. Combine egg, milk, and salad oil. Add all at once to dry ingredients. Add blueberries. Stir well. Fill greased muffin tins 2/3 full. Bake at 400° for about 25 minutes. Makes about 1 dozen.

The Simmons Homestead Inn

The Simmons Homestead Inn

288 Scudder Avenue
Hyannis Port, MA
02647
(508) 778-4999

While the Simmons Homestead Inn is old, the spirit here is young. The decorations are bright and cheerful. Papermaché, brass, and ceramic are in every nook and cranny. The guest rooms are all completely different. One is decorated with all white wicker, one features a hand-made canopy bed, another features a brass bed, and others are appointed with canopies and antique settings. All are simply delightful.

A full breakfast is served either in the dining room or on the porch. If you are catching a morning boat to the islands, the meal will be ready early. Wine and cheese are served every afternoon.

Innkeeper: William B. Putman, Jr.

Open all year. 10 rooms/10 baths.

Rates: 6/1 to 10/15, $100-$125 (for two). No credit cards accepted.

Amenities: No children. No pets. Five working fireplaces. 10-minute walk to the beach. Rate includes wine and cheese in the afternoon.

Simmons Homestead's French Dipped Cinnamon Apple or Pear Waffles

Prepare your favorite waffle batter from scratch or from a ready-mix package. Add ground cinnamon to taste. In a food processor or blender, finely chop skinned and cored apples or pears. Add cinnamon to batter, to taste. Cook in waffle iron to a point where they are light tan color — NOT COMPLETELY COOKED. Refrigerate or freeze until ready to use. To serve, dip pre-cooked waffles in beaten mixture of raw egg and cinnamon. Cook on griddle or pan as you would French toast, until completely cooked and deep brown. Top with confectioner's sugar and serve with hot syrup.

Directions: Route 6 to Exit 6, Route 132 South. Go 1 ½ miles to the Sheraton and bear right onto Bearses Way. Go 100 yards and bear right again onto Pitchers Way. Take this road to the end. At the stop sign at the intersection of Scudder Ave, the inn is on your right.

Potter-Smith House

80 Tansy Circle
Osterville, MA 02655
(508) 428-4606

Innkeepers: Mildred &
Roger Smith

Open April to
December.
3 rooms/2 baths.

Rates: 5/15 to 10/15,
$45-$52 (for two). No
credit cards accepted.

Amenities: Children
welcome. No pets.
Fireplace. Television in
each room. 5-minute
drive to the beach.

Directions: Route 6 to
Exit 5. Turn right
(south) on Route 149.
Proceed 500 feet to
fork. Left at fork on
Osterville-West
Barnstable Road.
Follow to Route 28.
Turn left on Route 28
and proceed almost .3
mile to Tanglewood
Drive on your right (a
green sign also says
Hickory Hill). Follow
Tanglewood 300-400
yards to Tansy Circle
on left to Potter-Smith
House at the foot of
the hill.

Potter-Smith House

Sitting on the rear deck of the Potter-Smith House in Osterville is like being in the middle of a pine forest. The Smiths like introducing newcomers to Cape Cod including their own wooded area of the village, as well as other sites. One guest wrote, "We were grateful for Mr. Smith's history lessons, suggestions of sights to see and restaurants to visit, and enjoyed each of them." During the cocktail hour, guests are invited to have a complimentary "Cape Codder" or something else cold and refreshing.

A full breakfast is frequently served, and may include bacon and eggs, blueberry pancakes, fresh fruit, and a variety of bagel spreads.

Potter-Smith House's
Cream Cheese a la Raisin-Nut

1 pkg. cream cheese, softened   **¼ C. chopped walnuts**
½ C. raisins   **1 T. maple syrup or honey**
¼ t. cinnamon
Blend all ingredients thoroughly; pack into jars and refrigerate.

Village Bed & Breakfast

The Village Bed & Breakfast, a "Nantucket barn" house is situated among huge pines and a bird habitat at the end of a quiet lane. The rooms are in country French decor with accents of wicker. Innkeepers Ann and Bill Stralevich are warm and gracious in their hospitality. During the day a variety of beverages, hot and cold, are available to guests. A bay cruise with your hosts is a wonderful treat when the weather permits.

Breakfast is ample and home-cooked, served overlooking the pool or in the great room.

Village Bed & Breakfast's Baked Apricot Rice Custard

2 C. milk	¼ C. currants
3 eggs, beaten	1 t. vanilla
½ C. dark brown sugar	¼ t. nutmeg
½ t. salt	½ C. quality apricot jam

1 C. cooked rice

Scald milk, combine next 3 ingredients in 1½ qt. baking dish, and gradually stir in milk. Add cooked rice, currants, vanilla, and jam. Sprinkle nutmeg on top. Bake in a pan set in water at 325° for 50-60 minutes.

Village Bed & Breakfast

45 Woodland Avenue
Osterville, MA 02655
(508) 428-7004

Innkeepers:
Ann & Bill Stralevich

Open all year.
4 rooms/3 baths.

Rates: 5/30 to 10/12, $45-$60 (for two). No credit cards accepted.

Amenities: No children. No pets. Swimming pool. 5-minute walk to the beach.

Directions: Route 6 to Exit 5. Bear right, proceed to fork (500 feet). Left at fork to end (second stop sign). Turn left and follow through town to fork; bear right onto Wianno Avenue. After intersection at the Post Office, take the fourth street on the right (Sylvan Lane), then turn right immediately to #45 Woodland.

The Gentleman Farmer

886 Main Street
West Barnstable, MA
02668
(508) 362-6955

Innkeepers:
Gloria & Alan Clarke

Open 5/1 to 10/30.
5 rooms/3 baths.

Rates: $45-$60 (for
two; 10% discount for
single). No credit cards
accepted.

Amenities: No
children. No pets.
Fireplace in the living
room. 5-minute drive
to the beach.

Directions: Route 6 to
Exit 5. North on
Route 149 toward
West Barnstable to the
end. Left at
intersection with
Route 6A to the inn
on your right.

The Gentleman Farmer

The Gentleman Farmer is a 19th-century restored farmhouse offering charming accommodations in a country setting. The main house and its outbuildings overlook spacious grounds once used for grazing and country fairs. Over the years, the original house has been expanded to the rambling farmhouse/inn which welcomes guests today. There is also a quaint, very private hideaway on the third floor.

In the morning, breakfast is served on the sunporch. It features wonderful homemade breads such as the inn's Mandel bread.

Gentleman Farmer's Mandel Bread

1 C. sugar	3½ C. flour
¾ C. vegetable oil	2 t. baking powder
1 t. vanilla	½ t. salt
2 oz. orange juice	ground almonds or walnuts
3 eggs	cinnamon sugar

Cream sugar and oil together. Add eggs, vanilla, and orange juice. Sift dry ingredients and add slowly, mixing by hand. Refrigerate for at least two hours. Then place on a greased cookie sheet in long columns—no more than 2" wide (should make 4 columns). Bake at 350° for about 20 minutes. Cut diagonally into ½" pieces while still hot. Turn each piece on its side. Sprinkle with cinnamon sugar and bake 10 minutes longer, or until lightly brown.

Honeysuckle
Hill
591 Main Street
West Barnstable, MA
02668
(508) 362-8418

Innkeepers: Barbara &
Bob Rosenthal

Open all year.
3 rooms/ 3 baths.

Rates: 5/1 to 11/1,
$90-$105 (for two).
AMEX/VISA/MC

Honeysuckle Hill

One hundred years ago, guests enjoyed Honeysuckle Hill as an inn. It reopened in 1984 with all the niceties and pampering of a bygone era. All beds are fitted with featherbeds and down comforters. Terry cloth robes for guests hang on bathroom doors. Guests may even luxuriate with breakfast in bed. The master suite has a fireplace and the other two rooms are large bed/sitting rooms, beautifully decorated. The inn is surrounded by trees, shrubs, and flowers to be enjoyed from the big screened porch.

Afternoon tea features homemade cakes, cookies, and scones for which the innkeepers are famous. A full country breakfast is included each morning.

Amenities: Children
over 12 welcome. No
pets. Rates include
afternoon tea. 5-
minute drive to the
beach. Free pickup at
train or airport. Beach
towels, chairs,
umbrellas, and bicycles
are available.

Directions: Route 6 to
Exit 5. North on
Route 149 toward
West Barnstable, to
the end. Left at the
intersection with
Route 6A, to the inn
on your left.

Honeysuckle Hill's Breakfast Souffles

1 roll hot breakfast sausage	salt and pepper
1 can cream of mushroom soup (undiluted)	10 eggs
2 C. grated cheddar cheese	½ C. butter (melted)
4 C. cubed bakery bread	2½ C. milk

Brown crumbled sausage, add cream of mushroom soup. Butter 8 individual souffle dishes, and layer bread, sausage mix, cheese, bread, mix, cheese, and end with bread. Beat 10 eggs, add milk, salt, pepper, and melted butter. Pour over the mix in the souffle dish. Cover each with a small square of wax paper. Refrigerate overnight. Next morning sprinkle with parmesean cheese, pop them in the oven at 350° to 375° and bake for about 45 minutes until puffed and golden. Serve immediately.

Bourne

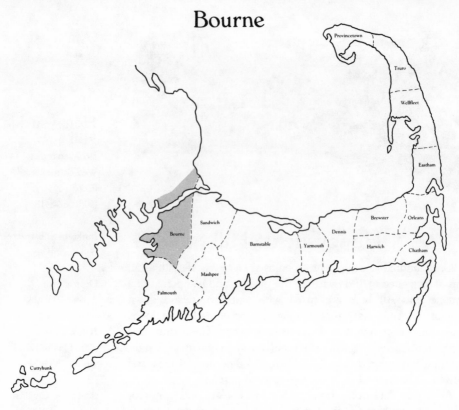

Bourne is the "gateway" to Cape Cod. Two of its villages are Buzzards Bay and Sagamore Beach. **Buzzards Bay** is very busy with many attractions: the Cape Cod Canal, the Massachusetts Maritime Academy, the famous "up and down" railroad bridge, and one of the Cape's most popular herring runs.

A quaint area in the northern part of town is **Sagamore Beach.** On a clear day there are wonderful views of Cape Cod Bay even to Provincetown on the very tip of the Cape. There are approximately 13 miles of service road along the Canal on both sides, and if you bring your bike, you can enjoy the drama of spotting freighters, tankers, and barges making their way through this inland waterway. Children will enjoy the boat watching, and if you bring your fishing rod you have a chance to catch a dinner of bass, flounder, cod, or mackerel. You can walk the service road south to the U. S. Army Corps of Engineers Visitor Center where there is a photographic exhibit and slide presentation on the building of the Canal and bridges.

Bed & Breakfast

  The inn is a private, peaceful home overlooking Cape Cod Bay. Relax in the casual atmosphere in front of the fireplace. John is a food stylist and operates mainly out of New York, so sometimes guests are on their own. Large porches and decks surround the house.

  Host John Carafoli is a gourmet cook and the kitchen shows it. What an honor to be a guest at his breakfasts! The home has been featured in *Bon Appetit* and *Better Homes and Gardens*.

Carafoli's Lemon Cloud

4 egg yolks	5 egg whites
3 T. sugar	1 T. confectioner's sugar
juice of ½ large lemon	½ t. cream of tartar
1 t. lemon extract	pinch of salt
zest of lemon	

  Preheat oven to 425°. Put eggs yolks in a bowl and beat on high for 1 minute. Add sugar slowly. Beat yolks until light colored and foamy and they form a ribbon. Add lemon juice and extract. (The acid in the juice will break down the foam momentarily, but it will come back.) Set aside.

  In another bowl, beat the egg whites at low speed for 1 minute; add the cream of tartar and salt. Beat on high until egg whites form stiff but not dry peaks. Add the sugar and lemon zest, and continue beating thoroughly. (Do not overbeat.) Fold whites into the yolk base. Pour the mixture into a 10½" cast iron skillet that has been buttered and lightly coated with sugar. Bake 12-14 minutes at 400°. Squeeze juice of the other ½ lemon over the souffle and dust with confectioner's sugar; serve immediately. Serves four.

Bed & Breakfast

One Hawes Road
Sagamore Beach, MA
02562
(508) 888-1559

Innkeeper:
John F. Carafoli

Open all year. 3
rooms/shared bath.

Rates: $75-$85 year-round (for two). No credit cards accepted.

Amenities: No children. No pets. Working fireplace. Walk for miles on the quiet sandy beach.

Directions: At the rotary *before* Sagamore Bridge, take the road marked "Scusset Beach." Proceed on this road. You will see a sign marked "Sagamore Beach Highlands." Turn left at the next road, Williston Road, and proceed about 2 miles, going through the stop sign at Clark Road. Turn right onto Hawes Road (the first right after the post office), to the inn on your left.

Brewster

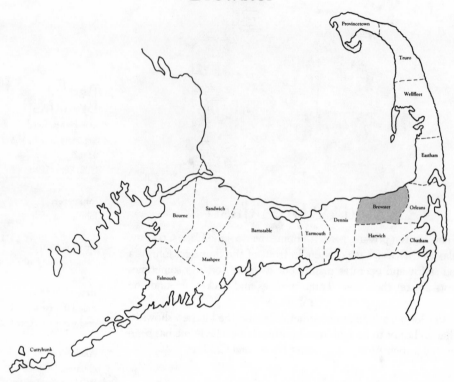

Located on the north side of the Cape between Dennis and Orleans, **Brewster** has several select inns, antique shops, and museums, including the Drummer Boy Museum, the New England Fire and History Museum, the Cape Cod Museum of Natural History, and the Brewster Historical Society Museum. It is reported that there were more deepwater sea captains per square inch in Brewster than anywhere else in America, and the homes they built are among the most impressive on the Cape.

Other points of interest are the Bassett Wild Animal Farm, Sealand of Cape Cod, Century Smock Windmill, and Stoney Brook Mill. The mill itself, circa 1874, is on the site of the Cape's first grist mill, built in 1663. Two ponds and a fish ladder for migratory alewives are popular with nature lovers for viewing the herring run in April and May.

Brewster is also the location of the 1,750-acre Nickerson State Park containing four trout fishing ponds and seven and a half miles of bicycle trails. The country store here provides leisurely sitting on a Sunday morning to watch the comings and goings of the town.

Beaches are on Cape Cod Bay at Crosby Lane, Ellis Landing, Linnell Road, Saint's Landing, and Robbins Hill. Freshwater sites include Long Pond, Pine Pond, Paine's Creek, Sheep Pond, Slough Pond, and Walker's Pond.

In August, the Annual Arts and Crafts Fair is sponsored by the Society of Cape Cod Craftsmen at the Brewster Community Center. The Ocean Edge Golf Club is the official host of the New England PGA Championships.

Beechcroft Inn

Beechcroft
Inn
1360 Main Street
Brewster, MA 02631
(508) 896-9534

Innkeepers: Krista and
Christopher Diego

Open all year.
9 rooms/9 baths.

Rates: $59-$89 (for
two). VISA/MC

Amenities: "Well
traveled children
only." No pets.
Friendly household
pets on the premises.
Bikes available for
guest use. Picnic lunch
by arrangement. 1 mile
to bay beach.

Directions: Route 6 to
Exit 10. Take Route
124 North to Route
6A. Travel west on
Route 6A, and proceed
approximately 1 mile
to the inn on the left.

Beechcroft Inn, a former church meeting house, has been operated as an inn since 1852. Third floor rooms have an expansive view of the bay and a charming deck in the tree tops. Bedrooms are cozy, comfortable, and carpeted in a lovely rose shade. Flowers are everywhere.

Afternoon tea and cocktails are served at a tiny bar with a fire burning in the fireplace. "Seems more like 'Old England' than New England," said one guest. A hearty buffet breakfast is served in the morning.

Poppy Seed Lemon Bread

Serve at breakfast in a large loaf or for afternoon tea in mini-loaves.

2¼ C. flour
1¼ C. sugar
1½ t. baking powder
1 T. grated lemon peel
½ t. salt
¾ C. milk
2 T. poppy seeds
1 C. butter
3 eggs

Heat oven to 350°. Grease bottom only of loaf pans. In a large bowl, mix all ingredients. Beat at medium speed until mixed, about 2 minutes. Pour into prepared pans. Bake 30-40 minutes (in minipans) or until wooden pick comes out clean. In a small bowl stir glaze ingredients. Pour over warm bread. Cool 10 minutes. Loosen edge with a knife and remove.

Glaze: ½ C. sugar, 1 ½ T. lemon juice, 3 T. melted butter.

The Bramble Inn & Restaurant

2019 Main Street
Brewster, MA 02631
(508) 896-7644

Innkeepers:
Ruth & Cliff
Manchester

Open 4/1 to 12/31.
11 rooms/11 baths.

Rates: 6/15 to Labor
Day, $75-$95 (for
two). VISA/MC
AMEX/DC/Carte
Blanche

Amenities: Children
over 8. No pets.
Tennis courts across
the street. ½-mile walk
to the beach. 10-
minute drive to The
National Seashore.

Directions: Route 6 to
Exit 10. Take Route
124 North to Route
6A. Turn right on
Route 6A to the inn
on your left.

The Bramble Inn

The Bramble Inn consists of three antique homes. The main inn, built in 1861, has four guest rooms and a restaurant. The rooms are decorated with floral papers, wicker, oak, brass, and iron furnishings and there is a decided tilt to the floors, adding to the fun of staying here. The 1849 house has 5 guest rooms with country furnishings and wallpapers. A favorite room with honeymooners is the gardener's shed, which is a tiny room off the back of the 1849 house with its own entrance and hidden deck. The Captain Bangs Pepper House, built in 1793, is a Federal-style colonial. Rooms in this house are stately with queen canopy beds and more formal surroundings.

Dinner at the inn is a must. There are five small dining rooms each seating six to twelve people. The menu is continental. An informal breakfast is served from 8:30 to 9:30 and includes fresh fruit, homebaked muffins, and cereal. Some items are seasonal, such as baked apples, frittatas, winter fruit compote, or oatmeal.

Bramble Inn's Raspberry Grand Marnier Muffins

1 stick unsalted butter, melted	½ C. milk
1 C. sugar	2 t. baking powder
2 eggs	3 T. Grand Marnier
2 C. flour	1 T. grated orange peel

Mix all ingredients together until smooth. Fold 1 ½ C. raspberries into above. Bake in muffin tins at 375° for 30 minutes. Dust with powdered sugar.

The Captain Freeman Inn

The Captain Freeman Inn faces Brewster's town green which makes for a lovely setting. Built in 1860 by a wealthy sea captain, the house has 10' ceilings and nine over nine windows reaching almost to the floor. Memorabilia belonging to the captain are on display in the parlor. Six rooms have canopy beds.

On warm summer mornings breakfast is served on the side porch overlooking the pool.

Captain Freeman Inn's Peach Muffins

2 C. flour	½ C. brown sugar
1 T. baking powder	¼ t. baking soda

¼ t. allspice

Combine above ingredients.

1 C. sour cream	1 egg
¼ C. vegetable oil	1 C. peaches, pureed

Combine wet and dry ingredients and spoon into muffin tins. Bake at 400° for 15 minutes. Makes 1 dozen muffins.

The Captain Freeman Inn

15 Breakwater Road
Brewster, MA 02631
(508) 896-7481

Innkeepers:
John & Barbara Mulkey

Open all year.
10 rooms/8 baths.

Rates: 7/1 to Labor Day, $50-$88 (for two).
VISA/MC/AMEX

Amenities: Children over 12 welcome. No pets. There is a resident cat. Swimming pool. Working fireplaces in the public rooms. 5-minute walk to the beach. No smoking in the inn.

Directions: Route 6 to Exit 10. Take Route 124 North to Route 6A. Turn right on Route 6A to Breakwater Road. Turn left to the inn.

High Brewster

964 Satucket Road
Brewster, MA 02631
(508) 896-3636

Innkeeper: Ron Patak

Open all year.
4 rooms, 1 with private
bath/3 with shared
bath.

Rates: 7/1 to Labor
Day, $35-$85 (for
two). VISA/MC

Amenities: Children
in the cottages only.
No pets. Fireplace in
one cottage. 5-minute
drive to the beach.
Seasonal gourmet
American cuisine
restaurant (no liquor
license; bring your own
spirits).

Directions: Route 6 to
Exit 9. Take Route
134 North to Route
6A. Turn right on
Route 6A to the town
of Brewster. Take the
first right, Stoney
Brook Road, to the
intersection and war
memorial. Turn right
on Satucket Road to
the inn immediately on
your left.

High Brewster

A four-star restaurant occupies the first floor of this early American restoration. The home, built in 1738, was originally the Nathaniel Winslow Homestead and offered to the Winslows through a king's grant. Three dining rooms — the Living Room, the Sitting Room, and the Borning Room — are decorated with bold print floral wallpaper, colonial green trim, and an assortment of colorful French posters. The hand-hewn beamed ceiling and the red-painted wide floor boards add to the charming colonial atmospher. Diners may bring their own bottle of wine or spirits to enjoy with dinner.

Upstairs, four restored rooms are decorated with antiques of the period. There are two cottages, both overlooking the Lower Mill Pond.

A continental breakfast is included.

High Brewster's Grilled Scallops served over Lime Chutney

2 lbs. bay or sea scallops	1 bunch coriander
1 T. lemon juice	½ C. olive oil

salt and pepper

Clean the scallops, then place them on a double skewer and lay them flat in a pan. Chop fresh coriander and blend with olive oil, lemon juice, salt, and pepper. Completely cover scallops with marinade and let sit for two hours.

Lime Chutney:

1 C. rice vinegar	1 C. brown sugar

Combine vinegar and brown sugar and bring to a boil. Add:

1 arm of fresh ginger, finely chopped	3 shallots, thinly sliced
2 small hot peppers, finely chopped	1 T. mustard seed
3 garlic cloves, finely chopped	1 dash white pepper

Simmer for 2-4 minutes. Peel and cut 6 limes into small pieces and add to the pot. Cook for 15 minutes. Add honey to taste (approximately 4 T.) to cut the tartness of the limes. Place a small amount of chutney on a plate. Grill the scallops for approximately 2 minutes on each side. Serve over chutney. Chutney should be at room temperature.

Isaiah Clark House

Guests are pampered at Isaiah Clark House. Beds with patchwork quilts are turned down at night, and guest bathrobes hang in every closet. Furnishings are simple and thoughtful, with stenciling artfully applied. Many times the bed is kitty-corner in the room, creating the focus, and one room has a skylight over the bed.

The beautiful Rose Cottage was added in 1988. It has an additional five rooms, one with a private bath, four with shared baths.

A hearty continental breakfast is served.

Isaiah Clark's Special Recipe for Lily Clark's Spice Cookies

¾ C. butter
1 C. brown sugar
1 egg
¼ C. molasses
2½ C. flour

1 t. finely chopped fresh ginger
1 t. cinnamon
2 t. baking soda
½ t. ground cloves
¼ t. salt

Cream butter with sugar; then add beaten egg and molasses. Sift together all remaining dry ingredients three or four times. Mix all ingredients. Roll into small balls and place on an ungreased cookie tray. Press ball with thumb. Cookies may be dropped in to granulated or powdered sugar after cooking. Bake in pre-heated 350° oven for 10 minutes.

Isaiah Clark House

1187 Old King's
Highway
Brewster, MA 02631
(508) 896-2223

Innkeepers: Charles De Caesare & Richard Griffin

Open 2/1 to 12/31.
7 rooms/7 baths.

Rates: 6/15 to 10/15, $75-$89 (for two).
VISA/MC/AMEX

Amenities: Children over 12 welcome. No pets. Working fireplaces. ¾-mile walk to the beach. Rates include afternoon tea, juice, and cookies.

Directions: Route 6 to Exit 9. Take Route 134 North to Route 6A. Turn right on Route 6A to the inn on your left.

Ocean Gold

74 Locust Lane
Brewster, MA 02631
(508) 255-7045

Innkeeper:
Marge Geisler

Open all year.
3 rooms/2 baths.

Rates: May to
October, $60-$85 (for
two). No credit cards
accepted.

Amenities: No
children. No pets.
Resident cats. No
smoking. Secluded
fresh water pond for
guests. 3-minute drive
to the ocean and bay
beaches.

Directions: Route 6 to
Exit 9. Turn left onto
Route 134 to Route
6A. Turn right on
Route 6A to
Nickerson State Park.
The inn is across the
road from the park.

Ocean Gold

Ocean Gold is across the road from Nickerson State Park with its miles of bike and walking paths and country setting. A beautiful secluded fresh water pond is available to guests. A two-room suite on the ground level with a kitchen unit, color television, full bath and whirlpool tub is delightful for long stays.

Breakfast is a full-country style meal, featuring homemade breads and fresh eggs from the inn's own chickens.

Ocean Gold's Pecan Pancakes

Follow the recipe for pancakes on the Bisquick box, but add ½ C. extra milk and ¾ C. chopped pecans to the batter, stirring well. When serving on a platter, place sautéed banana slices on top and sprinkle with more chopped pecans. Dust with a little confectionery sugar. Heat maple syrup before serving and offer heated apple or peach slices, cooked with a little cinnamon and nutmeg, in a side dish. Also offer bacon, ham, or breakfast patties.

The Old Manse Inn

The Old Manse Inn

1861 Main Street
Brewster, MA 02631
(508) 896-3149

Innkeepers:
Sugar & Doug
Manchester

Open 3/1 to 12/31.
9 rooms/9 baths.

Rates: 7/1 to Labor
Day, $75-$80 (for
two).
VISA/MC/AMEX

Amenities: Children
over 6 years welcome.
No pets. Full service
restaurant offers
gourmet dining from
May 15 to October 15.
10-minute walk to the
beach.

Directions: Route 6 to
Exit 9. Turn left onto
Route 134 North to
Route 6A. Turn right
onto Route 6A to
Brewster. The inn is
on the left, about 3
miles after entering
town.

It isn't often that you find innkeepers successful at innkeeping AND operating a full service restaurant. But Sugar and Doug Manchester, who own The Old Manse Inn, are. Two intimate dining rooms seat 26 by reservation only. Balloon valances dress the windows which surround one dining room. Several round tables are set with fine china and crystal from the innkeeper's private collection.

Bright colors are used throughout the guest rooms creating a light and airy feeling among the lovely antiques which furnish this stately sea captain's home. All but one room have queen-size beds with headboards made by a local craftsman, and patchwork quilts made by the ladies of the guild at the Baptist church across the street.

A full breakfast is included. Entrées served in the restaurant include sautéed soft shell crabs with maple bourbon sauce, and grilled quail on a tomato coulis with marinated black bean sauce.

The Old Manse Inn's Tomato Ginger Soup

2½" peeled and minced ginger root   1 C. homemade chicken stock
4-5 large tomatoes, peeled and seeded   1 T. sugar
1 stick (¼ lb.) unsalted butter   1 medium onion
                               ¾ C. heavy cream

Purée onion and ginger in processor. Melt butter in pan on medium heat. Add onion-ginger purée anc ook until onion softens. Process tomatoes using on/off pulse to chop them. Add onion and ginger. Add chicken stock, sugar, salt, and pepper to taste. Add cream and simmer until slightly thickened.

Old Sea Pines Inn

2553 Main Street
Brewster, MA 02631
(508) 896-6114

Innkeepers:
Michele & Stephen
Rowan

Open 4/1 to 12/22.
14 rooms/9 with
private baths/5 with
shared baths.

Rates: 7/1 to 9/6, $36-
$78 (for two).
VISA/MC/AMEX/DC

Amenities: Children
over 9 welcome. No
pets. Full service
restaurant. Working
fireplaces serviced by
the staff. 1-minute
walk to the beach.

Directions: Route 6 to
Exit 10. Follow signs
for Brewster. At the
end of Route 124, turn
right on Route 6A.
Proceed one mile to
the inn on the left.

Old Sea Pines Inn

Who can resist an inn which was once the Sea Pines School of Charm and Personality for Young Women? That was from 1907 to 1970, but the first floor still has the spaciousness of an exclusive school lobby with a grand sweeping stairway. Rooms are decorated with old wicker, old fashioned country print wallpapers, priscilla curtains, and brass and iron beds.

A full breakfast is served in the elegant mirrored dining room or on the porch. A large new addition to the inn provides more dining room seating.

Old Sea Pines Inn's Chicken Lindy

Trim a skinless, boneless, chicken breast to a heart shape and bake with no spices in white wine and water. Sauté small chunks of crabmeat with fingernail cuts of broccoli florets. Make fresh hollandaise sauce with white pepper, egg yolk, and clarified butter. Slice a ripe tomato ½″ thick, bake with fresh basil and parsley next to the chicken for 2 minutes. Mix hollandaise, crabmeat, and broccoli and spoon over chicken breast. Serve with tomato.

Chatham

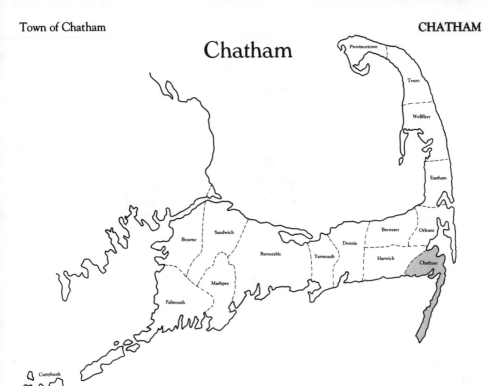

Located at the "elbow" of Cape Cod, **Chatham** is one of the most scenic towns on the Cape, overlooking the vastness of the Atlantic Ocean to the east and the serenity of Nantucket Sound to the south.

Chatham has a distinctive shopping district with fine specialty shops and restaurants, and there is also the 1797 Godfry Windmill (where corn is still ground), the historic Atwood House and the Railroad Museum to visit.

Monomoy Island, which was connected to mainland Chatham until a 1956 hurricane, is a wildlife refuge, home to over 300 bird species and considered one of the more important ornithological sites on the "Atlantic Flyway." The Chatham Coast Guard Station and the Chatham Radar Weather Observatory Station provide vital support to both recreational and commercial boating and are interesting places to visit.

The Chatham Harbor Run, a 6.2-mile road race along the seaside, takes place in June. In July, Chatham celebrates Under Chatham Blue, a professional arts and crafts exhibition, on the grounds of Chatham High School. Three ocean beaches invite your swimming.

At the end of Bridge Street, vistas of Nauset Spit, Chatham Light and Chatham Harbor await. On the bluff, one of the finest views of the Atlantic can be surveyed through public telescopes. At the Chatham Fish Pier at Aunt Lydia's Cove, fishing boats off-load daily catches for the trip to market.

Activities to be enjoyed in Chatham include golf, fishing, shellfishing, and tennis. Sailboat races take place Tuesday, Thursday, and Saturday at Pleasant Bay, and every Tuesday, Thursday, and Sunday at Stage Harbor. The Cape Soccer League begins in June, and the Cape Cod Baseball League plays in Chatham as well.

The Barnstead

22 Lorenzo Buck Way
Chatham, MA 02633
(508) 432-2685

Innkeeper:
Betsy Bloomer

Open all year.
5 rooms/3 baths.

Rates: 7/1 to Labor
Day, $55 (for two). No
credit cards accepted.

Amenities: Children
welcome. No pets.
Working fireplaces in
the main rooms. 15-
minute walk to the
beach.

Directions: Route 6 to
Exit 11. Take Route
137 South to Route
28. Turn right on
Route 28 to Lorenzo
Buck Road. Turn left
to the inn on your
right.

The Barnstead

The Barnstead is a traditional Cape Cod main house located on a secluded cul-de-sac two miles from downtown Chatham. Although it was built in 1968, the house has old-style nails in the patined wide-plank floors and sparse colonial decor that gives it the feel of an older inn. Furnishings are comfortable and tastefully done in colors of the Southwest. A converted barn with a vaulted ceiling and fireplace is open during the the summer season. It has three guest rooms and a large living space—quite private for wedding guests or others traveling together.

A continental breakfast is included.

The Barnstead's Banana Bread

2 C. flour	1 C. sugar
1 t. baking soda	2 eggs
½ C. margarine	1 C. ripe mashed bananas

1 T. vinegar and enough milk to make ½ C. liquid

Sift flour and baking soda, and then cream margarine, and sugar. Add the eggs and beat until fluffy. Add flour mixture alternately with the bananas and liquid. Pour into a well-greased loaf pan and bake for 1 hour at 350°. Cool before serving. This recipe makes one loaf.

Bradford Inn & Motel

There are seven buildings in the Bradford Inn & Motel complex. The Captain Elijah Smith House, circa 1860, is the oldest. Others, such as the Jonathan Gray House, imitate an older time. Most of the inn and motel rooms are on ground level. They are all decorated in a style reminiscent of Williamsburg, Virginia, with canopy beds and fireplaces.

Just opened is the Lion's Den, a large fireplaced living room for guests to visit, relax, or perhaps get acquainted with one of the resident cats. At the rear of the Captain's House, nestled within the garden area near the pool, is a two-bedroom cottage. It is cozy and private, a perfect place to spend a romantic evening.

A full breakfast with New England favorites is served, along with specialties of the house. Your are invited to take your coffee by the pool.

Bradford Inn's Baked Stuffed Quahogs

1 small loaf of dry bread, crumbled
4 strips bacon, cooked and crumbled
    save drippings
                1 T. Romano cheese

1 T. parsley
few drops Tobasco
enough milk to wet bread

Mix all of above together and set aside.

Sauté in 2 T. bacon drippings: **1 small onion, minced**
                                      1 small green pepper, minced
                                      1 stalk celery, minced
                                      1 carrot, minced

When tender, add 3 T. sherry. Combine bread mixture with sautéed vegetables. Stir in 1 pint chopped quahogs and enough clam juice to moisten. Fill clean clam shells and drizzle stuffing with oil. Sprinkle with paprika. Microwave 3 minutes or bake in 375° oven for 12-15 minutes. Broil top slightly if desired. Garnish with lemon slices.

Bradford Inn & Motel
26 Cross Street
Chatham, MA 02633
(508) 945-1030

Innkeepers: William & Audrey Gray

Open all year.
25 rooms/25 baths.

Rates: 6/30 to 9/3, $105-$162 (for two). AMEX/DIS/VISA/MC

Amenities: Children over 8 welcome. No pets. Outdoor heated pool. Full service restaurant and liquor license. Eight fireplaces. All rooms are equipped with refrigerators, televisions, and telephones. 4-minute walk to the beach.

Directions: Route 6 to Exit 11. Take Route 137 South and proceed approximately 3 miles to Route 28. Turn left on Route 28 towards Chatham Center. At the rotary, go straight through to Main Street. Cross Street will be on your right.

Captain's House Inn of Chatham

369 Old Harbor Road
Chatham, MA 02633
(508) 945-0127

Innkeepers:
Cathy and Dave Eakin

Open 2/1 to 12/1.
14 rooms/14 baths.

Rates: 6/1 to 10/23,
$95-$135 (for two).
VISA/MC/AMEX

Amenities: No
children. No pets.
Working fireplaces. 10-
minute walk to the
beach.

Directions: Route 6 to
Exit 11. Take Route
137 South to Route
28. Turn left on Route
28 to Chatham
Center. At Chatham
Center follow the
rotary out of town on
Route 28 toward
Orleans. The inn is
about ½ mile ahead on
your left.

Captain's House Inn of Chatham

The elegant Captain's House Inn of Chatham has been awarded Four Diamonds by AAA. Built in 1839, the inn is a white Greek Revival style home with handsome tavern green shutters. Innkeepers Cathy and Dave Eakin have maintained the elegance of early American life by decorating with furnishings reminiscent of Williamsburg, Virginia. A crackling fire in the fireplace greets you as you enter the reception room which still has the original random width pumpkin pine floors and period wallpapers. Guest rooms have a variety of furnishings, including four-poster beds with pineapple finials, lacy white fishnet canopies, plush velvet wing chairs, braided rugs, and fireplaces in three of the rooms.

Additional lodging is provided in the Captain's Cottage and the Carriage House. The cottage, a full Cape with three guest rooms, boasts the features of a 200-year-old home. A white picket fence borders the cottage's garden of lady slippers, forget-me-nots, and heather.

An extensive continental breakfast is served.

The Captain's House Inn's Apple Bread

½ C. butter
1 C. sugar
2 large eggs
1 t. vanilla extract
2 C. flour
1 T. baking soda

½ t. salt
1 t. grated lemon rind
¼ t. cardamom (optional)
1/3 C. orange juice
2 C. coarsely chopped apples
1/3 C. chopped walnuts

Cream the butter and sugar. Add the eggs and vanilla extract and beat. Sift dry ingredients and add them alternately with the orange juice, then fold in the apples and nuts. Top with Streussel Topping. Bake in a buttered loaf pan at 350° for 55 minutes or until loaf tests done.

Streussel Topping: ¼ C. melted butter   ¼ C. flour
                     ¼ C. sugar   ½ t. cinnamon

Rub butter into mixed dry ingredients. Mix well and sprinkle on top of bread before baking.

Chatham Village Inn

Chatham Villiage Inn is a quaint guest house, part of a complex of three buildings in the "Old Village" area of Chatham. The inn building is a 75-year-old Cape Cod home decorated with country antiques and hand-stenciled borders on bedroom walls. A fireplace and a baby grand piano are in the parlor. The brick patio and an old fashioned herb garden make a lovely spot to sit. A recent guest commented that the innkeepers "have captured the spirit of Cape Cod."

The continental breakfast features homemade blueberry buckle, molasses bread, or cranberry walnut muffins, and gourmet Swiss chocolate almond coffee.

Chatham Village Inn's Molasses Bread

Sift together: ¾ C. granulated sugar
2½ C. flour
½ t. salt

Add to the above ingredients: 1 C. cooking oil
1 C. dark molasses
1 egg
1 C. boiling water to mix
with 1 t. baking soda

Pour batter into a greased and floured bundt or angelfood cake pan. Bake at 350° for 1 hour. Serve warm with whipped cream cheese. Any of the following can be added to the bread batter: ¾ C. chopped walnuts, ¾ C. golden raisins, ¾ C. peeled chopped apples.

Chatham Village Inn
207 Main Street
Chatham, MA 02633
(508) 945-0792

Innkeepers: Ellen & Walter Ripley

Open all year.
11 rooms/7 baths.

Rates: 5/30 to 10/30, $80-$90 (for two).
VISA/MC/AMEX

Amenities: Children over 10 years welcome. No pets. Full breakfast, lunch, and dinner available at The Tavern restaurant. Working fireplace. 2-minute walk to the beach.

Directions: Route 6 to Exit 11. Turn left onto Route 137, and proceed 3 miles to Route 28 (Main Street). Turn left and proceed through Chatham center to the stop sign at the intersection of Main Street & Shore Road. Turn right to the inn on your right.

The Cranberry Inn at Chatham

359 Main Street
Chatham, MA 02633
(508) 945-9232

Innkeeper:
Peggy DeHan

Open all year.
14 rooms/14 baths.

Rates: Memorial Day
to Columbus Day, $98
(for two).
VISA/MC/AMEX

Amenities: Children
over 12 years welcome.
No pets. Working
fireplace. 10-minute
walk to the beach.

Directions: Route 6 to
Exit 11. Turn left on
Route 137 and proceed
to Route 28. Turn left
on Route 28 and
follow to rotary. At
the rotary go straight
to Main Street and
follow to the inn.

The Cranberry Inn

The Cranberry Inn has provided lodging for more than a century. However, 1989 will be mark its first season under new management. Peggy DeHan has refurbished and restored the inn to its former beauty and charm. The guest rooms are tastefully decorated with attractive window and wall coverings, and antique and reproduction furnishings.

Continental breakfast is served in the dining room or on the patio or porch.

The Cranberry Inn's Walnut Breakfast Pastries

1 pkg. dry yeast	¾ C. milk, scalded
¼ C. shortening	1 egg beaten
3 T. sugar	3 C. sifted all-purpose flour
1½ t. salt	¾ C. chopped walnuts
melted butter	strawberry or apricot preserves
1 C. sifted confectioner's sugar	¼ t. almond extract

Soften the yeast in ¼ C. warm water. Add shortening, sugar, and salt to milk in a large bowl. Stir until shortening melts and sugar dissolves. Cool to lukewarm. Add egg and yeast, and mix well. Stir in half the flour, beat until smooth. Add walnuts. Blend in remaining flour gradually. Drop by heaping tablespoons onto lightly greased baking sheets. Brush with butter. Let rise for 1 hour or until doubled in bulk. With back of spoon, make indentation and place spoonful of preserve into the middle of each roll. Bake at 350° for about 25 minutes or until brown. Combine confectioner's sugar, 1 T. water, and almond extract in a bowl. Drizzle over cooled buns. Yield: 1 dozen. To make more (24 or 36), use teaspoons to drop batter onto baking sheet.

Cyrus Kent House

The old and the new coexist nicely at Cyrus Kent House. The living room combines a magnificent marble fireplace, ceiling rosettes, and elaborate plaster molding with modern over-stuffed couches and original art.

A continental breakfast is served buffet-style in the hall on a lovely antique breakfront. Guests carry their breakfast to the period-style dining room where they sit around a long table and discuss plans for the day.

Cyrus Kent House's
Currant-Cream Scones

1/3 C. margarine, butter, or shortening	½ t. salt
1¾ C. flour	1 beaten egg
3 T. sugar	½ C. currants or raisins
2½ t. baking powder	4-6 T. half-and-half

1 beaten egg (for brushing on scones)

Heat oven to 400°. Cut margarine into flour, sugar, baking powder, and salt until mixture resembles fine crumbs. Stir in 1 egg, the currants, and just enough half-and-half so dough leaves sides of bowl. Turn dough onto lightly floured surface. Knead lightly 10 times. Roll ½" thick. Cut dough into 2½" circles with floured cutter. Place on ungreased cookie sheet. Brush with egg. Bake until golden, 10-12 minutes. Immediately remove from cookie sheet. Yield: 10-12 scones. Enjoy!

Cyrus Kent House

63 Cross Street
Chatham, MA 02633
(508) 945-9104

Innkeeper: Richard T. Morris

Open 3/15 to 12/20. 8 rooms/8 baths.

Rates: 5/27 to 10/12, $98 (for two). All major credit cards accepted.

Amenities: Children over 12 welcome. No pets. Working fireplaces. Telephone in room. 5-minute walk to the beach.

Directions: Route 6 to Exit 11. Take Route 137 South to Route 28. Turn left on Route 28 to the center of town. Turn right at Cross Street to the inn on your left.

The Inn at the Dolphin

352 Main Street
Chatham, MA 02633
(508) 945-0070

Innkeepers:
The Kennedys

Open all year.
7 rooms/7 baths.

Rates: 6/30 to 9/5,
$105-$145 (for two).
VISA/MC/AMEX/DIS

Amenities: There is a
charge for breakfast.
No children. No pets.
Hot tub. Color TV in
all rooms. Working
fireplaces. Swimming
pool. 2-minute walk to
the beach. Full service
restaurant providing
breakfast and lunch
daily, dinner by
reservation, brunch on
Sunday. The
restaurant is
occasionally made
available for special
private functions.

Directions: Route 6 to
Exit 11. Take Route
137 South to Route
28. Turn left on Route
28 to the inn on your
left.

The Inn at the Dolphin

The Inn at the Dolphin has been awarded Three Diamonds from AAA and the Mobil Guide. This 1805 captain's inn in the historic district of the village has been restored with m odern conveniences. Most guest roms have a water view. Some rooms have jacuzzis in the bath. The swimming pool and hot tub in the garden are a wonderful treat. In addition to the inn, there is a motel on the grounds.

A full breakfast is available at the restaurant.

The Inn at the Dolphin's Veal Bontemps

4 oz. of medallions of veal   **Apple Jack Brandy**
heavy cream   **green apples and raisins**

Sauté veal with Apple Jack Brandy then reduce in a demi-glaze and heavy cream. Finish off with apples and raisins.

The Old
Harbor Inn
22 Old Harbor Road
Chatham, MA 02633
(508) 945-4434

Innkeepers: Sharon &
Tom Ferguson

Open all year.
6 rooms/6 baths.

Rates: April to
October, $95-$125 (for
two).
VISA/MC/AMEX

Amenities: Children
over 14 welcome. No
pets. Working fireplace
in the Common Room.
Conferences welcome.
3-minute walk to the
beach.

Directions: Route 6 to
Exit 11. Take Route
137 South to Route
28. Turn left on Route
28 and proceed 3.4
miles to the rotary.
Stay on Route 28
South, which is Old
Harbor Road. The inn
will be immediately on
your right.

The Old Harbor Inn

Innkeepers Sharon and Tom Ferguson have retired from the corporate life and are in their second season at The Old Harbor Inn. They now help others to kick off their shoes and escape the "rat race." The inn has been graciously and carefully renovated in an elegant country style. Antique furnishings and Laura Ashley linens blend nicely with modern conveniences creating a pleasant, relaxed ambience.

Homemade breakfast is a special treat outside on the deck, weather permitting. Otherwise it is served in the sunroom, a pretty room with wicker furniture and a stenciled floor.

Old Harbor Inn's
Scottish Oat Scones

2/3 C. butter, melted	¼ C. sugar
1/3 C. milk	1 T. baking powder
1 egg	1 t. cream of tartar
1½ C. all-purpose flour	½ t. salt
1¼ C. quick Quaker Oats, uncooked	½ C. raisins

Combine dry ingredients. Add butter, milk, and egg and mix just until dry ingredients are moistened. Stir in raisins. Shape dough to form a ball; pat out on lightly floured surface to form 8" circle about ¾" thick. Cut into 8-12 wedges. Bake on greased cookie sheet in preheated 425° oven for 12-15 minutes or until light golden brown. Serve warm with butter, honey or preserves, as desired. Yield 8-12 scones.

Queen Anne Inn

70 Queen Anne Road
Chatham, MA 02633
(508) 945-0394 or
(800) 545-INNS

Innkeepers: Guenther
& Nickie Weinkopf

Evelyn Simek,
Manager

Open 4/15 to 11/30.
30 rooms/30 baths.

Rates: $96-$196 (for
two).
AMEX/VISA/MC

Amenities: Children
welcome. No pets.
Tennis courts. Spa.
Whirlpools. Air
conditioning. Working
fireplaces. All rooms
have telephones. $3.00
daily housekeeping
service charge. Full
service restaurant. 2-
minute walk to the
beach.

Directions: Route 6 to
Exit 11. Turn South
on Route 137 to Route
28. Turn left on Route
28 toward Chatham
Center. At your first
traffic light, turn right
on Queen Anne Road
to the inn on your
right.

Queen Anne Inn

The furnishings at Queen Anne Inn are beautiful, elegant, and massive — there are magnificent carved poster beds with matching dressers and desks. Some rooms have balconies overlooking the garden or Oyster Bay. Some have working fireplaces and private whirlpools. The public rooms are comfortable and papered with a colonial-style wallpaper.

The inn has the charm and amenities of a small European hotel: new clay tennis courts, boats for guests' use, and a spa, in addition to a full service restaurant. A continental breakfast is served to inn guests.

Queen Anne Inn's Apple Pie

Pastry Crust:

2¾ C. flour	1 pinch salt
1 C. butter	1 drop vanilla extract
1 C. and 3 T. confectioner's sugar	½ t. each finely chopped
	lemon zest and orange zest

Sift flour into a bowl. Make a depression in the center. Dice the butter and place it in the center. Mix flour and butter into a fine, well blended mixture using finger tips. Add all other seasonings. Knead the mixture into a medium firm dough. Let the dough rest for a minimum of one hour. While dough is resting, begin filling preparation.

Preheat oven to 380°. Set 1/3 of dough aside for top of pie. Roll dough into flat square (⅛" thickness). Place the dough in a 9" metal pie pan which has been greased and lightly sprinkled with flour.

Mix together: 1/3 C. sliced almonds, ¼ C. bread crumbs. Place in pie pan over bottom of pie crust dough.

Pie Filling:

5 large Macintosh apples, peeled and sliced into ¼" pieces.

1 t. cinnamon	¼ C. granulated sugar (to taste)
2 T. lemon juice	1 T. rum
1 drop vanilla extract	

Mix ingredients well and let sit for 30 minutes. Place filling in pie shell, over almond and bread crumb layer. Cover with remaining dough. Trim and decorate crust and rim. Brush crust evenly with egg wash (1 egg yolk lightly beaten). Bake at 380° for 40 minues. Serve fresh and warm with whipped cream.

The Ships Inn at Chatham

364 Old Harbor Road
Chatham, MA 02633
(508) 945-5859

Innkeeper:
Peggy DeHan

Open all year.
6 rooms/6 baths.

Rates: Memorial Day
to Columbus Day, $95
(for two).
VISA/MC/AMEX

Amenities: Children
over 12 welcome. No
pets. Three working
fireplaces. 15-minute
walk to the beach.

Directions: Route 6 to
Exit 11. Take Route
137 South to Route
28. Turn left on Route
28 towards Chatham
Center. At the rotary,
proceed to Route 28
South, which is Old
Harbor Road. The inn
is about ½ mile ahead
on the right.

The Ships Inn at Chatham

The 1989 season will be the second one for this newly restored whaling captain's home. Innkeeper Peggy DeHan is experienced, though, and she has decorated the inn to enhance the history and charm of a grand old New England home. The house features wide planked floors, stencilled walls, original Sandwich window glass, and Barnstable brick. The guest rooms are furnished with antiques and reproductions. Some have brass and four-poster beds, and all have telephones.

The atmosphere is friendly and informal. The hearty continental breakfast includes homemade breads and house specialties and is served out on the porch or terrace, in nice weather.

Ships Inn at Chatham's English Muffin Loaf

For 2 loaves:

6 C. unsifted bread flour	¼ t. baking soda
2 pkgs. dry yeast	2 C. milk
1 T. sugar	½ C. water
2 t. salt	cornmeal

Preheat oven to 400°. Combine 3 C. flour, undissolved yeast, sugar, salt, and baking soda. Heat milk and water until warm. Add to dry ingredients and beat well. Stir in remaining flour to make a stiff batter. Pour into two 8" x 4" greased loaf pans that have been spinkled with cornmeal. Sprinkle tops with cornmeal. Cover and let rise for 45 minutes in a warm place. Bake for 25 minutes. Remove from pans and cool.

Ye Olde Nantucket House

2647 Main Street
South Chatham, MA
02659
(508) 432-5641

Innkeeper:
Peggy DeHan

Open all year.
5 rooms/5 baths.

Rates: Memorial Day
to 9/15, $60-$72 (for
two). VISA/MC

Amenities: Children
over 8 welcome. No
pets. Non-working
fireplaces. 10-minute
walk to the beach.

Directions: Route 6 to
Exit 11. Take Route
137 South to Route
28. Turn right on
Route 28. The inn is ¾
mile ahead on the left.

Ye Olde Nantucket House

Ye Olde Nantucket House was originally built on Nantucket before its prosperous whaling industry began to fail. In about 1867 the inn was floated to its present location. It is in Cape Cod farmhouse style, one room leading into another, bookcases built into doors, a narrow staircase, pine floors, nooks and crannies. The stencilling and window and wall coverings create a "country Victorian" ambience.

A hearty continental breakfast is served in the bright dining room.

Ye Olde Nantucket House's Blueberry Bread

This recipe was given to the innkeeper by a guest, and has become a favorite of many guests.

2 T. butter/margarine	2 C. sifted flour
¼ C. boiling water	1 T. baking powder
½ C. orange juice	¼ t. baking soda
1 egg	½ t. salt
1 C. sugar	1 C. blueberries (fresh or frozen)

Melt butter in boiling water. Add ½ C. orange juice. Beat eggs and sugar until light. Add sifted dry ingredients and liquid to beaten eggs and sugar. Beat until smooth. Add blueberries. Pour into greased and floured loaf pan (9″ x 5″ x 3″). Bake at 325° to 350° for about 1 hour. For a variation, add streusel topping before cooking; mix 2 T. each of margarine, sugar, and flour. Add cinnamon to taste and mix until crumbly. Sprinkle on top of batter.

Dennis

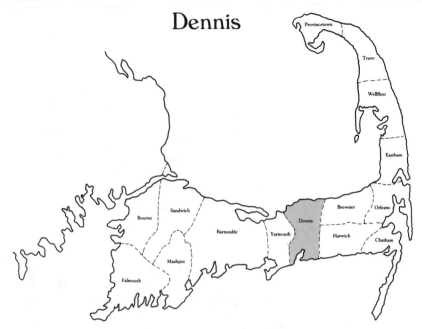

Dennis crosses the Cape from Cape Cod Bay to the Nantucket Sound. From its quieter village along Route 6A, to the hustle and bustle of **Dennis Port** on Route 28, to **South Dennis** and **West Dennis**, this is a microcosm of the entire Cape.

A small white church and cemetery are the first sights you see upon entering Dennis from Route 6A. Nearby Scargo Hill is one of the highest points on Cape Cod. Legend has it that Scargo Lake was dug by Indians using clam shells. The lake is known for containing some of the finest black bass.

The world-famous Cape Playhouse is the oldest professional regional theatre in the country. In the same complex is the Cape Cod Museum of Fine Arts. Nationally known auctions take place regularly at Eldred's Auction House in East Dennis. The Old Sound Phonograph Museum has a collection of antique phonographs, radios, and recordings.

Packet and clipper ships were built in Shiverick Shipyard. Salt production in the marshes was a major enterprise in former days. Dennis has beaches on both sides of the Cape at Bay View Road, Chapin Beach, Cold Storage Road, Corporation Road, Glendon Road, Haigis Beach, Harbor View Beach (Sesuit Neck), Howes Street, Inman Road, Mayflower Beach, and West Dennis Beach off Route 28.

Deep sea fishing boats leave from Sesuit Harbor. Excellent golfing is available at Dennis Pines Golf Course. For jogging enthusiasts, there is a one-and-a half mile trail called the "Lifecourse," at the corner of Access and Old Bass River Roads. The winding path through the woods is open to the public free of charge. Nearby, off Route 143, are handball and basketball courts.

The Josiah Dennis Manse, a restored 1736 saltbox home, has an exhibition of artifacts describing the maritime history of Dennis, the building of clipper ships, the salt works, light ships, and whaling.

The Four
Chimneys
Inn

946 Route 6A
Dennis, MA 02638
(508) 385-6317

Innkeepers: Christina
Jervant & Diane
Robinson

Open 3/1 to 1/1.
9 rooms/8 baths.

Rates: July 1 to Labor
Day, $45-$85 (for
two). MC/VISA

Amenities: Children
over 8 welcome. No
pets. 10-minute walk
to the beach. Working
fireplaces.

Directions: Route 6 to
Exit 8; turn left on
Union Street. At the
end of this street, turn
right onto Route 6A
for 3/8 mile to the inn
on your left.

The Four Chimneys Inn

The first thing guests notice, after the pink geraniums everywhere, is that there are no curtains on the windows in the common rooms of The Four Chimneys Inn. High windows that reach from ceiling to floor show off their Victorian molding and give a cool, spacious feeling. Fireplaces warm the living room and dining room on cool evenings. Guest bedrooms are equally grand, bright, and airy. The third floor room has a deck for sitting. Other rooms in the front of the house have wonderful views of Scargo Lake.

Breakfast is served on the screened-in summer porch at individual tables or around the big table in the dining room.

The Four Chimneys Inn's
Cranberry Coffee Cake

Cream ½ C. margarine and 1 C. sugar. Add 2 eggs and mix dry ingredients separately:

1 t. baking powder   ¼ t. salt
1 t. baking soda   2 C. flour

Mix with sugar mixture. Blend in 1 t. almond extract and 1 C. sour cream. Pour ½ mixture into a greased tube pan. Place ½ can (8 oz.) cranberry sauce and ½ C. walnuts on batter. Repeat. Cut through mixture with a knife to swirl. Bake at 350° for 55-60 minutes.

Isaiah Hall
B & B Inn
152 Whig Street
Dennis, MA 02638
(508) 385-9928

Innkeepers:
Marie & Dick Brophy

Open mid-March to
mid-November.
11 rooms/10 baths.

Rates: 6/16 to Labor
Day, $48-$80 (for
two).
VISA/MC/AMEX.

Amenities: Children
over 8 welcome. No
pets. One fireplaced
room. 15-minute walk
to the beach. Cable
TV. Smoking limited
to carriage house.

Directions: Route 6 to
Exit 8. Turn left on
Union Street and
proceed 1.2 miles to
Route 6A. Turn right
on Route 6A for 3.4
miles to Hope Lane
(opposite church and
cemetery). Turn left
on Hope Lane to the
end, then turn right
on Whig Street to the
inn on the left.

Isaiah Hall B & B Inn

Innkeepers Marie and Dick Brophy deserve their Three Diamonds from AAA and more. They see to every comfort of their guests in the great Cape Cod tradition at their Isaiah Hall B & B Inn. The inn exudes a casual country warmth with antiques, Oriental and braided rugs, scrubbed pine beds and magnificent handmade quilts from Nova Scotia. The parlor of the main house looks like a typical antique New England room, complete with coal stove.

The carriage house has a more casual atmosphere — white wicker in the great room, and rooms decorated in knotty pine and stenciling. Some rooms have decks overlooking the garden or an extra single bed. Terry cloth robes and hair dryers are provided for guests.

A long table with eight leaves is the setting for a breakfast that includes homemade breads and muffins.

Isaiah Hall's Any Fruit Coffee Cake

**4 C. chopped apples, apricots, peaches, pineapple,
blueberries, blackberries, or raspberries**

1 C. water	1 t. salt
2 T. lemon juice	1 C. margarine/butter
1¼ C. sugar	2 slightly beaten eggs
1/3 C. cornstarch	1 C. milk
3 C. flour	1 C. sugar
1 t. vanilla	1 T. baking powder
1 t. cinnamon	

Topping:
½ C. sugar	½ C. flour
¼ C. butter/margarine	1 C. chopped walnuts

In a saucepan, combine fruit and 1 C. water and simmer for 5 minutes until tender. Stir in lemon juice, 1 ¼ C. sugar, and cornstarch. Cook and stir until thickened, then cool. Mix together 3 C. flour, 1 C. sugar, baking powder, cinnamon, and salt, then cut in butter until mixture is fine crumbs. Combine eggs, milk, and vanilla. Add to flour mixture and mix well until blended. Spread ½ of the batter in a 13" x 9" x 2" baking pan or two greased 8" x 8" x 2" pans. Spread fruit mixture over batter. Spoon rest of the batter over fruit and spread. Combine the ½ C. sugar and ½ C. flour. Cut in ¼ C. butter until crumbly. Stir in nuts and sprinkle over batter. Bake at 350° for 40-50 minutes (13" pan) or 40-45 minutes (8" pans).

Ocean View Lodge & Cottages

5 Depot Street
Dennis Port, MA
02639
(508) 398-3412

Innkeepers:
Mr. & Mrs. Valente

Open May to October.
3 rooms/2 baths.

Rates: 6/30 to Labor
Day, $30-$35 (for
two). No credit cards
accepted.

Amenities: Children
welcome in the
cottages only. No pets.
1-minute walk to the
beach.

Directions: Route 6 to
Exit 9. South for 2
miles on Route 134.
Turn left on Route 28
for 1 mile to Depot
Street. Turn right and
proceed almost to the
end of the street. The
lodge is on your right.

Ocean View Lodge & Cottages

A real family-style lodge near the ocean, the Ocean View is immaculately clean. There is a spacious knotty pine-paneled TV lounge. Guest bedrooms are bright and comfortable with a view of the ocean. For those who prefer cottage accommodations, there are two-and four-bedroom cottages, each having a living room, kitchen, and porch. They are fully equipped for housekeeping except for linens. The cottages are ideal for young families with children of all ages. Guests have commented on the relaxing and pleasant atmosphere.

A continental breakfast is offered every morning.

Ocean View Lodge's Banana-Nut Bread

1/3 C. shortening	1 t. baking powder
½ C. sugar	½ t. baking soda
2 eggs	½ t. salt
1¾ C. sifted all-purpose flour	1 C. mashed ripe banana
½ C. chopped walnuts	

Cream together shortening and sugar; add eggs and beat well. Sift dry ingredients together, add to creamed mixture alternately with bananas blending well after each addition. Stir in nuts. Pour into well-greased 9½" x 5" x 3" loaf pan. Bake in moderate oven (350°) for 40-50 minutes or until done. Remove from pan, cool on rack.

The Rose
Petal Bed &
Breakfast

152 Sea Street
Dennis Port, MA
02639
(508) 398-8470

The Rose Petal Bed & Breakfast

Innkeepers Dan and Gayle Kelly have completely restored and decorated their 1872 Cape house, which is set in the middle of other century-old houses and cottages on the way to the beach at Nantucket Sound. There is a television and a piano in the guest parlor and a refrigerator on the enclosed back porch. Guest rooms have big fluffy terry robes, color coordinated with the bath towels.

Dan Kelly is a baker by profession and bakes all the breads. Even the French toast is made with home-baked bread. A full breakfast is served, featuring items like Eggs Benedict and coffee cakes.

The Rose Petal's Coffee Cake

Mix: 1 ¾ C. sugar   2 2/3 C. cake flour
     ¾ C. shortening   2 t. salt
     ¼ C. margarine   1 t. baking powder

Nut Mixture: Combine **1 C. pecans, ¼ C. sugar, and 2 T. cinnamon**

Add ½ C. milk and mix for five minutes. Add 5 eggs and mix five more minutes. Spread ¼ batter into a well greased 8″ cake pan. Cover with ¼ of the topping mixture. Pour the remainder of the batter into the pan and top with nut mixture. Bake at 350° until done, about 30-35 minutes. Makes two cakes.

Innkeepers:
Dan & Gayle Kelly

Open all year.
4 rooms/2 baths.

Rates: Mid-June to Labor Day, $47-$50 (for two). VISA/MC

Amenities: Children welcome. No pets. 7-minute walk to the beach.

Directions: Route 6 to Exit 9. Turn right onto Route 134. Follow to the end, then turn left onto Lower County Road. Proceed 1 ½ miles to Sea Street. Turn right to the first house on the left.

Country Pineapple Inn

370 Main Street
South Dennis, MA
02660
(508) 760-3211

Innkeepers:
Barbara & Tracy Olsen

Open all year
3 rooms/2 baths.

Rates: 5/15 to 10/15,
$60-$75 (for two). No
credit cards accepted.

Amenities: Chldren
over 10 welcome. No
pets. Two working
fireplaces. Bike trail is
a 5-minute ride away,
as is the beach.
Smoking permitted
outdoors only.

Directions: Route 6 to
Exit 9. Turn right onto
Route 134. At the
third traffic light,
immediately past the
intersection, turn right
onto Duck Pond Road.
Follow to the end.
Turn left to the first
white house on your
left.

Country Pineapple Inn

Guests pass a neatly tended herb garden as they approach Country Pineapple Inn. This is the second seasons for the charming bed and breakfast and there is a real appreciation for authenticity here. The guest quarters occupy the second floor. Rooms are beautifully decorated with antiques as well as fine reproductions. The formal sitting room with a fireplace is done in Queen Anne and Chippendale period decor.

The Wedgewood room is more formal, with its antique Oriental rug, crewel wing chair, and period double bed. The Ashley room is in white wicker and pink roses. The Bayberry room has white iron twin beds covered in green ticking bordered with country ducks, which complement the scrubbed pine dresser.

A continental breakfast features home baked breads, served in the country-style "Keeping Room."

Country Pineapple Inn's Blueberry Coffee Cake

¼ C. shortening	½ C. milk
2 C. flour	½ t. salt
¾ C. sugar	1 egg
2 t. baking powder	2 C. blueberries

Sift dry ingredients. Cream shortening and sugar. Add egg to milk and mix together until smooth and then add dry ingredients. Fold in blueberries. Put in greased 8″ pan. Sprinkle crumb topping on top, and bake at 375° for 40-45 minutes.

Crumb Topping
Mix: ½ C. **sugar**	¼ C. flour
½ t. **cinnamon**	¼ C. butter

The Lighthouse Inn

Soon after the Stones bought The Lighthouse Inn in 1938, they started a dining room as a service to their guests, since the West Dennis area was so isolated. Their son was recruited to manage the dining room. He hired a college student waitress for the summer who captured his heart. A short while later they were married, and now the third generation, Jonathan Stone, is active in running the inn. The Lighthouse Inn is a rustic family lodge on the shores of Nantucket Sound, with the protection and care reminiscent of those found in the Catskills or the Poconos. The center section of the main house was the Bass River Lighthouse from 1850-1914; it is full of tradition yet equipped with all the comforts of today. There are a few rooms in the main house, but most are in private cottages on a knoll or on the waterfront.

The view of the ocean is spectacular from the library, common room, or dining room. A children's director plans activities for the kids. Miniature golf, putting, shuffleboard, tennis, horseshoes, ping pong, billiards, and a private beach are all on the property. Specialties of the inn include Sunday night buffets and luncheons served outdoors at the pool and by the sea.

A full breakfast is included.

The Lighthouse Inn's Fresh Strawberry Soup

2 T. cornstarch
½ C. water
2 C. Port wine

1 qt. fresh strawberries
1/3 C. sugar
1 C. sour cream

juice of 1 fresh lemon

Blend cornstarch with water in a saucepan. Simmer and add Port wine. Wash, hull and cut up fresh strawberries, and add to simmering ingredients. In a separate bowl, blend together sugar, lemon juice, and sour cream. When well-blended, add to the rest. Bring soup to boil and continue boiling for 1 minute. Chill and serve in frosted champagne glasses.

The Lighthouse Inn
Lighthouse Road
West Dennis, MA
02670
(508) 398-2244

Innkeepers:
The Stone Family

Open mid-May to late October.
60 rooms/60 baths.

Rates: 6/30 to Labor Day, $65-$90 per person per day (incl. breakfast/dinner).
VISA/MC

Amenities: Children welcome. No pets. Two tennis courts. Solar heated pool. Fireplaces. All rooms have televisions, refrigerators, and hair dryers. Full service restaurant. Private beach.

Directions: Route 6 to Exit 8. Turn right onto Union Street. Follow Union Street to Route 28. Turn left onto Route 28, follow for about a mile, and turn right at the Texaco station onto School Street. Follow School Street about a half mile and watch for signs to the Lighthouse Inn on the right.

Eastham

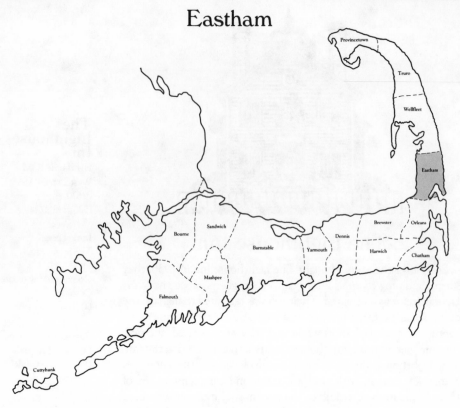

The villages of **Eastham** and **North Eastham** are located on the Lower Cape and are a more tranquil part of Cape Cod. Beaches include Campground Beach, Coast Guard Beach, Cooks Brook Beach, First Encounter Beach, Great Pond Beach, Nauset Light, Sunken Meadow, and Wiley Park.

The Cape Cod National Seashore, which protects 27,000 acres of beaches and dunes, runs through Eastham. The Salt Pond Visitors Center is the orientation center for the National Seashore, with a nature museum, gift shop, and film auditorium. The Visitor's Center is the starting point for many nature paths and the Cape Cod Rail Trail which offers miles of bicycle trails to explore the dunes.

There are artisan galleries to browse through, and fine restaurants and accommodations to enjoy in the village of North Eastham and Eastham itself. The Eastham 1896 Schoolhouse Museum is a one-room schoolhouse preserving Indian artifacts and farming and nautical implements. Another restoration open to the public is the Captain Edward Penniman House on Fort Hill Road, a 19th century Victorian home of a whaling captain.

The Over Look Inn

This restored Victorian sea captain's house is presided over by innkeepers Ian and Nan Aitchison, who are Scottish. Queen-size brass beds, claw foot bathtubs, wicker, lace, and a lovely Victorian parlor with a life-size doll all retain the original charm of the era. Big, puffy "duvets" grace each bed. They are stuffed with down and are removed each day for laundering. Each room carries out a different pastel color scheme with imaginative use of color accents.

Guests are offered many amenities, but the most unusual is the billiard room. A full breakfast is served at a leisurely pace in the Andrew Wyeth dining room. Afternoon tea is in the parlor, and guests are invited to special holiday dinners.

The Over Look Inn's Country Breakfast

6 slices bacon, diced
4 C. cooked potatoes, cubed
½ C. chopped green pepper

2 T. chopped onion
6 eggs
1 C. shredded cheddar cheese

Cook the bacon in a skillet until crisp; remove from the skillet and pour off the excess fat. Add the potatoes, green pepper, and onion to the skillet. Cook until lightly browned. Break the eggs over the potato mixture. Cover and cook until the eggs reach the desired firmness. Sprinkle with cheese and bacon. Cover and heat until the cheese is melted. Serves 6.

The Over Look Inn

Route 6, County Road
Eastham, MA 02642
(508) 255-1886

Innkeepers:
Ian & Nan Aitchison

Open all year.
8 rooms/8 baths.

Rates: 6/15 to 9/15,
$80 (for two).
VISA/MC/AMEX

Amenities: Children over 12 years welcome. No pets. Working fireplaces. Half-hour walk along the bike/nature trail to the beach (1 mile). Rate includes afternoon tea. Smoking permitted only in the library.

Directions: Route 6 to the Orleans rotary. The inn is on Route 6 in the town of Eastham on your left.

Whalewalk Inn

Whalewalk Inn
169 Bridge Road
Eastham, MA 02642
(508) 255-0617

Innkeepers: Ginny &
Norm de la Chapelle

Open April 1 to
December 1.
7 rooms/7 baths.

Rates: 7/1 to 9/30,
$95-$145 (for two). No
credit cards. Personal
checks accepted.

Amenities: No
children. No pets.
Bicycles available. Near
bike trails and bird
sanctuaries. Working
fireplaces. A few
minutes walk to the
beach.

Directions: Route 6 to
the Orleans rotary;
take the Rock Harbor
exit. At the end of the
exit, turn left toward
Rock Harbor. Bridge
Road is the first road
on the right. The inn
is 1 ½ blocks down on
the right.

Whalewalk Inn is a circa 1830 whaling master's home, but innkeepers Ginny and Norm de la Chapelle have added modern conveniences to provide an unusual setting for relaxation and enjoyment. No "imitation periods" here, just creative variations of furniture, fabrics, accessories, and art. The barn and the guest house are colonial. The guest house has cathedral ceilings and exposed beams. The saltbox cottage, decorated in pale blue and pink roses, white wicker, and a white iron bed, is an additional accommodation with living room, fireplace, kitchen, and private patio. It is remote and peaceful.

The gourmet breakfast may consist of Belgian waffles or crepes plus fresh baked muffins or cakes. The innkeepers provide a wonderful array of hors d'oeuvres and snacks for the happy hour, as well as ice, mixers, and a refrigerator. Former guests make up an "alumni association" who return for the nightly social hour. In nice weather this time is enjoyed on the patio, otherwise it is spent at the mini bar.

Whalewalk Inn's Chutney Cheese Paté

1 pkg of cream cheese (8 oz.)   1½ T. sherry
4 oz. shredded cheddar cheese   ¾ t. curry powder
⅛ t. salt

Mix all the above ingredients. Spread into a ¾" thick circle. Chill. Before serving, spread chutney on top and sprinkle with finely chopped green onions. Serve with date/walnut bread cut into small pieces.

The Penny House
Route 6
North Eastham, MA
02651
(508) 255-6632

The Penny House

Neat hedges, a garden, and a vine-covered trellis greet guests at The Penny House. The main house is a bow-roof Cape reflecting the shipbuilding techniques of the time. Original beams, wide-planked pine floors, and Oriental rugs carry out the theme. Main floor rooms have cathedral ceilings and double beds; one has a queen-size bed. The newer wing retains the older feeling of the main house. One room has a canopy bed. The upstairs bow-roof rooms are quaint and historic.

Two-hundred-year-old beams buttress the ceiling of the public room where the hearty country breakfast is served each morning at a large oak table. Breakfasts includes homemade breads or muffins plus a chef's choice entrée.

The Penny House's Apple Dutch Babies

Batter: 2 eggs
½ C. milk
1 t. vanilla
½ C. flour

3 t. butter
2 Golden Delicious apples (peeled, cored, and sliced)
½ t. cinnamon
1 t. sugar

Preheat oven to 425°. Mix eggs, milk, and vanilla in blender. Add sugar and flour while still blending. Blend 5 minutes. Place ½ t. of butter into each of six individual au gratin dishes. Put dishes into bottom rack of oven to melt butter. Divide apple mixture into dishes and pour batter over. Bake 10 minutes.

Innkeepers:
Paul & Barbara Landry

Open all year.
12 rooms/6 baths.

Rates: 6/25 to 9/5, $60-$65 (for two).
VISA/MC

Amenities: Children over 13 welcome. No pets. Working fireplaces. 1½ miles to the beach.

Directions: Route 6 to the Orleans rotary. The inn is on Route 6, five miles beyond the Orleans rotary on the left, directly across from The Sandpiper Restaurant in the Nauset Light Beach area.

Falmouth

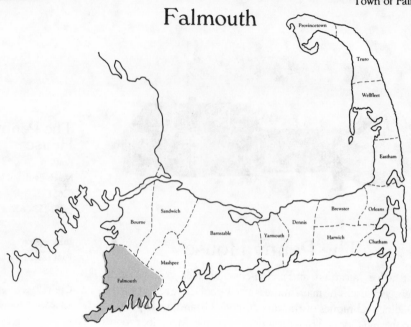

Falmouth is located at the southwest corner of Cape Cod where Buzzards Bay and Vineyard Sound meet, and includes the villages of **East Falmouth, Falmouth Heights, North Falmouth, West Falmouth,** and **Woods Hole.** This town is one of the "gateways" to the islands, especially Martha's Vineyard.

Special sites worth visiting are the Woods Hole Oceanographic Institute and surrounding area; the National Marine Fisheries Aquarium in Woods Hole; Nobska Light, on a bluff where you can see ships traveling between the mainland and the islands, and Ashumet Holly Reservation with its 45 acres of holly trees and an herb garden managed by the Massachusetts Audubon Society. Both the New Alchemy Institute, a non-profit research facility, and Washburn Island, a nature preserve, are worth seeing. On Falmouth's beautiful village green there is a bell cast by Paul Revere which rings for services and strikes the hours for the First Congregational Church, built in 1796.

The recently renovated and revitalized Falmouth Playhouse presents Equity theater productions. The Falmouth Historical Society maintains two restored houses and a colonial garden; Katherine Lee Bates' birthplace museum is on Main Street, and the Barnstable County Fair is held in July, as is the Arts and Crafts Street Fair which features 200 exhibitors.

Some beaches to be enjoyed are Menauhant Beach, Old Silver Beach, Bristol Beach, Falmouth Heights Beach, Nobska Beach, and Surf Drive Beach.

Falmouth has 10 harbors with boating facilities in all. You can watch polo games at Boxberry Hill Farm in Hatchville and there are several facilities for horseback riding in Falmouth. Cape Cod League baseball is played at Guv Fuller Field on Main Street. Golf may be enjoyed at several excellent golf courses. The Falmouth Road Race, considered "the best non-marathon road race in the country," is held in August.

About a half mile west of Falmouth Center on the road to Woods Hole is the start of a truly spectacular bike path. It follows the old railroad right-of-way for a leisurely three-plus miles to the Steamship Authority parking lot in Woods Hole.

Falmouth offers one of the best shopping districts as well.

Peterson's
Bed &
Breakfast
226 Trotting Park
Road
East Falmouth, MA
02536
(508) 540-2962

Innkeepers: Joel &
Anna Marie Peterson

Open all year.
2 rooms/1 bath.

Rates: 6/1 to 10/31,
$50 (for two). No
credit cards accepted.

Amenities: "Our
children will welcome
your children." Pets
accepted by pre-
arrangement, if they
will tolerate the two
cats in residence. No
smoking. Laundry
available. Working
fireplaces.

Directions: Route 28
South to Brick Kiln
Road Exit towards
East Falmouth. Go 1.4
miles to first traffic
light at Gifford Street.
Continue on Brick
Kiln Road to next
right, 3/10 mile to
Locustfield Road.
Follow Locustfield
Road 4/10 mile to
gravel driveway, just
before new Day Care
Center.

Peterson's Bed & Breakfast

The specialty of Peterson's Bed & Breakfast is children: human, canine, and feline. For that reason it is quite unique among B & Bs. The inn is small and informal, set within a quiet residential neighborhood full of pine trees. Guests often say how delightful it is to be able to travel with their children. One room is called Grandma's Garret: it has old-fashioned comfort and decor, as well as all the modern conveniences. A queen-size bed and crib are available. The other room is The Greenhouse: it has an airy garden atmosphere with a huge skylight, double bed, and homemade quilt.

A full breakfast is served every morning. The recipe of Welsh Griddle Cakes was one Anna Marie learned in the Mexican Jungle while in missionary survival training. "We would take our cold lake bath each day and then come back for tea and cakes," she says. "They were welcomed by us then and please our guests now."

Peterson's Bed & Breakfast's Welsh Griddle Cakes

2 C. flour
½ C. sugar
1 t. baking powder
½ C. wheat germ (optional)

¼ t. salt
½ C. butter or margarine
(1 stick)
½ c. raisins

1/3 - 1/2 C. milk

Blend dry ingredients with wire whisk. Cut in butter with pastry blender or two knives — stir in raisins. Add milk to create a stiff dough. Knead and form cakes about 2" in diameter. Bake at medium heat on a floured griddle until brown and crusted. Turn over and brown the other side. Serve with butter and marmalade. Also makes a welcome snack for cold or weary new arrivals!

Sea Shell Inn

88 Menauhant Road
East Falmouth, MA
02536
(508) 548-6941

Innkeepers: Sean &
Sheila Regan

Open Memorial Day to
Columbus Day.
5 rooms/5 baths

Rates: 6/20 to 9/5,
$52-$75 (for two),
$450-650/week for
apartments. No credit
cards.

Amenities: Children
welcome. No pets.
Working fireplace.
Located right on the
beach. Color cable
television.

Directions: Route 28
South toward
Falmouth. Left on
Brick Kiln Road to
Route 28 again. Left
on Route 28 to
Acapesket Road. Right
on Acapesket to the
water, and left to the
inn.

Sea Shell Inn

The Sea Shell Inn is located right on the beach with all the amenities you would want for an enjoyable beach holiday. There are two apartments for longer stays; one with two bedrooms, a fully equipped kitchen and dining area, the other with one bedroom containing a double bed and a single bed, a kitchen, dining area, and separate entrance. Both apartments have color cable televisions and bay windows providing a constant ocean breeze. Guest rooms are on the first floor and enjoy ocean views. One guest room has an enclosed porch, as well. The rooms are casually furnished with wall-to-wall carpeting and white wicker furniture. The two guests rooms share a shower.

The inn has picnic tables, cookout equipment, boat moorings, and a beautifully landscaped lawn. Breakfast, including the inn's homemade Irish bread, is served to guests who do not have kitchen facilities. Sheila Regan guards her recipe carefully, but has allowed it to be published here.

Sea Shell Inn's Irish Bread

4 C. flour
½ C. sugar (or more to your taste)
1 t. salt
1 t. soda
½ qt. buttermilk

2 t. baking powder
1 stick margarine (cut up)
raisins (to your taste)
caraway seeds (optional)
2 eggs

Mix together all ingredients except buttermilk and eggs. In separate bowl, beat buttermilk and eggs. Add wet ingredients to dry ones and stir to get a moist but not mushy batter. Grease a large black frying pan and pour in batter. Cut a cross on top (a blessing). Put a pat of margarine in each corner and sprinkle the top with sugar and buttermilk. Bake at 350° for 50-60 minutes or until a knife comes out clean. Enjoy!

Captain Tom Lawrence House

The Captain Tom Lawrence House is a Victorian whaling captain's home built in 1861. Each guest room is in a corner of the house and all are cheerfully decorated with antiques and four-poster canopy beds.

The large living room of the inn has comfortable chairs, a warm fire in the fireplace, a piano, and a 200-year-old cupboard from Germany. The gracious circular stairwell, original hardwood floors, and high ceilings recall the time when the Captain himself lived there. The full breakfast may be the highlight of your stay. Entrées range from Quiche Gisela, to crepes, to Black Forest bread made with homeground flour.

Captain Tom Lawrence House Inn's Whole Wheat and Bran Belgian Waffles

1 1/3 C. whole wheat flour	4 eggs
1 1/3 C. all-purpose flour	3/4 C. brown sugar
1½ C. unprocessed bran	3 C. milk
3 T. baking powder	2/3 C. butter or margarine, melted
	1½ t. salt

Mix all ingredients in a blender except for the flour and bran. Mix liquid mixure with flour and bran. Bake waffles in preheated waffle iron. Serve hot with warm strawberry sauce and whipped cream or your favorite topping.

Captain Tom Lawrence House

75 Locust Street
Falmouth, MA 02540
(508) 540-1445

Innkeeper:
Barbara Sabo-Feller

Open all year.
6 rooms/6 baths.

Rates: 6/15 to 10/30, $60-$85 (for two). No credit cards.

Amenities: Children over 12 welcome. No pets. Working fireplace. 10-minute walk to the beach. Within walking distance to bird sanctuary. Shining Sea Bike Path is a block away.

Directions: Route 28 South to Falmouth Center (approximately 15 miles). In Falmouth, follow the sign toward Woods Hole to the fifth house on the right. Locust Street is the beginning of Woods Hole Road.

Gladstone Inn

219 Grand
Avenue South
Falmouth, MA 02540
(508) 548-9851

Innkeepers:
Jim & Gayle Carroll

Open May to October.
16 rooms/4 baths

Rates: 5/15 to 10/15,
$45 (for two). No
credit cards accepted.

Amenities: Children
over 14 welcome. Pets
welcome. Working
fireplace. The beach is
just across the street.

Directions: Route 28
South toward
Falmouth. At first
traffic light turn left
onto Jones Road. Stay
on Jones Road to the
ocean (road becomes
Worcester Park). Turn
left to the inn on your
left.

Gladstone Inn

For 18 years, the Carrolls have anticipated every need of the traveler at their oceanfront Gladstone Inn. Rooms are furnished in simple beach style with some nice period pieces. There are lots of books, bicycles, a barbecue, sand chairs, and a pay telephone available. There are also discount tickets for some boats and refreshments. Although there are no private baths, there is a sink in each guest room.

A nautical theme decorates the enclosed porch where breakfast is offered buffet-style from 7:00-10:00 a.m. Note the early hour, another thoughtful accomodation to boat catchers. The newly renovated carriage house, a second floor apartment, offers a complete kitchen, private bath, color television, and a deck for spectacular views of the Sound and Martha's Vineyard.

Gladstone Inn's Breakfast Pizza

Spread two cans of crescent rolls on a cookie sheet to make a crust. (If a heavier and thicker crust is desired, use Country Man biscuits.)
Sprinkle dough with:

1 C. shredded cheese (cheddar or Swiss)   ¼ C. chopped onions
½ C. chopped peppers   ½ C. chopped tomatoes
1 C. sliced sausage or crumbled bacon

In a blender, mix 6 eggs, ½ C. milk, salt, and pepper. Beat, then pour over cookie sheet. Toss on freshly chopped parsley and any herb you enjoy (dill is nice), for color and flavor. Bake at 350° for 12-14 minutes until done. Cut in squares. Any topping can be used; use your imagination. Serves 10.

King's Inn by the Sea

**King's Inn
by the Sea**
Central Park Avenue
Falmouth, MA 02540
(508) 548-9086

Innkeepers: Sam &
Barbara Getzie

Open all year.
4 rooms, all shared
baths.

Rates: 6/20 to 9/10,
$55 (for two).
MC/VISA

Amenities: Children
welcome. No pets.
"Barefoot walk to the
beach." Near the
Shining Sea Bikeway.
Bicycles for rent.

Directions: Route 28
South to Falmouth.
At the first set of
traffic lights, turn left
on Jones Road.
Continue through two
more traffic lights
until you come to a
flashing red light.
Turn right and
immediately left
around Worcester
Court. Go straight
ahead to the water.
Turn right on Grand
Ave. to Central Park
Ave. Turn right on
Central Park Ave. to
the inn on your right.

The King's Inn overlooks the town green in Falmouth, at the edge of Vineyard Sound. Long term rentals are a specialty in the comfortable, clean atmosphere of a seaside home. King-size beds are available. Your hosts offer mini-tours of Cape Cod, as well as bicycle rentals.

Breakfast is served buffet-style in the dining room. This provides a time for mingling with other guests, as does the afternoon snack time in the living room or on the front porch with its view of the Sound.

King's Inn by the Sea's
Banana Bread

Preheat oven to 350° and grease a loaf pan 9" x 5" x 3".

1¼ C. flour	½ C. margarine or butter
1 C. sugar	1 C. bananas, mashed
½ t. salt	2 eggs

1 t. baking soda

In a large bowl, sift dry ingredients. Add margarine with a pastry cutter. Add bananas and eggs. Pour into the greased pan and bake for 50-65 minutes.

Mostly Hall
B & B Inn

27 Main Street
Falmouth, MA 02540
(508) 548-3786

Innkeepers: Caroline
& Jim Lloyd

Open mid-February to
January 1.
6 rooms/6 baths.

Rates: May to
October, $90-$95 (for
two). No credit cards
accepted.

Amenities: Children
age 16 and over
welcome. No pets. No
smoking. Working
fireplace. 15-minute
walk to the beach.

Directions: Route 28
South into Falmouth
Center. The inn is
directly across from
the village green.

Mostly Hall B & B Inn

Elegant southern hospitality in New England! The Mostly Hall
B & B Inn is surrounded by more than an acre of beautiful gardens
and rolling lawn. It looks like a southern plantation with wide center
hallways and shuttered windows. Oriental rugs and a variety of
antiques are scattered throughout. Each of the six large corner guest
rooms is furnished with queen-size, four poster "rice" or canopy beds
and other thoughtful touches typical of southern hospitality. There is
a delightful sitting room in the enclosed widow's walk on top of the
house — a great place to enjoy a peaceful retreat.

A full breakfast includes a special entrée such as stuffed French
toast or cheese blintz muffins with warm blueberry sauce. In the
summer, breakfast is served outside on the wrap-around veranda
overlooking the gazebo. Otherwise, you will enjoy it around the big
dining room table. Complimentary bicycles are available for use on
the "Shining Sea Bikeway."

Mostly Hall B & B Inn's
Cheese Blintz Muffins

1 lb. ricotta cheese	½ stick butter, melted
3 eggs	½ C. Bisquick
2 T. sour cream	1/3 C. sugar

Mix all ingredients together and bake at 350° for 30 minutes in greased
muffin tins. You can add chopped apple or light raisins if desired. Serve with
applesauce, jam, or blueberry sauce. This recipe makes 12 muffins.

Palmer House Inn

Palmer House Inn has a Victorian feeling with warm, rich woodwork, hardwood floors, period furniture, stained glass windows and old photos, books, and memorabilia everywhere. Grandpa's Room offers an impressive sleigh bed; the Tower Room has a four-poster bed and antique wicker. Quilts and lace doilies are all about, along with baskets of silk flowers creating a warm and inviting atmosphere.

The innkeepers' gourmet cooking has been featured in several publications. A full beakfast is served in the dining room at tables set with fine china and crystal. Entrees include cheese blintz with blueberry compote, Finnish pancake and strawberry soup, and pain perdue with orange cream—heavenly!

Palmer House Inn's Finnish Oven Pancake

1 T. butter	4 eggs
1/3 C. sugar	½ t. salt
2½ C. milk	½ C. flour

Heat oven to 425°. Heat 9″ glass pie pan in the oven for 10 minutes. Melt butter in hot plate to coat bottom and sides. Beat together the eggs, sugar, salt, and milk. Stir in the flour. Pour into prepared pie plate. Do not stir. Bake 25 minutes at 425° until puffed and lightly brown. Serve immediately with the following soup.

Strawberry Fruit Soup

Defrost and purée a 12 oz. package of frozen strawberries. Stir in 1 T. cornstarch, 1/3 to ½ C. sugar, and a splash of lemon juice. Heat to boiling—continue to boil for 1 minute, stirring frequently. Serve hot!

Palmer House Inn

81 Palmer Avenue
Falmouth, MA 02540
(508) 548-1230

Innkeepers: Phyllis Niemi-Peacock and Bud Peacock

Open all year.
8 rooms/8 baths.

Rates: July 4th weekend to Labor Day, $75-$95 (for two).
VISA/MC

Amenities: Children over 12 welcome. No pets. Working fireplaces. 20-minute walk to the beach. Bicycles available for your use. Two bedroom cottage available.

Directions: Route 28 South toward Falmouth, until divided highway ends. Continue 1.7 miles past Jones Road intersection, then turn left onto Palmer Avenue. The inn is ½ block ahead on the left.

Village Green Inn

40 West Main Street
Falmouth, MA 02540
(508) 548-5621

Innkeepers: Linda &
Don Long

Open all year.
5 rooms/5 baths.

Rates: 5/15 to 10/15,
$80-$95 (for two). No
credit cards accepted.

Amenities: No
children. No pets. 5
decorative fireplaces.
15-20-minute walk to
the beach.

Directions: Route 28
South to Falmouth.
When you get to Main
Street, turn left. The
Village Green Inn is
on the village green.

Village Green Inn

The Village Green Inn is a Federal-style home originally built in 1804 and extensively renovated as a Victorian in 1894. Guest rooms are large, immaculately clean, and tastefully decorated in soft pastels, creating a restful and comfortable atmosphere.

A fragrant, hot spiced fruit dish is a specialty of the hearty Cape Cod breakfast served every morning. Breakfast is served outside on large open porches furnished in white wicker surrounded by red geraniums. Afternoon sherry and lemonade are also served. This is a gracious inn with lots of charm.

The Village Green Inn's Hot Spiced Fruit

**1 one-lb. can each of peach slices, pear halves, pineapple chunks,
pitted dark sweet cherries, and apricot halves**
2 tart apples   **3 T. lemon juice**
½ t. each nutmeg and cinnamon   **¼ t. cloves**
1/3 C. brown sugar

Drain and combine syrup from fruits and reserve 1 ½ C. liquid. Turn drained fruit into a 2 ½ quart baking dish. Core and cup up apples. Mix with lemon juice and toss with other fruit. Stir together syrup, nutmeg, cinnamon, cloves, and brown sugar. Pour over fruit. Bake at 350° for 25-30 minutes or microwave for 10-20 minutes on high.

The Worcester House

The
Worcester
House

9 Worcester Avenue
Falmouth, MA 02540
(508) 540-1592

Innkeepers:
Janet and Bob Conlon

Open May to October.
3 rooms/2 baths.

Rates: $45-$60 (for
two). No credit cards
accepted.

Amenities: Children
over 16 welcome. No
pets. One block walk
to the ocean; great for
board sailors. Working
fireplace.

Directions: Route 28
South to Falmouth. At
the first set of traffic
lights in Falmouth,
turn left onto Jones
Road. Continue
straight through two
sets of traffic lights
onto Worcester Court,
which continues onto
Worcester Avenue.
The house is white
stucco and on your
right.

Only a block from the ocean, The Worcester House is ideally located for swimming or enjoying a scenic view of Martha's Vineyard from an old fashioned porch. Your hosts are friendly and like to advise their guests of local happenings, museums, and nearby attractions. The house was built in the 1920s and is decorated in casual "House Beautiful" tradition.

The innkeepers serve a delicious continental breakfast with homemade muffins and fruit jams.

The Worcester House's Walnut Prune Muffins

1 C. wheat bran cereal
¾ C. milk
1 large egg
¼ C. vegetable oil
2 ½ t. baking powder

½ C. chopped prunes
½ C. walnuts
1 C. all-purpose flour
¼ C. granulated sugar

Mix cereal with milk in a medium-size bowl, and let stand 3-5 minutes until milk has been absorbed. Heat oven to 400°. Grease muffin tins. Beat egg and oil into soaked cereal. Stir in the chopped prunes and walnuts. Thoroughly mix flour, sugar, and baking powder in a large bowl. Pour in the liquid ingredients. Fold in with a rubber spatula, just until dry ingredients are moistened. Place batter into muffin cups. Bake 15-20 minutes or until springy to the touch in the center. Turn out onto a rack to cool thoroughly. Let stand several hours for flavor to develop. May be reheated.

Wyndemere House at Sippewissett

718 Palmer Avenue
Falmouth, MA 02540
(508) 540-7069

Innkeeper:
Carole Railsback

Open 5/15 to 10/15
6 rooms/5 baths.

Rates: $75-$95 (for two). No credit cards accepted.

Amenities: Children over 14 welcome. No pets. Working fireplace. Cable television in the living room. 10-minute walk to the beach.

Directions: Route 28 South four exits to Sippewissett exit, onto Palmer Avenue. Take the third right onto Goodings Way.

Wyndemere House At Sippewissett

In 1797, Lord Wyndemere left Sussex, England under mysterious circumstances relating to his wife's disappearance. He built an old English manor in Falmouth and became known for his reclusive lifestyle.

In 1980, an architect tripled the size of the house and completely remodeled it. Now, guests are welcomed into a two-story living room with skylights and a balcony overlooking the living/dining room. The rooms are furnished with English antiques, chintz, and lace curtains. There is an elegant but relaxed atmosphere in this charming inn full of amenities and adventures. Try one of the frequent murder mystery weekends.

A full breakfast is served on the European-style terrace, weather permitting. High tea is served on the terrace between 4:00-5:00 p.m.

Wyndemere House's Peach Crepes

Sauce: 1/2 peach per person, peeled, pitted, and sliced
1 large T. margarine per peach

Sauté sliced peaches and add: ¼ t. nutmeg
½ T. lemon juice
¼ C. maple syrup per peach
(You can use fresh raspberries or blueberries instead of peaches.)

Crepes: May be made ahead and reheated in microwave or conventional oven. The innkeeper uses a good pre-packaged pancake mix. Batter will be thin. 12 crepes, 3-4 to a person.

1 C. pancake mix
1½ C. water
1 egg
1 T. oil

Use a soup ladle 2/3 full and a good cast iron skillet 8"-10" in size (this is better than a crepe pan). Roll batter quickly around pan on high heat and turn, cooking 3 minutes. Cool and stack on plate. Roll up and pour peach sauce over them.

The Amherst

The two guest rooms are on the first floor and are simply and comfortably furnished with hand-quilted items made by Shirley Smith. One room has a water view. The Smiths have operated the inn as a guest house for 31 summers and enjoy helping people have a nice holiday. Mel is a retired railroad engineer.

The living room and a large porch with a view of Vineyard Sound are relaxing places to sit. No need for air conditioning here, as the breeze from the Sound is cool and refreshing. The continental-plus breakfast is served at guests' convenience and features homemade jams.

The Amherst's Rhubarb Jam

5 C. finely diced rhubarb   **½ jar pineapple preserves**
3 C. sugar   **1 small package strawberry gelatin**

Mix rhubarb and sugar together and let stand overnight. In the morning, stir well and add pineapple preserves. Cook all ingredients for 12-15 minutes. Remove from heat and thoroughly stir in the small package of gelatin. Seal in sterilized jars at once.

The Amherst
30 Amherst Avenue
Falmouth Heights,
MA 02540
(508) 548-2781

Innkeepers: Mel & Shirley Smith

Open April to October. 2 rooms/1 bath

Rates: June to September, $45 (for two). No credit cards accepted.

Amenities: Children welcome. No pets. Working fireplace. Vineyard Sound beach across the street.

Directions: Route 28 South to Falmouth. At the first set of traffic lights, take a left on Jones Road. Continue through two more traffic lights until you come to a flashing red light. Turn right and immediately left around Worcester Court. Go straight ahead to the water, then left onto Grand Avenue, five blocks to Amherst Avenue.

The Moorings Lodge

207 Grand
Avenue South
Falmouth Heights, MA
02540
(508) 540-2370

Innkeeper:
Shirley Benard

Open 5/15 to 10/15. 8
rooms/7 baths.

Rates: 6/15 to 10/15
$45-$65 (for two). No
credit cards.

Amenities: "Some"
children welcome. No
pets. Working
fireplace. Beach is
across the street.

Directions: Route 28
South toward
Falmouth. The road
will change from a
four-lane road to a
two-lane street. At the
first traffic light, turn
left onto Jones Road.
Stay on the same road
until you come to the
ocean. The name of
the street changes to
Worcester Park but it
is a continuation of
Jones Road. Turn left
at the ocean to The
Moorings on your left.

The Moorings Lodge

Built in 1905, The Moorings Lodge is typical of Falmouth Heights beach homes constructed in the early part of this century. Guest rooms are furnished in a clean, simple style. The inn has a lovely, large (43-foot) glass-enclosed porch that overlooks the Vineyard Sound and Martha's Vineyard. Falmouth Heights Beach is directly across the street and has lifeguards on duty all summer. The water temperature in July and August is about 73°-75° due to the warm gulf stream.

The breakfast buffet is served on the porch where guests will enjoy the view while meeting new friends. Homemade breads, coffee cakes, and granola are the standard fare.

The Moorings Lodge's
Cherry or Blueberry Square

3 C. flour	1 t. salt
½ lb. margarine (2 sticks)	1½ t. baking powder
1¾ C. sugar	1 t. vanilla
1/3 C. milk	½ C. chopped nuts
4 eggs	1 can cherry or blueberry
	pie filling (Comstock)

Cream butter, sugar, and eggs. Add dry ingredients with milk, vanilla, and nuts. Spread ½ the batter in a greased jelly roll pan or large cookie sheet. Spread 1 can of blueberry or cherry pie filling over the batter. Top with remaining batter (will not quite cover). Sprinkle with cinnamon and sugar. Bake at 350° for 35-40 minutes. Freezes well.

Captain's Inn
Bed &
Breakfast
237 Old Main Road
North Falmouth, MA
02556
(508) 563-6793

Captain's Inn
Bed & Breakfast

Once a country estate, Captain's Inn Bed & Breakfast has served many visitors as a tea room. Built in 1812, it is an elegant tea room again, as well as a B & B, and it attracts visitors looking for the gracious ambience and exceptional victuals provided here. Epicurean breakfasts with entrées of corn custard quiche, seafood crepes, or blueberry dumplings are all made at the inn.

There are lovely gardens, paddocks, and stables on the property, as well as several historic elm trees. This is the setting for lawn croquet and other sports. Guests have a private entrance through an indoor garden. Rooms are large and airy, elegantly decorated, appointed with queen-size four-poster beds of oak and mahogany. An ocean beach is just a walk down a quiet road.

Innkeepers:
Joan and George

Open all year.
4 rooms, some shared baths.

Rates: June to October, $80-$85 (for two). No credit cards accepted.

Amenities: Children welcome. No pets. Working fireplace in the common room. 5-minute walk to the ocean beach.

Directions: Route 28 South to Route 151. Left toward North Falmouth. Cross Route 28A and the railroad tracks to North Falmouth village and flashing "Caution." Turn left onto Old Main Road to the inn on the left.

Captain's Inn French Pancakes
Stuffed With Seafood A La Creme

Pancake Preparation

In a bowl mix: 2 eggs beaten, 1 C. milk (or half milk/half cream), ¼ t. salt, 1 C. all purpose flour.
Stir vigorously until completely smooth, then set aside for ½ hour. The batter needs to be thin, just thick enough to coat the bowl of a spoon. Thin with milk if necessary. Heat a 6 inch skillet greased with corn oil. Pour in enough batter to form a very thin layer. Spread batter by tilting pan back and forth. Cook side until batter is set, then flip and lightly brown other side.

Place in a greased shallow baking dish: 1 salmon steak, ½ lb. sea scallops, ½ lb. boned cod fillet.
Scald 1½ cups all purpose cream and/or milk, 1 small bay leaf, 2 sprigs parsley, 2 med. slices each onion & shallots, ¼ t. ground white pepper, 1 t. minced fresh dill, dash of nutmeg. Pour over fish, bake at 350° until done (approx. 40 min.). Remove fish, reserving liquid and discarding vegetable bits. Cut into bite-sized pieces. Wrap 2 T. fish mixture in each pancake. Cover and keep warm until ready to serve.

Place reserve liquid in sauce pan with 1 T. dry sherry. Bring to simmer. Thicken with 1 t. of corn starch mixed with 1 T. water. Spoon over stuffed pancake in each dish. Garnish with tomato and avocado.

Yellowbird House
P.O. Box 492
Falmouth, MA 02541
(508) 563-6892

Innkeeper:
Chris Arnold

Open all year.
3 rooms/2 baths.

Rates: 4/30 to 11/30,
$35-$65 (for two). No
credit cards accepted.

Amenities: No
children. No pets. 10-
minute walk to the
beach. "This is a non-
smoking house. We do
not refuse smokers.
We just ask them to
smoke outside."

Directions: Route 28
South toward Falmouth.
After approximately 4
miles, there is a rotary
at Otis Air Force Base.
Take the second exit
to Falmouth and Woods
Hole (Route 28). Take
the first exit off Route
28 (marked as North
Falmouth, Mashpee,
and New Seabury).
Turn left at the
bottom of the ramp
onto Route 151.
Proceed to the traffic
light. Turn right to
the first right, Pebble
Lane in the Silver
Pointe development.

Yellowbird House

Chris Arnold is an experienced traveler to B & B's, having stayed in them as she traveled for four years in Europe, with her four children. Her experiences there and in the Far East are reflected in her hostess style. Yellowbird House is a small cottage in a quiet residential neighborhood. The accomodations are secure for women traveling alone, secluded and private for honeymooners, and the area is ideal for runners.

Chris pays careful attention to special dietary needs. She loves to cook and serves a full breakfast Saturday, Sunday, and holidays from 8:00-9:00 a.m., but an earlier time can be arranged if you wish. There is a large deck for sunbathing and many other nice touches.

Yellowbird House's Pumpkin Pancakes

Mix and let stand 5 minutes: ½ C. **coarse ground cornmeal**
                                1 C. **boiling water**

Stir in and mix well: 1 C. **milk**
                        ½ C. **pumpkin purée**
                        1 **egg**

Sift together these ingredients: 1 C. **all-purpose flour**
                                   1 T. **sugar**
                                   2 ½ t. **baking powder**
                                   1 t. **allspice**
                                   ½ t. **salt**

Add to wet ingredients. Pour scant ¼ C. of batter on the griddle. Cook 1-2 minutes. Turn and cook 1 minute more. Serve with fruit, butter, and hot syrup. Best made with fresh baked pumpkin or butternut squash. Makes 24 pancakes.

The Elms

The Elms
495 W. Falmouth
Highway (Route 28A)
West Falmouth, MA
02574
(508) 540-7232

Innkeepers: Betty and
Joe Mazzucchelli

Open all year.
9 rooms/8 baths.

Rates: 5/31 to 10/11,
$65-$75 (for two). No
credit cards accepted.

Amenities: No
children. No pets.
Working fireplace in
the living room. 10-
minute walk to the
beach. Dinner on
request.

Directions: Route 28
South toward
Falmouth to Route
151. Left at the
bottom of the ramp
onto Route 151, to the
first traffic light. Turn
left at the light onto
Route 28A South, to
the inn on your left,
just after Brick Kiln
Road.

A specialty of The Elms is their winter "stressless" weekends, which feature a gourmet dinner on Saturday night and brunch on Sunday — a great getaway. Each spacious room is decorated in an elegant Victorian manner, furnished with lovely antiques and plants. Beautifully landscaped grounds feature an old English herb garden, a Saints garden, and a Victorian gazebo surrounded by a variety of roses. It is a refreshing spot to sit and enjoy the cool breezes of Buzzards Bay. The Mazzuchelli's have received many awards for maintaining the gardens in the same period of the house.

A Victorian library is the setting for the gourmet breakfast and for the social hour with complimentary sherry at 4 p.m.

The Elms' Bananas Foster on French Toast

Per serving:

2 eggs
1 T. heavy cream
½ C. maple syrup
1 T. butter

½ banana
2 slices of white bread
chopped walnuts
strawberry, to garnish

1 oz. Grand Marnier and brandy

Beat eggs and cream and soak bread in the mixture. Grill in buttered pan. In a heated sauce pan, pour maple syrup, butter, and Grand Marnier and brandy. Simmer sauce for 3 minutes. Cut a banana in half and then in quarters. When toast is done, sautée bananas in syrup for 1 minute. Place toast in dish and serve bananas on center of toast with syrup and chopped walnuts. For garnish, serve with a strawberry or banana slice on top.

The Inn
at West
Falmouth

66 Frazer Road
West Falmouth, MA
02574
(508) 540-6503

Innkeeper:
Lewis Milardo

Open all year. 9
rooms/9 baths.

Rates: $135-$185 (for
two). All major credit
cards accepted.

Amenities: No
children. No pets. Clay
tennis court. Heated
outdoor swimming
pool. Several fireplaces.
10-minute drive to the
beach.

Directions: Route 28
South to Brick Kiln
Road exit. Turn right
at end of ramp. Follow
Brick Kiln Road ¼
mile, then turn right at
the yellow blinking
light (Route 28A).
Follow Route 28A 1/3
mile, then turn right
onto Blacksmith Shop
Road (just before the
fire station). Take the
first right to the inn.

The Inn at West Falmouth

The luxurious rooms in The Inn at West Falmouth are furnished with English, Oriental, or French antiques. Each one is graciously decorated and architecturally unique. Every room has a telephone with direct outside access, a wall safe, and a private marble bath with a whirlpool tub. Most rooms have a fireplace and a balcony to enjoy the view of Buzzards Bay. Guests can pamper themselves by requesting the hairdresser or masseuse on staff.

The inn also caters to business meetings and seminars with four meeting rooms located on the main floor. At guests' request, the inn will supply audio-visual or other equipment for business presentations. The main dining room seats eighteen and is attractively decorated with fresh flowers everywhere. The chef is happy to prepare your favorite dish if requested in advance.

The Inn at West Falmouth's
Morning Muffins

2½ C. sugar
4 C. flour (unbleached) or 2 C.
   white, 2 C. whole wheat
6 t. cinnamon
1 t. nutmeg
½ t. cloves
4 t. baking soda
1 t. salt
6 eggs

1 C. raisins plumped in
   ¼ C. Grand Marnier overnight
1½ C. shredded coconut
4 C. shredded carrots
2 shredded apples
1 small shredded zuchini
1½ C. toasted pecans
2 C. vegetable oil
2 t. vanilla

Sift dry ingredients into a bowl. Add the coconut, fruit, nuts, zucchini. Add the eggs, oil, and vanilla. Stir gently until mixed. Spoon the batter into cupcake tins and bake at 375° for 20-25 minutes. Muffins should be made one day in advance for maximum blending of flavors. Makes 24 large muffins.

Old Silver Beach B & B

This small, country-style guest house offers privacy and comfort. It is a fairly new half-Cape house, casually and tastefully decorated, and furnished with country antiques. Rooms are on the second floor and feature a private entrance. One room has twin beds; the other has an antique double spool bed. Electric blankets are available for those cool Cape Cod evenings. There is an outside hot and cold shower to use after a day on the beach.

Afternoon tea is served on the deck. Set-ups for cocktails are provided. Homemade breads are featured in the daily continental breakfast.

Old Silver Beach B & B's Pumpkin Muffins

1 ½ C. flour	4 T. butter, melted
2 t. baking powder	1 egg
¾ t. salt	½ C. cooked, mashed, and
2/3 C. sugar	well-drained pumpkin
½ t. ground cinnamon	½ C. milk
½ t. grated nutmeg	½ C. seedless raisins

Sift together flour, baking powder, salt, and ½ C. of the sugar, cinnamon, and nutmeg into a bowl. Combine the butter, egg, pumpkin, milk, and raisins. Add to the sifted dry ingredients. Stir enough to mix. Pour into the buttered cups of a muffin pan. Sprinkle a little of the remaining sugar over each muffin before placing in the oven. Bake at 400° for 20 minutes. Makes 9 large muffins.

Old Silver Beach B & B

3 Cliffwood Lane
West Falmouth, MA
02574
(508) 540-5446

Innkeeper:
Beverly A. Kane

Open all year.
2 rooms/1 bath

Rates: July 1 to Labor Day, $55 (for two). No credit cards accepted.

Amenities: Children over 3 years welcome. No pets. Cable TV. Fireplace in the living room. 7-minute walk to Old Silver Beach.

Directions: Route 28 South to Route 151. Turn left at the bottom of the ramp onto Route 151 to the first set of lights. Turn left at traffic lights onto Route 28A to the rotary and then take an immediate right onto Curley Blvd. Follow this road past Old Silver Beach. About 4/10 of a mile past the beach on the left is Cliffwood Lane. Turn left to the first house on the right.

Sjoholm Bed & Breakfast Inn

**Sjoholm
Bed &
Breakfast
Inn**

17 Chase Road
West Falmouth, MA
02574
(508) 540-5706

Innkeeper:
Barbara Eck Menning

Open all year. 15
rooms/10 baths.

Rates: 6/15-9/15, $55-
$70 (for two). No
credit cards accepted.

Amenities: Children
over 4 years welcome.
No pets. Smoking in
designated areas only.
15-minute walk to the
beach.

Directions: Route 28
South to Thomas
Landers Road exit.
Right at the bottom of
the ramp. Turn left ½
mile ahead on Route
28A, to Chase Road
on the right.

Originally an old farmhouse, Sjoholm Bed & Breakfast Inn was converted to an inn 25 years ago. It is decorated in country motifs, with antiques and collectibles, and plants in each window. The five suites with private baths are new. The four "economy" rooms in the sail loft are priced for the budget traveler and share one large bath. There is definitely a family atmosphere, with two friendly dogs, a cat, and two high school age children.

Innkeeper Barbara Eck Manning is Swedish on her father's side and has kept family traditions alive. She does all the cooking using only natural ingredients for the full buffet breakfast which includes egg dishes, homemade muffins, fresh fruit, and cereal. The dining room will seat 20 people at a time. Other nice places to relax are the large porch and the oversized living room with cable television. There is also an outside shower for after the beach.

Sjoholm Bed & Breakfast Inn's Swedish Baked Pancake

Preheat oven to 400°. Place a 13″ x 9″ glass pan in oven with ½ stick of margarine/butter. Mix:

6 eggs, 1 C. milk, 1 C. flour, dash of salt

Pour batter over melted butter in pan. Bake 20 minutes until golden and fluffy. Cut into squares. Serve hot with toppings, such as maple syrup, orange butter, cranberry orange relish, powdered sugar, and sour cream.

Orange Butter:

1 stick butter, 3 oz. cream cheese.

Bring to room temperature. Add:

**1 T. orange juice (thawed concentrate),
1/3 C. powdered sugar, 1 T. grated orange rind.**

Beat until fully mixed. Store in refrigerator, serve at room temperature. Makes about 1 C. Delicious on muffins, toast, everything!

The Marlborough

Patricia Morris is a gracious innkeeper who takes obvious pride in making a stay at The Marlborough a memorable experience. Special accomodations for families are available. Two rooms on the main floor, the Chelsea and the Bryn Mawr, can be conveniently shut off from the rest of the inn to create a family suite. The Chelsea is a large room with a sitting area, which overlooks a quaint formal English herb and flower garden. The Bryn Mawr is smaller, with an iron and brass double bed and Persian rug. Other lovely rooms feature antique wicker and oak, and floral wallcoverings. Terry cloth bathrobes and a heated towel bar are provided for guests in "Kensington Gardens," as its private bath is located down the hall.

The common room is a comfortable place for relaxing and for taking tea or the gourmet breakfast. There are 2 seatings for breakfast, at 9 and 10 a.m. In winter, high tea is served at 4 p.m. as a fire blazes in the fireplace. The menu includes a variety of finger sandwiches, potted meats or patés, seasonal fruit, and homemade scones with clotted cream.

The Marlborough

320 Woods Hole Road
Woods Hole, MA
02543
(508) 548-6218

Innkeeper:
Patricia Morris

Open all year. 5 rooms/5 baths.

Rates: $85 (for two). No credit cards accepted.

Amenities: Children welcome. No pets. Swimming pool hours, 9 a.m.-3 p.m., children and parents. 3 p.m.-5 p.m., adults only. Air conditioning. Gift shop on premises. One mile to private association beach.

Directions: Route 28 South toward Falmouth. Route 28 becomes Woods Hole Road.

The Marlborough's Pineapple Casserole

½ C. sugar	1 can (#2 size) crushed pineapple
3 T. flour	4 slices white bread, cut in ½" cubes
3 eggs	½ C. melted butter

Combine sugar, flour, and eggs. Stir in pineapple with juice. Pour into buttered casserole (9" square or round). Top with cubed bread and drizzle with melted butter. Bake at 350° for 1 hour. Serves 6-8 people.

This is a breakfast side dish, served with a slice of cooked breakfast meat (Canadian bacon, ham slice, or thinly sliced pork chop), and a poached or soft-boiled egg, which makes an innovative, pretty breakfast combination.

Harwich

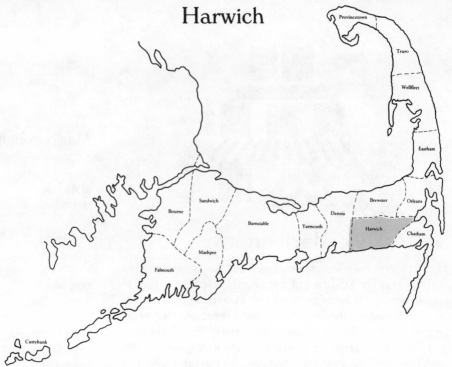

Harwich has seven small villages on the south shore of the Cape along Nantucket Sound with Harwich at the center surrounded by **East Harwich, West Harwich, North Harwich, South Harwich, Harwich Port,** and **Pleasant Lake.**

Harwich has been a leader in the Cape's cranberry industry and there are many miles of picturesque bogs in the area, clothed in their seasonal colors. The Cranberry Harvest Festival is held on the grounds of the Brooks Library in September.

Harwich Junior Theatre has offered quality entertainment for over 30 years with an emphasis on children's plays. The theatre conducts acting classes and workshops, and the arts are professionally taught here.

Eighteen John Rogers figurines are on display in the Brooks Academy, one of the first navigational schools in the country. It houses a significant collection of Indian artifacts, marine instruments, antique glass, and cranberry industry articles.

Free band concerts in the summer, an annual arts and crafts fair in July, golf at Cranberry Valley (rated excellent by *Golf Digest*), horseback riding at Deer Meadow Stable, and a Sailboat Regatta in August at Wychmere Harbor are just a few activities for your enjoyment. There are five ocean beaches and three fresh water sites for swimming.

Victorian Inn at Harwich

Victorian Inn at Harwich
102 Parallel Street
Harwich, MA 02645
(508) 432-8335

Innkeepers: Betty & Charlie Schneiderhan

Open all year.
5 rooms/4 baths.

Rates: $70-$80 (for two). VISA/MC

Amenities: No children. No pets. Two fireplaces. 3-minute drive to the beach.

Directions: Route 6 to Exit 10. South on Route 124 to Harwich Center. The inn is one block east of Route 124.

Each guest room here has its own flavor with a different period of furnishings represented; not all are Victorian, although the two-room parlor is. A Victorian fireplace features a two-tiered mantel with columns draped with carved laurels and bows. Dark wood floors are set off by Oriental rugs. Victorian sofas and chairs and a butler's table carry out the period. Other rooms are decorated in Southern colonial, Shaker, Williamsburg, or Early American style. Several rooms have distinctively elegant armoires. Each room has a vanity with a private bath located in the upstairs or downstairs hallway. The twin-bedded room has an in-room private bath. Personal touches such as fluffy bathrobes, turned down beds at niht, and picnic lunch baskets make for a pleasant stay.

A "gentle and proper" afternoon tea (prix fixe) is served to guests and the public in the "country English" tea room, which is also the site for the generous continental breakfast served every morning.

Victorian Inn's Chocolate Chip Cookies
(for the Picnic Basket)

1 C. shortening	2 t. baking soda
½ C. butter	1½ t. salt
1-1/3 C. granulated sugar	1 t. cinnamon
1 C. firmly packed brown sugar	½ C. quick-cooking rolled oats
4 eggs	3 C. all purpose flour
1 T. vanilla	2 C. chopped walnuts
1 t. lemon juice	2 pkgs. (12 oz. each) semi-sweet chocolate chips

In a large bowl, place shortening, butter, granulated sugar, and brown sugar. Using an electric mixer at high speed, cream until light and fluffy (5 minutes). Add eggs, one at a time, beating well after each addition. Beat in vanilla and lemon juice. In another bowl, stir together baking soda, salt, cinnamon, oats, and flour. Beat flour mixture into butter mixture until well blended. Stir in chocolate chips and nuts. Drop ¼ C. dough on lightly greased cookie sheet. Space cookies about 3" apart. Bake at 350° for 16-18 minutes or until golden brown. Transfer cookies to rack to cool. Makes about 3 dozen large cookies.

Captain's Quarters

85 Bank Street
Harwich Port, MA
02646
(508) 432-0337 or
800-992-6550 (outside
MA)

Innkeepers: David &
Kathleen Van Gelder

Open all year.
5 rooms/5 baths.

Rates: 6/10 to 9/5,
$75 (for two).
VISA/MC/AMEX

Amenities: No
children. No pets. Free
tennis privileges 1 mile
away. Swimming pool.
5-minute walk to the
beach.

Directions: Route 6
to Exit 9. Turn right
onto Route 134 and
follow it 3.2 miles to
the end (Lower
County Road). Turn
left and continue 3.7
miles. Look for the
Harbor Breeze sign on
the left. All check-ins
and check-outs are
processed at the office
located at Harbor
Breeze

Captain's Quarters

Captain's Quarters has charming gingerbread trim and an authentic Victorian turret room. Queen-size brass beds, bedside flowers, and eyelet-trimmed sheets reflect the warmth and comfort of a private home. The inn is ideally suited to couples seeking a leisurely quiet time away. A sitting room provides television or informal socialization.

Innkeeper David Van Gelder, a Coast Guard Captain, takes passengers by boat to Monomoy Island—an isolated spit of land that is part of the Cape Cod National Seashore. Since the area is accessible only by boat, its solitude is especially appealing to nature lovers, bird watchers, and snorkelers.

Breakfast is a help-yourself buffet to enjoy with other guests around the dining room table or on the porch.

Captain's Quarters' Apple Raisin Loaf

1½ C. flour	1 t. cinnamon
¾ C. baking soda	2/3 C. salad oil
1 C. sugar	1 egg
½ C. raisins	1½ to 2 C. peeled and sliced apples

Mix the flour, cinnamon, and baking soda in a small bowl and set aside. Mix the oil, sugar, and egg in a medium shallow bowl with a whisk. Add the flour mixture with a wooden spoon until stiff batter forms. Fold in the apples and raisins. Spoon into a greased loaf pan and lightly press the top to flatten. Bake at 350° for 1 hour or until bread tests done with a pick.

The Coach House.
74 Sisson Road
Harwich Port, MA
02646
(508) 432-9452

Innkeepers:
Sara & Cal Ayer

Open May to October.
3 rooms/3 baths.

Rates: $65 (for two).
VISA/MC/AMEX

Amenities: No
children. No pets.
Tennis court. 5-minute
drive to the beach.

Directions: Route 6 to
Exit 10. Turn right
onto Route 124. At
the stop sign in
Harwich Center, turn
right and then make a
quick left onto Sisson
Road. The inn is
exactly 1 mile from
that point. Watch for
the sign.

The Coach House

The Coach House was built in 1909 as a barn on a prominent old Cape estate. The conversion was done in the 1950s and the result is a lovely home turned into a bed and breakfast. There is a quiet, comfortable elegance found in the king- and queen-size bedded guest rooms.

Fresh fruit compote and home-baked muffins, coffee bread, or croissants make up the continental breakfast, set in the dining room.

The Coach House's "Morning Glories"
(Muffins)

Combine in a large bowl: **4 C. flour (unbleached)**
2 C. sugar
4 t. baking soda
4 t. cinnamon

Add: **4 C. grated carrots (approx. 1 lb.)**
1 C. seedless raisins
1 C. chopped pecans
½ C. shredded sweet coconut
2 large apples, peeled, cored, and grated

In a separate bowl, beat: **6 eggs**
1¾ C. vegetable oil
3 t. vanilla

Stir into the flour mixure until combined. Fill large muffin tins ¾ full. Bake at 350° for 25 minutes. Makes approximately 3-4 dozen. Serve with fresh unsalted butter and homemade elderberry or crab apple jelly.

Country Inn Acres

86 Sisson Road
Harwich Port, MA
02646
(508) 432-2769

Innkeepers:
Jim & Lois Crapo

Open all year.
8 rooms/8 baths.

Rates: 6/1 to Labor
Day, $75-$95 (for
two). VISA/MC/AMEX

Amenities: Children
welcome during the
off-season. No pets.
Three tennis courts.
In-ground swimming
pool. Full service
restaurant. Working
fireplaces. 1 mile to
the beach. 1 mile to
the Rail Trail (21 miles
of paved bikeways).
Cable TV. Public
telephone.

Directions: Route 6 to
Exit 10. Turn right on
Route 124 to Harwich
Center. Turn right,
then take a quick left
onto Sisson Road
(Route 39) and
continue one mile to
the inn on your right.

Country Inn Acres

Innkeepers Jim and Lois Crapo obviously enjoy the Country Inn. They have left the old wide plank floors natural and have decorated with a casual country charm. The spacious guest rooms are furnished with homey comfortable pieces. There are two rooms with double beds. The rest of the rooms have king- and queen-size beds. One lovely suite has a king-size bed and a separate living room with a sleeper couch. It also has cable television and a walk-out porch.

There is a two-night minium stay on all summer weekends.

There are 6½ acres of grounds around the inn. A nature trail through the woods starts at the inn's back door. Apple trees and a strawberry patch provide fresh fruit for breakfast and for the restaurant. The apple trees yielded thirty bushels a tree last season! In summer, fresh vegetables come right from the garden to the table in the colonial style restaurant.

Country Inn's Escalloped Oysters

2 pints of fresh shucked oysters, drained (save oyster liquid)

Crumbs: Mix together:
2 C. crushed cracker crumbs   **¼ C. melted butter,**
                         garlic powder to taste

Sauce: Mix together:
oyster liquor   **1 C. heavy cream**
freshly ground black pepper, to taste   **1/3 C. sherry**
                  dash of Worcestershire sauce

In a shallow baking dish or shallow individual casseroles, layer the following: 1/3 of the crumbs, ½ of the oysters in a single layer, ½ of the sauce, 1/3 of the crumbs, remaining half of the oysters, remaining ½ of the sauce, last 1/3 of the crumbs.

Bake at 425° for 15 to 20 minutes until oyster edges curl. May be used as an appetizer, side dish, or entrée.

Dunscroft by-the-Sea

Dunscroft by-the-Sea
24 Pilgrim Road
Harwich Port, MA
02646
(508) 432-0810

Innkeepers: Alyce &
Wally Cunningham

Open all year.
6 rooms/6 baths, plus 2
efficiency apartments.

Rates: 6/30 to Labor
Day, $90 and up (for
two).
VISA/MC/AMEX

Amenities: Children
limited. No pets.
Working fireplaces.
Private beach.

Directions: Route 6 to
Exit 9. Turn right on
Route 134 to Route
28. Turn left on Route
28 and proceed 5
miles. Turn right onto
Pilgrim Road to the
inn on the right.

Plants and flowers are everywhere around Dunscroft by-the-Sea, a comfortable and traditional inn that has been in operation for over 30 years. The inn has large, sunny rooms with double plump pillows and linens of eyelet, ruffles, and lace. Many areas of the inn are for guests' use, including a large, enclosed sun porch and a brick terrace. The efficiency apartments have separate entrances. In addition, there is a cozy fireplaced cottage.

Innkeeper Alyce Cunningham serves homemade breads, freshly ground coffee, cereals, and fruits for breakfast in the dining room or on the sun porch or terrace.

Dunscroft by-the-Sea's English Muffin Loaves

3 C. unbleached flour   2 t. salt
2 pkgs. dry yeast   ¼ t. soda
                        1 T. sugar

Combine all of the above ingredients. Heat 2 C. milk and ½ C. water to very warm. Add to above mix and beat well. Stir in 3 C. unbleached flour to make a stiff batter. Spoon into two 8 ½" x 4 ½" pans that have been greased and sprinkled with cornmeal. Sprinkle tops with cornmeal. Cover and let rise in a warm spot for 45 minutes (if using quick rising yeast, let rise about 30 minutes). Bake at 400° for 25 minutes. Remove and cool on a rack.

Harbor Breeze

Harbor Breeze

326 Lower County
Road
Harwich Port, MA
02646
(508) 432-0337 or
(800) 992-6550

Innkeepers: David &
Kathleen Van Gelder

Open April to
December.
9 rooms/9 baths.

Rates: 6/10 to 9/5,
$55-$75 (for two).
VISA/MC/AMEX

Amenities: Children
of all ages welcome. No
pets. Free tennis
privileges 1 mile away.
Swimming pool. Color
TV. 4-minute walk to
the beach.

Directions: Route 6 to
Exit 9. Turn right onto
Route 134 and proceed
3.2 miles to the end
(Lower County Road).
Turn left and proceed
3.7 miles to the inn on
your left.

Harbor Breeze, a rambling cedar shake inn with a garden courtyard is located across the road from Allen's Harbor. There is a main house and a separate guest wing. Walkways lined with flowers lead to the outside entrances for each guest room. These are arranged like a motel and each has a color television but no telephone in the room (a pay phone is available on the grounds). Some adjoining rooms form two bedroom-two bathroom suites offering both privacy and proximity to families and friends traveling together.

The innkeepers offer a limited number of boat trailer spaces to guests who would enjoy the use of their own boat while on the Cape. A public launch ramp is also available at the town harbor.

A buffet breakfast of juice, fresh fruit, cereals, and homemade breads, coffee cakes, or muffins is set out each morning in the common hospitality room.

Harbor Breeze's Banana Raisin Bread

1 1/3 C. flour	¾ stick (6 T.) margarine
1 t. baking soda	1 C. golden raisins
¾ t. baking powder	3 small to medium very ripe bananas
2 eggs	1 t. lemon juice
¾ C. sugar	1 t. vanilla

Mix first three ingredients in a small bowl and set aside. In a food processor with a metal blade, process the eggs and sugar for 2 minutes. With food processor running, add the margarine, bananas, lemon juice, and vanilla one at a time, mixing completely after each addition. Turn food processor off, remove top, and add flour mixture. Replace top and process just until mixed—do not overmix. Turn food processor off, remove top, add raisins. Replace top and process until just barely mixed—do not overmix. Pour into a greased loaf pan. Bake at 350° for 1 hour or until bread tests done with a pick.

The Inn on Bank Street

The Inn on
Bank Street
88 Bank Street
Harwich Port, MA
02646
(508) 432-3206

Innkeepers: Janet &
Arky Silverio

Open April to
November.
6 rooms/6 baths.

Rates: 6/24 to 9/15,
$70 (for two).
VISA/MC

Amenities: Children
welcome. No pets.
Working fireplace.
Cable TV. 5-minute
walk to the ocean
beach. 19-mile paved
bike trail at the door.

Directions: Route 6 to
Exit 10. Take Route
124 South to the stop
sign. Turn left on
Main Street and
proceed to the first
right, Bank Street.

Guests of The Inn on Bank Street frequently comment on its great location and the warm, helpful innkeepers. The living room and library of the inn offer a piano and a fireplace as well as cable television. All the guest rooms have private entrances.

Breakfast is leisurely here: fresh ground coffee, fruit, juice, granola, and homemade bread or muffins are served on the sun porch.

The Inn on Bank Street's Strawberry Nut Bread

20 oz. frozen strawberries with liquid
4 extra large eggs
1 C. vegetable oil
3 C. all-purpose flour
2 C. sugar — can mix brown and white.

3 t. cinnamon
1 t. baking soda
1 t. salt
1 C. chopped walnuts
¾ C. raisins

Combine and stir strawberries, eggs, and oil. Sift dry ingredients together. Add wet ingredients to dry ones and stir to blend. Stir in nuts and raisins. Pour into a large greased and floured tube pan. Bake in 350° oven for 1 to 1¼ hours, or until tester comes out clean. Cool on a rack. Cut bread when it is cool — the following day is fine. Makes 20 generous slices.

The Shoals Guesthouse

The Shoals Guesthouse
3 Sea Street Extension
Harwich Port, MA
02646
(508) 432-3837

Innkeepers: Dottie &
John Girard

Open all year.
8 rooms/8 baths.

Rates: 6/20 to Labor
Day, $70-$80 (for
two). No credit cards
accepted.

Amenities: Children
welcome. No pets.
Working fireplace.
Private beach.

Directions: Route 6 to
Exit 10. Take Route
124 South to the stop
sign. Turn left on
Main Street to Bank
Street. Turn right on
Bank Street to Route
28. Turn right on
Route 28 and proceed
one block to Sea Street
on the left. The inn is
at the end of the street
on the left.

The Shoals is tucked into the sand dunes on the south shore of
Cape Cod. The inn has its own private mile-long beach on
Nantucket Sound, a lovely spot for swimming, windsurfing, and
small sailboating. Guest rooms have recently been redecorated so all
are fresh and clean. Five of the rooms have a water view. If yours
doesn't, you can relax on the outdoor patio or, of course, on the
beach.

There are two large community rooms for guests' use. A breakfast
of muffins, breads or coffee cakes, fruit, juice, and tea or coffee is
served in the sun room. Innkeeper Dottie Girard has been
nicknamed "The Muffin Lady."

The Shoals' Donut Muffins

1/3 C. vegetable oil	2 t. baking powder
½ C. sugar	½ t. salt
1 egg	¼ t. nutmeg
½ C. milk	½ C. butter, melted
1½ C. flour	½ C. sugar/cinnamon mixture

Preheat oven to 400°. Cream oil, sugar, and egg. Sift together flour,
baking powder, salt, and nutmeg and add to creamed mixture alternately
with milk. Turn into greased tin and bake for 20-25 minutes. Immediately
remove from the pan and roll in melted butter, then into sugar/cinnamon
mixture.

The House on the Hill

"Christian doors" with handwrought latches and wide pine board floors date this lovely Federal style 1832 farm house. The living room has original paneling, beamed ceiling, and a fireplace for guests' use along with a television, VCR, and shelves of books. Guest bedrooms are large and airy. There is a three bedroom and bath suite for families and the innkeepers are happy to supply cribs and cots for children.

The inn also offers a quiet patio with a stonewall, flower garden, and deck.

The continental breakfast is served in a country dining room with its fireplace and beehive oven.

The House on the Hill's French Breakfast Muffins

1½ C. + 2 T. flour	1 egg, beaten with 1/3 C. melted butter
¾ C. sugar	1/3 C. melted butter (additional)
2 t. baking powder	½ C. sugar
¼ t. salt	1 t. cinnamon
¼ t. nutmeg	½ t. vanilla
	½ C. milk

Combine the first column of ingredients. Add milk and egg/butter mixture, and mix well. Grease and flour muffin pan cups. Fill ½ full. Bake at 400° for 15-20 minutes. Makes about 10 muffins. This recipe may be doubled. Remove from muffin pans and dip muffin into melted butter, coating tops thoroughly. Roll in mixture of sugar, cinnamon, and vanilla.

The House on the Hill

968 Main Street
(Route 28)
South Harwich, MA
02661
(508) 432-4321

Innkeepers: Carolyn & Allen Swanson

Open all year.
4 rooms/2 baths.

Rates: 7/1 to Labor Day, $50 (for two). No credit cards accepted.

Amenities: Children of all ages welcome. No pets. Working fireplaces. Cable TV. 15-minute walk to the Red River beach on Nantucket Sound.

Directions: Route 6 to Exit 10. Take Route 124 South to Route 39. Turn left on Route 39 to the first street on the right (Bank Street), to Route 28. Turn left and proceed 1.9 miles to the inn on the left.

Barnaby Inn

36 Main Street
West Harwich, MA
02671
(508) 432-6789

Innkeepers:
John & Victoria Lynch

Open May to October.
4 rooms/4 baths.

Rates: $50-$60 (for
two). MC/VISA

Amenities: "Children
are welcome if they
can respect the quiet
atmosphere we offer."
No pets. Full service
restaurant. Working
fireplaces in the dinner
house. 15-minute walk
to the beach.

Directions: Route 6 to
Exit 9. Turn right on
Route 134. At the
third traffic light, turn
left onto Upper
County Road. Merge
onto Route 28 at the
traffic light. The inn is
on your left about ⅛
mile ahead.

Barnaby Inn

The spacious guest rooms in the 200-year-old Barnaby Inn are located in a private guest wing. Each guest room has a sitting area and is decorated with pastel floral print wallpaper, handmade afgans, and lace doilies.

The dinner house has original details like wide-board pine floors and several fireplaces. Recipes are Innkeeper (and Chef) John Lynch's creations and include veal, beef, poultry, and seafood. Desserts are homemade and all dinners include a *complimentary* shrimp bowl.

In the New England tradition of hospitality, a light homemade breakfast is *delivered* to your room each morning. Talk about pampering!

The Barnaby Inn's Apple Crumb Pie

Filling:
**2 lbs. apples (Granny Smith,
  Cortland, or Macintosh)**
¾ C. brown sugar
¼ C. flour
¼ T. nutmeg

Topping:
1 C. flour
¾ C. brown sugar
½ C. softened butter
¼ t. cinnamon
¼ t. nutmeg
¼ T. cinnamon

Crust: 1 frozen pie crust, thawed and cooked at 350° for 15 minutes.

Peel, core, and slice the apples. Combine with the filling. Fill the pie shell. Put an even layer of topping over the pie. Cook at 325° for 1 hour.

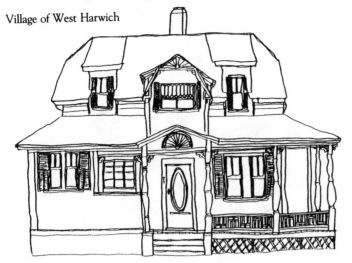

Cape Cod Sunny Pines B & B Inn

77 Main Street
West Harwich, MA
02671
(508) 432-9628

Cape Cod Sunny Pines B & B Inn

Irish hospitality abounds in this comfortable turn-of-the-century inn where Victorian ambience is felt in the furniture decorated with doilies, overstuffed beds, and dark wallpapers. All guest rooms include sitting rooms or adjoining areas, and a color television. A refrigerator in the second floor hall and one on the porch by the pool are for guests' use.

The history of the inn is rich with tales of the sea right up to its present "Captain Jack" who has sailed the world for twenty years researching the ocean floor with a famous oceanographic institute. "Queeny" is the friendly resident Doberman.

An authentic Irish breakfast is served in the dining room by candlelight, on fine china and Cape Cod glassware. You may have "bangers," eggs, soda bread, hot Irish oatmeal with cranberry conserve, or fresh fruit, yogurt and granola. Omelettes are a specialty.

Innkeepers: Eileen & Jack Connell

Open all year.
6 rooms/6 baths.

Rates: $60-$75, all year (for two).
VISA/MC/AMEX/DIS

Amenities: Children over 12 welcome. No pets. Working fireplace. Swimming pool. Cable TV in rooms. 15-minute walk to the beach.

Directions: Route 6 to Exit 9. Take Route 134 South to Route 28. Turn left and proceed approximately 2 miles to the inn on the right.

Sunny Pines' Eggs

Hollandaise Sauce

6 egg yolks
salt and pepper to taste

¼ C. lemon juice (freshly squeezed)
1 C. butter (2 sticks)

Place egg yolks, juice, salt and pepper in a blender. Blend on high for a full minute. Bring butter to a boil. Drizzle hot butter into egg mixture continuously blending on high. The hot butter actually cooks the egg mixture in the blender.

1 grilled English muffin
2 poached eggs

2 cooked sausage patties
cranberry marmalade

Place sausage pattie on grilled muffins and poached egg on pattie. Pour Hollandaise Sauce over the egg. Add a dollop of cranberry marmalade to top of egg.

Cranberry Marmelade

Mix 1 can of whole cranberry sauce with 1 C. of orange marmalade.

Cape Winds by the sea

28 Shore Road
West Harwich, MA
02671
(508) 432-1418

Innkeeper:
Catherine Scales

Open 5/15 to 10/1.
8 rooms/8 baths.

Rates: 6/15 to Labor
Day, $60-80 (for two).
No credit cards
accepted.

Amenities: Children
over 8 years welcome.
No pets. A working
fireplace in the
common room.
Refrigerator in each
room. Cable TV. 3
minute walk to the
beach (right across the
road).

Directions: Route 6 to
Exit 9. Turn right on
Route 134 and proceed
1 mile to the third
traffic light. Turn left
and proceed 3 miles to
Route 28 at West
Harwich. Cross the
Herring River Bridge;
½ mile beyond, turn
right on Grey Neck
Road to Shore Road.
The inn is on the
right.

Cape Winds by the sea

Each room in the colonial Cape Winds by the sea has a view of Nantucket Sound. The inn is decorated in a simple beach style. All rooms may be heated to take the morning chill out of the air, which comes even in the summer and early fall on Cape Cod. There are two patios and a pleasant common room with a fireplace and a color television.

A continental breakfast is served every morning.

The Cape Winds' Irish Soda Bread

3 C. flour   1 t. baking soda
½ t. salt   ¼ t. cream of tartar
¼ C. sugar   ½ t. baking powder

Sift all above ingredients together.

1/3 C. margarine
1 1/3 C. buttermilk
1/3 C. currants

Cut in margarine with a pastry blender to have mix resemble cornmeal. Add buttermilk, stir until moistened. Mix in currants. Shape into a ball and knead about 15 seconds. Place on lightly greased iron fry pan (6" to 7" diameter). Flatten with the palm of your hand until about 1 ½" thick. With a sharp knife, cut a cross on top, ¼" deep and about 5" long to prevent cracking. Bake for 45-50 minutes at 350°. Cool on wire rack. Serve with butter curls.

The Lion's Head Inn

The Lion's Head Inn is a delightful, romantic inn with a sense of history which comes from many of the original features of the house—the pine floors, root cellar, and "captain's stairs" leading to the second floor. Some furnishings are period antiques and some are reproductions, but they all reflect the warmth and hospitality of innkeepers Kathleen and Bill Lockyer.

Fresh local eggs and home-baked breads make up the full gourmet breakfast which is served every morning on a table beautifully set with long stem crystal glasses. The afternoon features a wine and cheese hour by the fireplace with a complimentary glass of wine or sherry.

The Lion's Head Inn's Apple Pancakes

1 egg	3 T. butter, melted
1 C. milk	1½ C. flour
2½ t. baking powder	¼ t. cinnamon
½ t. salt	dash of nutmeg
3 T. sugar	1¼ C. peeled, chopped apples
	(or 1 large Granny Smith)

Beat the egg, milk, and melted butter together with egg beater or whisk until well blended. Combine flour, baking powder, salt, sugar, cinnamon, and nutmeg together and stir into the liquid. Stir in the chopped apple. Cook in lightly greased frying pan. Turn once when bubbles form. Serve with butter and heated maple syrup.

The Lion's Head Inn
186 Belmont Road
West Harwich, MA
02671
(508) 432-7766

Innkeepers:
Kathleen & Bill
Lockyer

Open all year. 4-5
rooms/3 baths.

Rates: $64-$72 (for
two). No credit cards
accepted.

Amenities: Children
over 12 welcome in
the inn; children of
any age are welcome in
the cottages. No pets.
Working fireplace.
Wine and cheese hour.
10-12 minute walk to
the beach.

Directions: Route 6 to
Exit 9. Take Route
134 South to Route
28. Turn left,
proceeding into West
Harwich for 1.7 miles.
Turn right onto
Belmont Road. The
inn is just around the
corner.

The Tern Inn

91 Chase Street
West Harwich, MA
02671
(508) 432-3714

Innkeepers:
Jane & Bill Myers

Open April 1 to
November 15.
5 rooms/4 baths.

Rates: 6/15 to 9/15,
$60 (for two). No
credit cards accepted.

Amenities: Children
welcome. No pets.
Working fireplaces.
Barbecue facilities.
Basketball area. 10-
minute walk to the
beach.

Directions: Route 6 to
Exit 9. Take Route
134 South to Route
28. Turn left on Route
28 and proceed
approximately 2.3
miles. Turn right on
Chase Street to the
inn.

The Tern Inn

The Tern Inn, built in 1797, was originally an 18' x 20' post and beam Cape Half House. It has been expanded up, out, and back through the years and now, in addition to the guest rooms, it has two large common rooms. There are wonderful old wooden floors and antiques and period furniture in the large "Publick" room where there are occasional sing-alongs at the family organ.

Three-bedroom and one-bedroom cottages are available, each with a cable television hook-up for your television set. Grounds are extensive and restful; there are two acres of pine and oak. An outdoor grill and a basketball area are for the use of guests.

A full breakfast is included.

The Tern Inn's "Nest Eggs"

8 eggs   ½ C. grated cheddar cheese
8 slices of white bread   sprinkle of seasonings

Trim crusts from bread. Using a biscuit cutter, cut centers out and tuck them in the bottom of 8 greased custard cups. Cut remaining bread in four pieces and prop around edges of custard cups. Toast in oven at 350° for 8-10 minutes. Cool. Drop in one egg per cup and top with 1 T. grated cheddar. Sprinkle with Salad Supreme, or your favorite herb/salt blend. Return to 350° oven for another 10 minutes until the eggs are barely firm on top. Serve on a warm plate; garnish with a snip of parsley and a cherry tomato. Serves 4, two nests per guest.

Mashpee

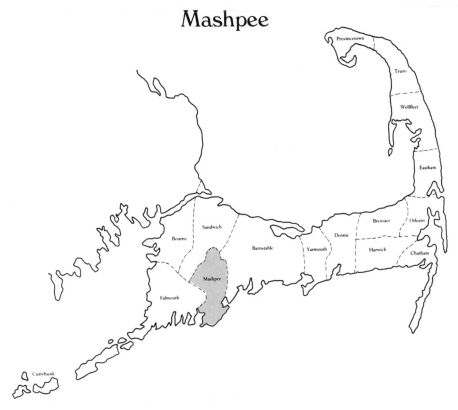

The town of **Mashpee** is located just east of Falmouth. Mashpee offers warm water beaches, excellent fishing, historical sites, and shopping centers.

The Wampanoag Indians maintain a strong community here. You can visit the Old Indian Meeting House and Burial Ground on Route 28, and the Mashpee Indian Museum on Route 130. Both are interesting and worth seeing.

The Lowell Holly Reservation is a 130-acre reservation with numerous trails, picnic, and swimming areas located at Mashpee Pond on South Sandwich Road off Route 130. Another area for sunning and swimming is South Cape Beach on Great Oak Road. Quashnet Valley Country Club provides the setting for great golf. The waterfront resort of New Seabury is also located in Mashpee, and features two 18-hole golf courses, 16 all-weather tennis courts, jogging trails, bicycle paths, and a marketplace with boutiques, galleries, and restaurants.

Mashpee Commons, located at the Mashpee rotary on Route 28, is a new and growing downtown shopping area that maintains the feeling of a New England village. The development has been designed with the pedestrian in mind, with spacious, tree-lined walkways and appealing, pastel storefronts. A variety of restaurants, gift shops, clothing stores, and other shops as well as a movie theater can be found at Mashpee Commons.

The authors did not receive any information regarding bed and breakfast inns in Mashpee to be included in this edition of the **Cape Cod Bed & Breakfast Guide and Innkeepers' Recipes.**

Orleans

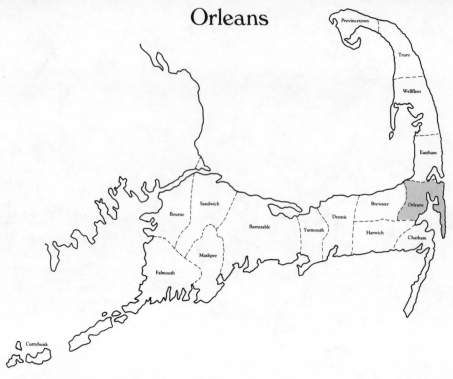

Orleans includes the villages of **East Orleans,** and **South Orleans**. Orleans is one of the few places anywhere from which you can watch the sun rise over the ocean and then, at the end of the day, just a few steps away, see it set again into the sea. Located near the elbow of Cape Cod, Orleans has waterfront on both the Atlantic Ocean and Cape Cod Bay. Rock Harbor was once the landing for packet ships traveling between the Cape and Boston.

Orleans is the only Cape town with the distinction of having a French name. The exiled Duke of Orleans, later to be King Louis-Philippe (1830-48), reportedly visited this area during the French Revolution in the 1790s.

Orleans is also a fisherman's paradise that offers sportfishing at its best, from early spring when the flounder start to stir until late fall when striped bass and bluefish start to swim south.

Libraries, and historical society houses and sites have excellent collections of Indian arrowheads and artifacts. The French Cable Museum commemorates the laying of the transatlantic cable from Brittany to Eastham in 1891; the Orleans Station became the terminal for the "direct" cable which covered the 3,000 miles in one length, laid in 1898-1899.

Windmills, the Cape Cod Rail Trail, the historic and heroically manned Coast Guard rescue boat CG 36500, and the site of Henry Beston's beloved Outermost House can add to a pleasurable stay in Orleans.

Nauset House Inn

**Nauset
House Inn**
143 Beach Road
East Orleans, MA
02643
(508) 255-2195

Innkeepers:
Diane & Al Johnson

Open April to
October.
14 rooms/11 baths.

Rates: $55-$85 (not
including breakfast)
VISA/MC

Amenities: No
children. No pets.
Working fireplaces. 10-
minute walk to the
beach.

Directions: Route 6 to
Exit 12. Bear right to
the second traffic light.
Turn right on Main
Street and proceed
approximately 2 miles
to Beach Road (left at
fork). The inn is on
your right.

Nauset House Inn is set on almost three acres of land, most of it an old apple orchard. There are three buildings used for guests: the farm house, carriage house, and storage shed, which is now a charming cottage set off by itself. The most spectacular room is the turn-of-the-century conservatory, which is filled with plants, flowers, a weeping cherry tree, and comfortable wicker furniture.

An old-fashioned country breakfast is served in a brick floored dining room that has an open hearth fireplace. Large doors open onto the terrace and gardens, a beautiful setting for a lovely inn.

The Nauset House Inn's Oatmeal Butterscotch Muffins

1 box (18 oz.) rolled oats
  (not quick)
1 qt. buttermilk
1 lb. dark brown sugar
3 sticks margarine,
  melted and cooled

3 C. flour
4 t. double acting baking powder
1 t. salt
1½ t. baking soda
2 C. butterscotch chips
6 eggs, slightly beaten

In a very large bowl, combine the oats and buttermilk. Let soak for 1 hour, then mix in sugar, margarine, and eggs. Sift flour, baking powder, salt, and soda together and add to oat mixture. Stir in butterscotch chips. Fill greased muffin tins ¾ full. Bake in a 400° oven for 15-20 minutes. Makes 3 dozen. The batter can be made the day before and kept in the refrigerator tightly covered.

The Parsonage

The Parsonage
202 Main Street
East Orleans, MA
02643
(508) 255-8217

Innkeepers: Chris &
Lloyd Shand

Open all year.
5 rooms/5 baths.

Rates: 5/15 to 10/15,
$55-$70 (for two).
VISA/MC

Amenities: Children
over 6 welcome. No
pets. 5-minute drive to
the beach.

Directions: Route 6 to
Exit 12. Bear right to
the second traffic light.
Turn right on Main
Street. The Parsonage
is 1 ½ miles ahead on
your left, at the corner
of Main Street and
Great Oak Road.

The Parsonage

The words "peaceful haven" have been used to express the atmosphere of The Parsonage, a 1770 Cape home operated as a bed and breakfast for the past five years. The picket fence with its hand-carved acorns, a Cape Cod tradition, is the first thing guests see. The Shands have preserved the history of the inn with early and mid-nineteenth century period pieces, old quilts, reproduction wallpapers, and stencilling. A cobbler had a shop over the kitchen at the turn of this century, and you can still see a depression in the floor where his bench was. Along with the historic appreciation, the innkeepers have provided a refrigerator available for guests' use, fans for the rooms in summer, and some air conditioning. There is a one-bedroom apartment and an efficiency apartment available for rental by the week.

A continental breakfast is served outside in the large courtyard in sunny weather. Guests gather here all day long in summer.

The Parsonage's Zucchini Bread

Group 1:
2 C. shredded zucchini
2 C. sugar
1 C. oil
3 eggs
1 t. vanilla

Group 2:
3 C. flour
¼ t. baking powder
1 t. baking soda
½ t. salt
1 t. cinnamon
½ t. ground cloves
1 t. ginger

Mix groups separately, then add Group 1 to Group 2. Add 1 C. chopped walnuts. Bake at 325° for 1 hour in a greased, floured pan. Makes 1 large loaf.

**Ship's Knees
Inn**
Beach Road
East Orleans, MA
02643
(508) 255-1312

Ship's Knees Inn

There is a nautical theme in the guest rooms and common room of Ship's Knees Inn. Ships' lanterns light the doorways. Woodwork is painted a colonial blue in some rooms, in others the walls are panelled. Many rooms have beamed ceilings, patchwork quilts, and old four-poster beds. Hallways wind around like the galley of a ship. Several rooms have an ocean view and the master suite has a working fireplace.

Continental breakfast is set out each day.

Ship's Knees Inn's
Buttermilk Biscuits and Honey

2 C. sifted all-purpose flour	¾ C. buttermilk
1 T. baking powder	1 T. sugar
½ t. salt	⅛ stick of butter, melted

Mix all ingredients together, roll out to ½" thickness, and cut into 2" biscuits. Brush tops with melted butter and place on cookie sheet. Cook 10 minutes at 450°. Serve immediately with butter and your favorite honey.

Innkeepers: Nancy & Carl Wideberg

Open all year. 19 rooms/12 baths, plus efficiency apartment and 2 cottages.

Rates: 5/2 to 10/30, $45-$95 (for two). No credit cards accepted.

Amenities: No children. No pets. Tennis court. Swimming pool. Working fireplaces. 5-minute walk to Nauset Beach.

Directions: Take Route 6 to Exit 12. Go to first stoplight and turn right. Go two stoplights, and turn right again. Follow signs for Nauset Beach. The inn is on your left.

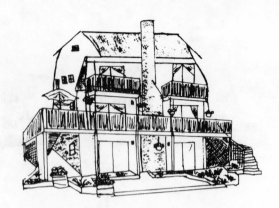

Arey's Pond Relais

16 Arey's Lane
Orleans, MA 02653
(508) 240-0599

Innkeepers: Susanne & Gilles Thibault

Open Memorial Day to Columbus Day.
1 room/1 bath.

Rates: 6/15 to Labor Day, $60 (for two). No credit cards accepted.

Amenities: Children welcome. No pets. Resident cat. No smoking. Refrigerator in room. Working fireplace.

Directions: Route 6 to Exit 12. Turn right to traffic light. Turn right to next traffic light (Route 28). Turn right again on Route 28 North (yes, north) for 1.8 miles to Arey's Lane on your left. Turn left to the third drive after the cranberry bog.

Arey's Pond Relais

This contemporary house is built right into the side of the hill, and the guest room is downstairs below the kitchen. You may enter through the country-style main rooms on one level or from an outside stairway off the patio. The home is in a very private wooded setting with a flowered terrace outside the guest room. A homemade quilt keeps the chill of the evening away.

Gourmet breakfast can be enjoyed in the dining room or on the large deck overlooking the pond. Your hosts are well traveled and are fluent in French and German. A beautiful grey cat roams the house and grounds.

Arey's Pond Relais' Buttermilk Raisin Scones

1¾ C. all-purpose flour   ½ t. baking soda
1 t. sugar   5 T. unsalted butter
½ t. salt   ½ C. buttermilk
2 t. baking powder   ½ C. raisins

Preheat oven to 450°. Combine and mix flour, sugar, salt, baking powder, and baking soda. Cut in butter until mixture resembles coarse crumbs. Add buttermilk and raisins to form a soft dough. Turn out onto a floured board and roll out ½" thick. Cut into 2" rounds. (This innkeeper uses her collection of antique heart shape cookie cutters to add a romantic touch). Place on an ungreased baking sheet. Bake 10-12 minutes until golden brown. Serve with strawberry jam and a fruit cup. This is a delectable alternative to muffins.

Bed & Breakfast
at Honeysuckle Lane

Bed &
Breakfast at
Honeysuckle
Lane
15 Honeysuckle Lane
Orleans, MA 02653
(508) 255-6400

Innkeepers: Cindy
Eagar & Susan Milton

Open all year.
1 or 2 rooms/1 bath.

Rates: Memorial Day
to Labor Day, $75 (for
two). No credit cards
accepted.

Amenities: No
children. No pets. A
few feet to Skaket
Beach.

Directions: Route 6 to
Exit 12. Turn right
onto Route 6A and
proceed to the second
traffic light. Turn left
on Main Street to the
sign for Skaket Beach.
Turn left to
Honeysuckle Lane, just
before the beach on
your left.

This contemporary salt box home will open as a bed and breakfast in the spring of 1989. Its modern design takes advantage of the heavily wooded setting with a deck catering to many species of birds and with windows providing beautiful views. The woods are a pleasant surprise just a block from Skaket Beach, popular by day for its swimming and sunning when the tide is in, and walks on the "flats" when the tide is out; by night, there are spectacular sunsets.

Owners live on the first floor; the queen-size guest room and bath are up the spiral stairway and overlook the marsh. The inn is operated by women and welcomes women as guests to share this lovely home. A full breakfast is served.

Honeysuckle Lane's
Cranberry Fruit Nut Bread

Coarsely chop 1 ½ C. cranberries in your processor. Add:

2 C. flour	1 t. salt
1 C. sugar	½ t. baking soda
1 ½ t. baking powder	¾ C. orange juice
2 T. shortening	1 T. grated peel
1 egg	½ C. nuts

Process all ingredients and pour into 9" x 5" greased loaf pan. Bake for 55 minutes at 350°. Cool for 15 minutes before serving.

The Farmhouse

163 Beach Road
Orleans, MA 02653
(508) 255-6654

Innkeepers: Dot &
Don Standish

Open all year.
8 rooms/5 baths.

Rates: June to
September, $42-$85
(for two). VISA/MC

Amenities: Children
over 8 years welcome.
No pets. Working
fireplace in the
common room. ½ mile
walk to the beach.

Directions: Route 6 to
Exit 12. Turn right to
first stoplight. Turn
right to the next
stoplight. Cross over
Route 28 to the next
stoplight. Turn right
on Main Street to the
fork in the road. Bear
left on Beach Road, to
the inn, 9/10 of a mile
ahead on the right.

The Farmhouse

Innkeeper Dot Standish's love for basket making is evident everywhere at The Farmhouse. There are many stunning examples, including some which are the same color as the towels in the guest bedrooms. Decoration in all rooms is nicely coordinated in charming 1870 farmhouse style; there are braided rugs, patchwork quilts, and white eyelet trim on colonial flowered curtains. Some rooms have ocean views.

Breakfast always features freshly baked muffins around the kitchen table with your friendly hosts.

The Farmhouse's Banana Cranberry Jam

12 oz. fresh cranberries, chopped (3 C.)   **7 C. sugar**
1½ C. water   **2 C. mashed banana**
½ of 6 oz. pkg. liquid fruit (pectin)

Combine cranberries and water in a 5-quart kettle. Simmer covered for 10 minutes. Stir in sugar and banana. Bring to a boil. Boil hard for 1 minute. Remove from heat. Stir in pectin. Skim. Spoon into ½-pint jars, leaving ¼" head space. Wipe jar rims and adjust lids. Process in boiling water bath for 15 minutes (from boiling point). Makes 6½ pints.

Hillbourne House

Hillbourne House, a lovely 1798 inn, commands a magnificent view of Pleasant Bay from all guest rooms and from the terraced garden. Since purchasing the house four years ago, innkeepers Barbara and Jack Hayes have put their personal stamp on this historic house, which served as a stop on the underground railroad during the Civil War. The trap door revealing this slice of the home's history is now covered by a circular braided rug in the common room. Baskets, plants, and dried herbs from Barbara's garden are carefully arranged around stuffed animals, making for a distinctive and relaxing atmosphere. A launching ramp is very close and the inn and provides moorings, a dock, and space to store your trailer.

A continental breakfast is served daily on the grass terrace overlooking the bay, on the back patio, or in the spacious country kitchen.

Hillbourne House's Rose Geranium Peach Crisp

5-6 C. peeled, sliced peaches (can use canned or frozen)

1 C. flour, divided	**1 t. baking powder**
¾ C. sugar, divided	**½ t. salt**
½ t. mace	**1 T. finely chopped rose geranium leaves**
1 egg	**1/3 C. melted butter cooled**
nutmeg to taste	**heavy cream**

Butter a 6" x 10" or 8" square baking dish. Gently toss peaches with mixture of 2 T. flour, ¼ C. sugar and mace. Place in baking dish. Combine the remaining flour and sugar, baking powder, salt, geranium leaves and egg with fork until crumbly. Spread over peaches. Pour butter over dough. Sprinkle with nutmeg. Bake on next-to-lowest rack in preheated 350° oven for 40 minutes. Remove from oven. Serve warm with pitcher of heavy cream. (May be made a day ahead — do not refrigerate. Cover with foil and re-warm in slow oven.)

Hillbourne House
Route 28
South Orleans, MA
02662
(508) 255-0780

Innkeepers:
Barbara & Jack Hayes

Open all year.
5 rooms/5 baths.

Rates: 6/15 to 9/15, $60-$80 (for two). No credit cards accepted.

Amenities: No children. No pets. Private beach on premises with dock and wharf.

Directions: Route 6 to Exit 11. Turn left onto Route 137 and almost immediately left onto Pleasant Bay Road to its end at Route 28. Turn left and proceed ½ a mile to Hillbourne House.

Provincetown

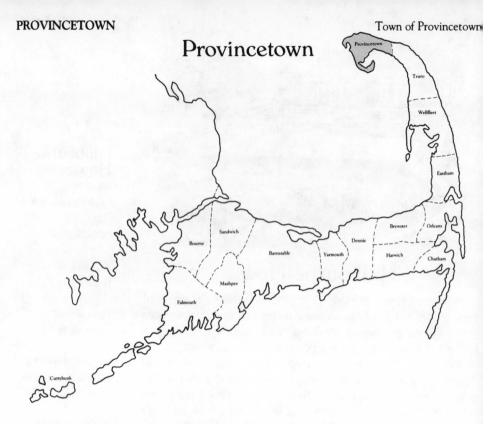

"Stand here and put all America behind you," Henry David Thoreau once said of **Provincetown.** Barely three miles three miles long and half as wide, the town is set like a sparkling diamond at the very tip of Cape Cod. It is surrounded by serene golden sand dunes and shimmering sapphire blue waters. There are magnificent sunrises and sunsets here, as well as a beautiful harbor and the Race Point area, for boaters, surfers, and bathers.

Provincetown is diverse and attracts people of all shapes, sizes, colors, and leanings, all here to enjoy the town's atmosphere. One block from the bay, Commercial Street is the core of the town. Walking is the recommended mode of travel here. This spot is one of parades, parties, festivals, and costume events that never seem to end. The night life is just as fun-filled with cabaret shows, comics, illusionists, and other live productions.

The east end is an art experience, most often described as the "quiet, charming side of town." Fine art, antiques, jewelry, and side-street restaurants are common.

Dune buggy tours are available, as are charter boats for deep-sea fishing, whale watching tours and two hour excursion sails.

On the last weekend in June, area fishermen enjoy a traditional celebration. The Blessing of the Fleet starts with High Mass, then proceeds with a parade through the streets, which begins a festive tribute to the patron saint of fishermen, St. Peter.

Provincetown Airport is a major source of transportation, as are the bus terminal and ferry service in summer between Provincetown and Boston, and Provincetown and Plymouth.

If Zen tennis is your thing, you can get instruction at Bissell's Tennis Courts on Bradford Street extension.

Bed 'n B'fast

Innkeeper Dick Knudson conducts an annual safari to Africa and there is evidence of his trips everwhere in the Bed 'n B'fast. Wild animals gaze at you from walls, and strong colors of that continent surround you. Each room has its own thermostat to control heat. The inn caters to men only on the second and third floor due to shared bath facilites. First floor rooms and apartments are available to women and couples. Rooms are comfortably furnished. You are invited to bring you own spirits to the safari bar. Dick and Bill supply ice, mixes, fruit, and glasses. There is a 5-night minimum in season, but guests are encouraged to call for space other than minimums in case rooms are available between reservations. By August, the inn is booked completely for the 4-night minimum Thanksgiving holiday, which includes a Thanksgiving dinner.

A full American breakfast is served until noon daily. Dinner can be arranged also. The innkeepers continue the custom started in the 1950s, of serving a bowl of chowder and a drink to anyone arriving after dinner.

Bed 'n B'fast
Linguica Cheese Omelette

This is for one serving:

1 T. chopped onion	2 large eggs
1 T. chopped green pepper	1 T. finely chopped linguica
1 t. water	1 T. mixed chopped Swiss and cheddar cheese

Sauté onion and green pepper. Add linguica. Crack 2 large eggs and mix with fork, adding the teaspoon of water. Pour over base. Add cheese to half omelette. Lifting that side with spatula, let egg run under, continuing until nearly done. Then fold in half and serve on a hot plate with blueberry or cranberry muffins.

Bed 'n B'fast
44 Commercial Street
Provincetown, MA
02657
(508) 487-9555

Innkeepers: Dick Knudson, Bill Gilbert

Open all year.
5 rooms/2 baths.

Rates: 5/19 to 9/24, $55-$85 (for two).
AMEX/DC/VISA/MC

Amenities: No children. No pets. Parking limited. 20-minute walk to the beach.

Directions: Route 6 into Provincetown to the last exit, Shank Painter Road (there's a blinking light there). Turn left on Shank Painter, then turn right on Bradford Street. At the top of the second hill, turn onto West Vine Street. Then turn left to Commercial Street. The inn is ahead on the right.

Bradford Gardens Inn

178 Bradford Street
Provincetown, MA
02657
(508) 487-1616

Innkeeper:
M. Susan Culligan

Open all year.
8 rooms/8 baths, plus 2
cottages and 1
efficiency apartment.

Rates: 6/24 to 9/6,
$89-$104 (for two). No
credit cards accepted.

Amenities: No
children. No pets. Six
working fireplaces;
rates include firewood.
In-room color TV.

Directions: Route 6
into Provincetown to
the Conwell Street
Exit. Follow Conwell
to Bradford Street.
Turn left on Bradford.
The inn is on your left,
the parking area is on
your right.

Bradford Gardens Inn

All the rooms in the Bradford Garden's main inn have a different character. The front hall has a white upright piano. Next to it is an old spinning wheel. Bold colors are used lavishly throughout the inn. Fuschia walls lead up the stairs. Woodwork is painted gold. One room uses red and white effectively; another surprises you with dark green; a third has a white eyelet canopy bed and yellow accents. One room on the second floor and an apartment on the first floor look out on a colorful Japanese cherry tree which blooms in mid-May.

The Morning Room, with its central fireplace and large bay window overlooking the garden, provides a delightful setting for guests to mingle and enjoy country breakfasts. The gardens are beautifully landscaped among flowering fruit trees and countless rose bushes. Guests are encouraged to broil their own dinner at the huge outdoor barbecue.

Bradford Gardens Inn's French Swiss Melt

Soak English muffins in egg, milk, and cinnamon. Then grill to a light golden brown. Top the English muffins with Swiss cheese and walnuts covered with maple syrup. Serve with a side dish of fresh fruit and yogurt.

The Cape Codder Guest House

The Cape Codder Guest House offers simple bedrooms in an old-fashioned guest house, neo-classical in style. Some smaller rooms are in the mid-1800s part of the house. The Bradford Street wing, added in the 1930s, contains larger rooms, and on the third floor, an apartment which is spacious and light. The apartment was added in the 1980s, and is fully equipped with dishwasher, phone, and cable television. All upstairs rooms are carpeted.

The inn is managed by the third generation of Mayos. They were trained as marine biologists and helped to start the Center for Coastal Studies in Provincetown.

Continental breakfast is available at the house for a small additional charge. The inn is open pre- and post-season, primarily for whalewatchers, with low rates, but has no central heat. For many this is no problem, but some guests prefer to bring a down comforter or a sleeping bag for chilly nights in the spring and fall.

The Cape Codder's
Whole Wheat Banana Bread

½ C. butter
¾ C. brown sugar or raw sugar
1 egg
1 C. unsifted stone ground whole
    wheat flour

½ C. unsifted, unbleached white flour
1 t. baking soda
¾ t. sea salt
1¼ C. mashed ripe bananas
    (2 large or 3 small)

¼ C. buttermilk or yogurt

Preheat oven to 350°. Cream butter and sugar together until very light and creamy. Beat in the egg. Sift together the whole wheat flour, white flour, baking soda, and salt. Combine the bananas and buttermilk, stirring just enough to mix. Add the dry ingredients alternately with the banana mixture to butter mixture, stirring just enough to combine well. Turn into an oiled 9″ x 5″ loaf pan. Bake for 50-60 minutes or until done. Cool in the pan for 10 minutes. Remove from pan and finish cooling on a rack.

The Cape Codder Guest House
570 Commercial Street
Provincetown, MA
02657
(508) 487-0131

Innkeeper:
Barbara May

Open April 15 to
October 31.
14 rooms/4 baths.

Rates: 6/15 to 9/15,
$25-$45 (for two). No
credit cards accepted.

Amenities:
"Reasonably quiet"
children welcome. Pets
by special advance
request. Private bay
beach across the street,
with sundecks and a
seaside garden. Small
additional charge for
continental breakfast.

Directions: Route 6 to
first Provincetown
exit. Turn left on
Howland to Bradford
Street. Turn left on
Bradford Street to the
back parking lot of the
Cape Codder.

The Courtland Guest House

14 Court Street
Provincetown, MA
02657
(508) 487-2292

Innkeepers:
S. Kerins & R.
Solomon

Open March to
December.
7 rooms, 1 with private
bath.

Rates: 5/26 to 9/8,
$30-$60 (for two).
VISA/MC

Amenities: No
children. No pets.
Limited parking for
cars; no trailers or large
vans. 10-minute walk
to the harbor beach at
the foot of the street.

Directions: Route 6 to
the first set of traffic
lights in Provincetown.
Turn left on Conwell.
Turn right on Bradford
to Court Street. Turn
left on Court Street to
the inn.

The Courtland Guest House

A restored Federal style captain's house, The Courtland Guest House offers a quiet, relaxed, and gracious atmosphere. The Common Room overlooks the yard and garden area and is equipped with a refrigerator for the use of all guests. The inn is a short walk from the craft shops, boutiques, galleries, and restaurants, as well as the cinemas and nightclubs. A continental breakfast of coffee, juice, and muffins is served in the Common Room in season.

The Courtland House's Apple Raisin Muffins

½ C. vegetable oil
½ C. sugar
2 eggs
2 C. all-purpose flour
1 C. raisins

1 T. baking powder
½ t. salt
1½ C. apples, peeled and chopped
½ C. walnuts
½ t. vanilla

Preheat oven to 350°. Combine the oil, sugar, eggs, and vanilla and whisk until smooth. In a separate bowl, combine the flour, baking powder, and salt. Add the egg mixture to the flour and mix until smooth. Fold in the apples, raisins, and walnuts. Bake for 25-30 minutes. Yield: 12 muffins.

Elephant Walk Inn

156 Bradford Street
Provincetown, MA
02657
(508) 487-2543

Innkeeper:
Len Paoletti

Open April 7 to
November 1.
8 rooms/8 baths.

Rates: 6/23 to 9/10,
$67-72 (for two).
VISA/MC/AMEX

Amenities: Children
welcome in the off
season only. No pets.
Color TV and
refrigerator in each
room. Ample parking.
2-minute walk to the
town beach. 5-minute
drive to the National
Seashore.

Directions: Route 6 to
first set of traffic lights
in Provincetown. Turn
left on Conwell Street
to Bradford Street.
The inn is on your left
at the corner of
Bradford and Conwell.

Elephant Walk Inn

The Elephant Walk Inn retains the romantic feeling of an Edwardian country house built at the turn of the century. A number of the rooms have refinished oak floors with Oriental carpets. Old captain's bureaus, antique tables, and brass lamps add to the ambience. The second floor rooms have ceiling fans. Rooms on the first floor have table fans.

A small sitting area off the second floor hall opens out onto a large deck at the rear of the house. You may sit here and enjoy a lovely view of the shady landscaped garden below. A continental breakfast is available in the large Sun Room on the first floor.

Elephant Walk Inn's Pineapple Walnut Cake

½ C. milk
4 eggs
1½ C. all-purpose flour
¼ C. sugar
confectioner's sugar

½ C. chopped walnuts
2 to 3 C. of fresh pineapple pieces
   (or wedges) or drained, canned pieces
2 t. vanilla

Preheat oven to 350°. To make the batter, stir the flour and eggs together in a large mixing bowl. Slowly stir in the milk, sugar, and vanilla extract. Beat with a whisk or an electric beater until the batter is smooth. Fold in the walnuts until they are evenly distributed. Pat the pineapple pieces completely dry with paper towels. Then spread them evenly in a shallow buttered baking pan that holds 5 to 6 cups and is about 2" deep. Pour in batter. Bake on the middle rack of the oven for 1 ½ hours until the top is golden brown and firm to the touch. Dust lightly with confectioner's sugar. This recipe serves six.

The Fairbanks Inn

90 Bradford Street
Provincetown, MA
02657
(508) 487-0386

Innkeeper:
Don Graichen

Open all year.
14 rooms/11 baths.

Rates: 6/20 to 9/15,
$45-$85 (for two).
VISA/MC/AMEX

Amenities: No
children. No pets.
Seven working
fireplaces. 2-minute
walk to the beach.
Ample parking. 7-night
minimum reservation
in July, August, and
Labor Day weekend.

Directions: Route 6 to
traffic lights at
Conwell Street in
Provincetown. Turn
left on Conwell to
Bradford Street. Turn
right on Bradford to
the inn on your right.

The Fairbanks Inn

The sense of 1770's history is clear at The Fairbanks Inn, and it is preserved by dark wallpapers, strong colonial colors, and lovely antiques. The furnishings are more Victorian in style but they fit nicely. The main house and carriage house have seven working fireplaces which were originally the only source of heat. In 1826, the owner sold the house to David Fairbanks, who founded the Seamens Savings Bank and became Provincetown's wealthiest resident. In fact, the bank operated in the two front rooms of the main house.

You enter the inn through a lovely garden into a covered patio/lounge which has comfortable furniture and a television for guests' use. Continental breakfast is served on the counter which separates the kitchen from the living room. A bar with ice and set-ups is available for cocktail hour.

The Fairbanks Inn's
Quick and Easy Baked Steak Casserole

3 lbs. sirloin steak, cut into narrow strips	1/3 C. flour
salt and pepper to taste	1 onion, sliced
1 green pepper, sliced	½ lb. sliced mushrooms
1½ lb. can Progresso crushed tomatoes	4 T. molasses
4 T. soy sauce	

Place meat in a 2½ qt. casserole. Sprinkle with flour, salt, and pepper. Toss to coat meat. Bake uncovered at 400° for 30 minutes. Add onion, green pepper, tomatoes, mushrooms, molasses, and soy sauce. Mix well. Cover and bake at 400° for 45 minutes. Serve over cooked rice or noodles. Serves 6 to 8.

Land's End
Inn
22 Commercial Street
Provincetown, MA
02657
(508) 487-0706

Innkeeper:
David Schoolman

Open all year.
14 rooms/12 baths.

Rates: 5/15 to 9/15,
$60-$100 (for two). No
credit cards accepted.

Amenities: Babes in
arms or children over
12 welcome. No pets.
Working fireplace. 20-
minute walk to the
beach. Ample parking.

Directions: Route 6
into Provincetown; ¼
mile after the Province-
town traffic light, bear
left at the blinking
light onto Shank
Painter Road. Contin-
ue to Bradford Street
and turn right. Follow
Bradford for .4 mile to
Dairy Queen on the
left. Turn left just
beyond Dairy Queen
parking lot onto West
Vine. Follow to Com-
mercial Street and
turn right. Continue
to Commercial Street,
four houses past the
municipal parking lot,
to Point Street on the
right. Turn into Point
Street, go to the dead
end, and follow Land's
End arrow up the
driveway.

Land's End Inn

Land's End Inn is a summer "bungalow" set on a high dune with a commanding panoramic view of Provincetown, the harbor, the upper and lower bay, the salt marshes, and the dunes. Inside, the inn has deep-hued walls, a collection of Oriental wood carvings, dark stained glass, Victorian pieces, and potted plants and flowers. Rooms are large; some accomodate five people comfortably. The "Tower Room," formerly the library, has a queen-size bed and windows which provide other views of Provincetown and the ocean.

The house encourages quiet socializing or solitude away from the bustle of downtown Provincetown. Continental breakfast is the central social event of the day.

Land's End Inn's
Strawberry Rhubarb Pie

Prepare: **1½ C. rhubarb cut into 1 inch pieces**
1½ C. fresh strawberries cut in half
(if using frozen strawberries, use 1 extra T. flour)

Mix: **1 C. sugar**
2 T. flour
1 egg (for a softer filling omit the egg)

Add mix to the rhubarb and strawberries. Line a 9-inch pie pan with plain pastry. Spoon in the filling. Put on top crust or a lattice top. Bake for 40 minutes at 425°.

Watership Inn

7 Winthrop Street
Provincetown, MA
02657
(508) 487-0094

Innkeepers: Jim Foss
& Bob Marcotte

Open March 1 to
November 15.
15 rooms/13 baths.

Rates: 6/18 to 9/12,
$38-$67 (for two).
VISA/MC/AMEX

Amenities: No
children. No pets.
Wood stove in the
lobby. Parking
available. 5-minute
walk to the harbor
beach. 5-minute drive
to the National
Seashore. 5-night
minimum stay over
July Fourth and Labor
Day weekends.

Directions: Route 6
into Provincetown; ¼
mile past the Province-
town traffic light, bear
left at the yellow
blinking light onto
Shank Painter Road.
Follow to the end
(approximately ½
mile). Bear left and
then take the first
right onto Winthrop
Street. The inn is the
second house on your
left.

Watership Inn

The Watership Inn is rustic, with barnside paneling in the large lobby. The second floor decks are great places for sitting and watching the world go by on the quiet residential side street. The rooms are furnished in rustic/nautical style and are named "Captain's Quarters," "Top Mast," and "Chart Room."

You are invited to meet and make new friends over the continental breakfast set out in the lobby. In summer, your innkeepers provide ice and mixers for the cocktail hour.

Watership Inn's Apricot Squares

1 C. sugar	½ C. ground walnuts
2 C. plus 1 T. flour	¼ t. salt
3 oz. margarine, melted	1 egg
1 ¼ C. grated coconut	1 t. vanilla extract

12 oz. apricot preserves

Mix dry ingredients well, including nuts and coconut. Make a well in the mixture and add the melted margarine, egg, and vanilla extract. Mix with a fork until a dough forms. Place half the dough in a square 9" pan. Spread apricot preserves over the mixture. Sprinkle remaining dough over the preserves. Bake at 350° for 35 minutes. When cool, cut into squares.

Windamar House

Windamar is one of the few properties in Provincetown that extends all the way from Commercial Street through to Bradford Street. It is surrounded by brick walks and spacious grounds consisting of beautifully manicured lawns and pristine English flower gardens, a sign of the immaculate housekeeping inside. The northwest side of the house boasts one of the oldest trumpet vines on the entire Cape, a magnificent sight when it is in bloom during the summer months. Guests are encouraged to spend time in the garden. A barbeque is provided for your use.

Each room is decorated with distinctive wallpaper and is furnished with antiques and original artwork. Some rooms have color-coordinated handmade quilts. The studio room has a cathedral ceiling and one entire wall of glass. It is furnished with a queen-size bed, antique clawfoot loveseat and matching armchair, armoire, and additional sofa. In the center of the house is the common room with a television, a sink, and a refrigerator. A continental breakfast is offered every morning.

Windamar House's Bread Pudding

Use left over muffins or breads. Crumble in a baking dish. Cover with condensed milk and half 'n half (just cover). Beat 3-6 eggs. Pour over the crumbled breads. Add cinnamon, nutmeg, raisins, and fresh fruit to taste. Bake at 325° until liquid is absorbed. Serve warm with yogurt.

Windamar House

568 Commercial Street
Provincetown, MA
02657
(508) 487-0599

Innkeeper:
Betty Adams

Open all year.
6 rooms/3 baths.

Rates: 5/26 to 9/15, $48-$72 (for two). No credit cards accepted.

Amenities: No children. No pets. 1-minute walk to the bay beach. 10-minute drive to the National Seashore. Ample parking off Bradford Street. Minimum 5-night stay over Memorial Day, July Fourth, and Labor Day weekends.

Directions: Route 6 to traffic light at Conwell Street. Left on Conwell to Bradford Street. Left on Bradford to the inn.

Sandwich

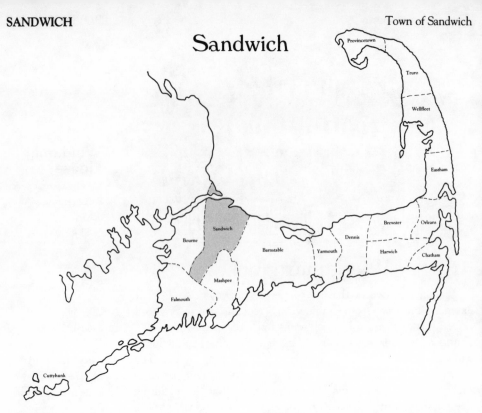

The oldest town of the Cape, **Sandwich** includes the villages of **Forestdale** and **East Sandwich**. The town was established in 1637 and yet is considered one of the best preserved in the nation. Sandwich celebrates its history in many interesting ways. Visitors can view boats from all over the world as they walk beside the famous Cape Cod Canal. You can visit the Green Briar Nature Center and Jam Kitchen, take a tour to the restored and authentically furnished Hoxie House, the operating Grist Mill, and the Thorton W. Burgess Museum (dedicated to the naturalist and children's author). At Yesteryears Doll Museum you will find a large display of rare old dolls, and on the site of the world famous Sandwich Glass Factory there is the magnificent Sandwich Glass Museum. Heritage Plantation features 76 acres where you'll find the Dexter collection of rhododendrons, antique cars, military artifacts, American folk art, a working grist mill, a working carousel, and many other historic sites.

There is an abundance of excellent restaurants, fine antique shops, and beautiful beaches along the Olde King's Highway (Route 6A) to the Great Marsh and Sandy Neck beach.

**Wingscorton
Farm Inn**
11 Wing Boulevard
off Route 6A
East Sandwich, MA
02537
(508) 888-0534

Wingscorton Farm Inn

Built in 1758, the inn is on an eight-acre working farm. The farm's eggs are sold to local markets, and you can visit the sheep and other farm animals.

The spacious rooms are decorated with authentic period pieces. Each guest room has a working fireplace and private bath. An antique carriage house offers a luxury bath, a kitchen, a woodstove, and a spiral staircase that leads to the bedroom. A private sunning deck and a brick patio complete the setting.

Guests enjoy farm-fresh produce from the livestock and gardens in the full country breakfast.

Innkeepers: Dick
Loring & Sheila
Weyers

Open all year. 4
rooms/4 baths, plus
carriage house and
cottage.

Rates: $115-$150 (for
two).
VISA/MC/AMEX

Wingscorton Farm Inn's Carrot Cake

2 C. flour	2 t. cinnamon
2 C. sugar	4 eggs
2 t. soda	1 C. cooking oil
1 t. salt	4 C. grated carrots

¾ C. chopped nuts

Mix the flour, sugar, baking soda, salt, and cinnamon together. Set aside. In a large bowl beat eggs until foamy. Slowly beat in oil. Add flour mixture slowly, beat until smooth. Mix carrots and nuts. Pour battter into 3 greased and floured 9" round pans. Bake in 350° oven for 35 minutes or until a wooden toothpick comes out clean. Allow to cool 10 minutes before removing from pans.

Cream Cheese Frosting

4 T. butter	2 t. milk
2 C. coconut	3½ C. confectioners sugar
8 oz. cream cheese	½ t. vanilla

Mix all of the above together and spread evenly. Coconut is optional.

Amenities: Children
welcome. Well-
behaved pets welcome.
Working fireplaces in
each room. 10-minute
walk down the back
path to a private
beach.

Directions: Route 6 to
Exit 3. Turn left at the
end of the ramp onto
Quaker Meetinghouse
Road, and proceed 1.5
miles to the end. Turn
right onto Route 6A
and proceed 2.5 miles
to the farm on your
left.

Academy Hill Bed & Breakfast

4 Academy Hill Road
Sandwich, MA 02563
(508) 888-8083

Innkeepers: Louise & Ed Stupack

Open all year. 3 rooms/2 baths

Rates: $60 (for two). No credit cards accepted.

Amenities: Children 12 years and older welcome. No pets. 5-minute drive to the beach.

Directions: Route 6 to Exit 1. Follow signs to Route 6A and then take Route 130 into Sandwich village. Turn right at Grove Street, which is right alongside the Sandwich Town Hall, and then take another quick right up Academy Hill.

Academy Hill Bed & Breakfast

Appropriately, this inn is set high up on Academy Hill, a picturesque and private country setting overlooking the village. It is a beautiful private home with no outward signs of being a bed & breakfast inn. The Stupacks offer spacious second floor bedrooms, one with a queen-size bed, tastefully decorated in white wicker, another comfortably furnished with twin-size beds. A large full bath serves both rooms. Another room has twin beds, a sky window, and a private bath.

A very special continental breakfast is served in the formal dining room or on the outside patio in season. The grist mill-ground corn bread uses cornmeal ground locally. Cable television is available in the common room. The innkeepers provide literature, brochures, and maps and menus to look over before you set out for the day.

Academy Hill's Cornbread

1 ¼ C. flour	¾ C. cornmeal
5 t. baking powder	2 eggs, beaten
½ t. salt	1 C. milk
½ C. sugar	½ C. corn oil

Sift dry ingredients. Add eggs and milk (beaten together), then add oil. Bake in a greased 8" square pan for 20 minutes at 425°. Serve warm.

The Barclay Inn

Antique brass and iron beds, firm mattresses, and feather pillows welcome you in both "bed chambers" in the Barclay Inn. 1988 was the first season for innkeepers Pat and Gerry and their historic house in the center of Sandwich village. They have created a pleasing atmosphere with an eclectic mix of furniture, hand-hooked rugs, and hand-stenciled walls.

The inn's location is ideal for touring Sandwich on foot. The inn offers a nice haven at the end of the day. A continental breakfast features home-baked goods every morning.

Barclay Inn's Glazed Orange Rolls

1 C. milk	4½ C. sifted all-purpose flour
3 T. butter	6 T. butter
½ C. sugar	½ C. sugar
½ t. salt	1½ t. orange peel
3 eggs	2 C. sifted confectionery sugar
3-4 T. orange juice	1 pkg. active dry yeast

Scald milk and place in a mixing bowl; cool to lukewarm. Add 3 T. butter, the first ½ C. of sugar, the salt, and the yeast. Let stand 3 minutes. Add the eggs and 1 C. flour, beat well, then add enough flour to make a moderately stiff dough, beating well. Turn out onto a floured surface, knead well until smooth and let sit for 10 minutes. Place in a greased bowl turning to coat surface, cover, let rise until double — about 2 hours. Divide dough in half. Roll each into a 12″ x 8″ rectangle. Stir together the softened butter, ½ C. sugar and orange peel. Spread over the dough, roll up each piece of dough starting with the long side, seal seams. Slice each section into 18 rolls. Place cut side down into muffin pans (greased) or use three 9″ round baking pans. Let rise until double (1½ hours). Bake at 375° for 15 minutes. Combine confectionery sugar and enough orange juice to make a glaze. Drizzle over warm rolls. Makes 3 dozen.

The Barclay Inn

40 Grove Street
Sandwich, MA 02563
(508) 888-5738

Innkeepers: Pat and Gerry Barclay

Open all year.
2 rooms/2 baths.

Rates: 5/1 to 10/30, $70 (for two). No credit cards accepted.

Amenities: No children. No pets. Working fireplace in the common area. 5-minute drive to the beach.

Directions: Route 6A to Tupper Road. Right on Tupper Road to the Sandwich Glass Museum. The inn is across the street on your right.

Captain
Ezra Nye
House

152 Main Street
Sandwich, MA 02563
(508) 888-6142

Innkeepers: Harry and
Elaine Dickson

Open all year.
6 rooms/5 baths.

Rates: Memorial Day
to Columbus Day, $45-
$75 (for two).
VISA/MC/AMEX

Amenities: Children 6
and up welcome. No
pets. 15-minute walk
to the beach. Cable
TV in the common
room.

Directions: Route 6 to
Exit 2. Turn left at the
end of the exit ramp
onto Route 130.
Proceed approximately
1 mile to the fork at
Route 130 and Main
Street, bear right onto
Main Street to the inn
on your right.

Captain Ezra Nye House

Built in 1829 by a noted clipper ship captain, The Captain Ezra Nye House is bright and romantic, with museum quality antiques and fine art throughout. The rooms are large and formal, yet comfortable. Guests are encouraged to play the piano in the parlor or watch cable television if they wish.

Breakfast, though basically continental, is sumptuous, with special treats and surprises served family style around a long table in the dining room. The raspberry strudel will melt in your mouth!

Captain Ezra Nye House's
Raspberry Strudel

Mix: **2 C. flour**
     1 C. sour cream
     1 C. margarine

Form a ball and wrap in plastic wrap to be refrigerated overnight. The next day, divide into two portions. Roll out on floured wax paper; each portion should be length of a standard cookie sheet and 9″ in width. Fill center of each with:

     ½-1 C. raspberry preserves, as desired
     ½ C. shredded coconut
     ½ C. coarsely chopped pecans

Roll, tucking in ends, into a long cylinder. Place seam side down on a greased cookie sheet. Bake at 350° for 45 minutes. May be dusted with powdered sugar. Cut into 2″ strips, or as desired. Delicious!

Hawthorn Hill Bed & Breakfast

The spacious guest rooms at the Hawthorn Hill Bed & Breakfast are in a separate wing of this recenlty built home. The rooms provide privacy for guests, yet are close to town and all the attractions of Sandwich. Rooms are comfortable, pretty, and nicely decorated.

The Carons serve a continental breakfast in the solarium which has a wonderful, ever-changing view of Shawme Pond.

Hawthorn Hill's
Quick Applesauce Muffins

2 C. Bisquick	1 egg
¼ C. sugar	2 T. cooking oil
1 t. cinnamon	¼ C. brown sugar
½ C. applesauce	¼ t. cinnamon
¼ C. milk	2 T. butter, melted

Preheat oven to 400°. Combine Bisquick, ¼ C. sugar, 1 t. cinnamon, applesauce, milk, egg, and oil. Beat vigorously for 30 seconds. Fill greased muffin pans 2/3 full and bake 12-15 minutes. Cool slightly and remove from pans. Mix remaining sugar and cinnamon. Dip tops of muffins in melted butter, then in sugar/cinnamon. Makes 12 muffins.

Hawthorn
Hill Bed &
Breakfast
P.O. Box 777;
off Grove Street
Sandwich, MA 02563
(508) 888-3336

Innkeepers: Roger & Maxime Caron

Open all year.
2 rooms/2 baths.

Rates: $60 (for two). No credit cards accepted.

Amenities: Children welcome. No pets.

Directions: Route 6A to Tupper Road. Turn right on Tupper Road to the Sandwich Glass Museum. Turn right on Grove Street to the inn on Shawme Pond.

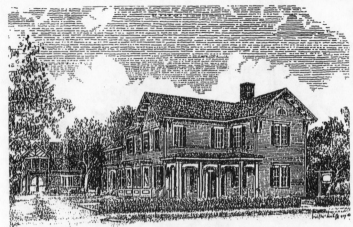

Isaiah Jones Homestead

165 Main Street
Sandwich, MA 02563
(508) 888-9115

Innkeepers: Steven
and Kathleen Catania

Open all year.
4 rooms/4 baths.

Rates: 5/12 to 10/28,
$80-$110 (for two).
VISA/MC/AMEX

Amenities: Children
over 12 welcome. No
pets. Fireplace in the
gathering room. 7- to
10-minute walk to the
beach. No smoking.

Directions: Route 6 to
Exit 2. Turn left at the
end of the exit ramp
onto Route 130.
Approximately one
mile to the fork at
Route 130 and Main
Street, stay right onto
Main Street to the inn
on your left.

Isaiah Jones Homestead

Dramatic high Victorian throughout, this inn was built in 1849 by Sandwich's doctor, Jonathan Leonard. In 1868-69, the Isaiah Jones family bought it and one of the descendents lived in the home until 1954. Period antiques, Oriental rugs, and attention to detail are visible everywhere. The house has been completely renovated with queen-sized beds, lovely sitting areas in all the bedrooms, and new ceramic tile in the bathrooms. One room has an antique Victorian ½ canopy bed, a large cheval mirror, and a whirlpool tub.

On cool mornings, breakfast is served in the Gathering Room before the fireplace. Afternoon tea is delightful.

Rhododendrons are a beautiful part of the landscaping that surround the elegant inn.

Isaiah Jones Homestead's Baked Apples

Core apples and pierce each apple four times. Add to each apple:

1 t. brown sugar
¼ t. butter
a few raisins
ground nuts

Add water to bottom of dish, about ¼" worth. Microwave at high temperature for 1 minute for each apple, or bake in conventional oven for 10 minutes at 400° in a covered dish. Apples are soft when served. Baste with juice before serving.

The Quince Tree

The Quince Tree
164 Main Street
Sandwich, MA 02563
(508) 888-1371

Innkeepers: Kathleen & Steven Catania

Open all year. 3 rooms/2 baths.

Rates: 5/15 to 10/31, $55-$75 (for two). No credit cards accepted.

Amenities: Children over 12 welcome. No pets. Two fireplaces are in guest rooms, and there is one each in the library and dining room. No smoking. 7- to 10-minute walk to the beach.

Directions: Route 6 to Exit 2. Turn left at the end of the exit ramp onto Route 130. Proceed approximately 1 mile to the fork at Route 130 and Main Street. Stay right onto Main Street, to the inn.

The Quince Tree was named for the vegetation which surrounds the home. Small and romantic, even breakfast is served by candlelight at the inn. The music room with baby grand piano and the library with a fireplace provide lovely spots for relaxing. They are beautifully furnished with antiques.

All three guest rooms are on the second floor. The wine room with its lace canopy queen-size bed is charming, a wonderful getaway. The blue room has a full bath. The green room shares a shower located right next door. The innkeepers supply fluffy terry velour bathrobes to guests.

At breakfast there is a choice of homemade quince jelly or grape jam made from fruit grown in the yard. The coffee is a unique house blend.

Quince Tree Inn's Surprise Muffins

Mix: **2 C. flour**
1/3 C. sugar
3 t. baking powder

In a separate bowl, beat: **1 egg**
¾ C. milk
½ C. oil

Add dry ingredients to wet. Spoon into greased muffin tin. Drop 1 t. strawberry preserves in each muffin. Add remainder of batter to each muffin. Bake at 350° for 18-20 minutes.

Six Water Street Bed & Breakfast

6 Water Street
Sandwich, MA 02563
(508) 888-6808

Innkeepers: Daphne &
Michael Sher

Open all year.
3 rooms/3 baths.

Rates: 6/1 to 10/31,
$75-$90 (for two). No
credit cards accepted.

Amenities: Children
over 12 welcome. No
pets. 5-minute drive to
the beach. No smoking
allowed in the inn.

Directions: Route 6 to
Exit 2. At the bottom
of the ramp turn left
toward Sandwich
village. The inn is a
mile and a half ahead
on the right.

Six Water Street Bed & Breakfast

Six Water Street was built in the mid-1800s as the home of a Sandwich craftsman. The detail in the home has been carefully preserved and enhanced by the renovations. The skylight room features a brass and white iron bed. French doors open to reveal an antique clawfoot tub in the bathroom. In the pond view room there is a queen-size sleigh bed. The Rose room has a queen-sized white iron bed and white cane and wicker furniture, as well as handcrafted brass fixtures in the private bath.

The grounds of this lovely, intimate inn border Shawme Pond, and the innkeepers offer rowboats for relaxing rides. In the words of a recent guest: "Our row with the swans, ducks, and waterfall was like something out of another century."

Breakfast is served on a table set with white linen and fine china in a setting overlooking the pond. Daphne's Finnish Baked Pancakes are very special.

Six Water Street's Finnish Baked Pancakes

6 large eggs	1 t. salt
1 quart milk	1 C. flour
4-5 T. sugar	¼ lb. butter

Melt and slightly brown the butter in a 12" x 16" pan (the innkeeper uses the oven for this). Mix the milk and eggs lightly. Add sugar, salt, and flour. Pour into the pan with butter. Bake at 450° for 20-23 minutes. Serve with hot maple syrup or confectioner's sugar and butter. Other toppings, such as canned pie fillings (apple, pineapple, or strawberries), can be served at room temperature.

The Summer House

The
Summer
House
158 Old Main Street
Sandwich, MA 02563
(508) 888-4991

Innkeepers: Dave &
Kay Merrell

Open April to
November. 5 rooms/3
baths.

Rates: 6/1 to 9/12,
$60-$70 (for two).
VISA/MC

Amenities: Children
10 years and older
welcome. No pets.
Seven fireplaces. 15-
minute walk to the
beach.

Directions: Route 6 to
Exit 2. Turn left at
end of exit ramp onto
Route 130, to
Sandwich village.
Proceed about 1.3
miles and bear right
onto Old Main Street.
The inn is .2 of a mile
ahead.

The Summer House is an exquisite example of Cape Cod Greek Revival architecture in an area of many equally stunning historic homes and public buildings. Newly restored and renovated, the inn was built in 1835 and owned until 1980 by the Hiram Dillaway family. Hiram Dillaway was employed by the Boston & Sandwich Glass Company for fifty years and was an innovator in the technique of molding and blowing glass.

The bedrooms are carefully decorated to evoke the spirit of the 19th century. Antique furniture, fireplaces, Cape Cod painted hardwood floors, original woodwork, and hardware are found throughout the house.

The continental breakfast is served in the plant-filled breakfast room. Originally a formal parlor, the room features Chinese red walls with white window molding, paneling, and interior shutters. The floor is black and white checkerboard, the fireplace black marble, and the bookcases are laden with the books you always meant to read.

The Summer House's Applesauce Streusel Cake

½ C. butter or margarine
2/3 C. sugar
1 egg
¾ C. applesauce
½ C. crushed branflake cereal
¾ C. all-purpose flour

¾ C. whole wheat flour
2 t. baking powder
1 t. salt
½ t. ground cinnamon
¼ t. ground cloves
1 t. vanilla

Heat oven to 375°. Cream butter and sugar until light and fluffy. Beat in eggs and stir in applesauce and cereal. Mix dry ingredients. Stir gently into applesauce mixture. Stir in vanilla and pour into a greased 8″ square baking pan. Bake 25-30 minutes. Make streusel topping while cake is baking. When cake has baked 25-30 minutes, sprinkle with topping and bake 5 minutes more.

Streusel Topping:
½ C. powdered sugar, 2 T. butter or margarine, 1 t. ground cinnamon
Mix all ingredients until mixture resembles coarse crumbs.

Wing-
Howland
House

8 Morse Road
Sandwich, MA 02563
(508) 888-1947

Innkeeper:
Janet Garnier

Open all year.
2 rooms/2 baths

Rates: 4/15 to 11/30,
$60 (for two). No
credit cards accepted.

Amenities: Children
welcome. Pets welcome
with prior notification.
Six fireplaces. 15- to
20-minute walk to the
beach.

Directions: Route 6 to
Exit 2. Turn left off
the exit, proceed
approximately 1 mile,
then turn right onto
Morse Road. Follow
around the curve (past
MEWS Condos) to the
first road on the right,
a country lane. The
house is set back in the
woods.

Wing-Howland House

Built in 1734, this inn is one of four "Wing" houses on Cape Cod.
It was known as the "old abandoned house" when Janet Garnier
purchased it in 1984, exactly 250 years after it was built by Jashub
Wing. Lovingly restored to its original charm, the inn boasts
pumpkin pine floors, hand-carved raised paneling, and six fireplaces.
Antique laces and linens accent the second floor guest rooms along
with wicker and collectibles. A quiet country lane leads visitors to its
tranquil setting.

You may choose to have your continental breakfast brought to
your room, or be served in the dining room. The conservatory
overflows with flowering plants. An original wainscotted sitting
room with a fireplace is available for relaxing. The feeling is that of a
quaint tree house tucked away in another time in history.

Wing-Howland House's
Breakfast Scones

2 C. flour	8 oz. sour cream
3 T. sugar	1 egg yolk
2 t. baking powder	1 slightly beaten egg white
½ t. baking soda	½ C. currants
5 T. butter	cinnamon and sugar

Combine flour, sugar, baking powder, and baking soda. Cut in butter
until mixture resembles coarse crumbs. Add currants, blend sour cream
and egg yolk. Add to the flour mixture. Knead on lightly floured surface
(10-15 strokes). Pat into 10" circle 1½" thick. Cut into 4" circles. Slice
each circle through into quarters—do not separate! Place on ungreased
cookie sheet. Brush with egg white. Sprinkle cinnamon-sugar over top.
Bake at 425° for 15-18 minutes. Cool for 5 minutes, then serve warm.

Truro

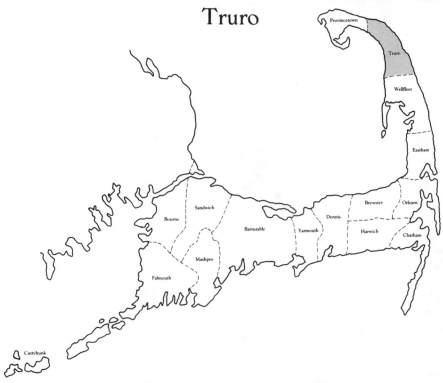

"The narrow land" of the town of **Truro** and its village of **North Truro** stretch fourteen miles along the Cape's forearm and are less than a half mile wide in some areas. Truro's first houses were built along Long Nook Road. Much of the populace made a living by "wrecking" — salvaging cargo and equipment of ships broken up along the treacherous Peaked Hill Bars. Religion flourished in the 1800s and there were so many meetinghouses atop each of the town's five hills that seamen used them to navigate by. A shipyard was built at the mouth of the Pamet River and Truro became one of the first whaling towns on the Cape.

The Pilgrim Heights Interpretive Shelter in the highlands of this town offers hikes through marshes and dunes to the ocean. This is the area the Pilgrims explored prior to their Plymouth landfall. From Corn Hill in North Truro you can see the tip of Cape Cod as well as the marker where the Pilgrims found Indian Corn, thus giving the hill its name. Highland Light (Cape Cod Light) dates from 1795 and is one of the most powerful lights on the Atlantic coast. Also at Highland Light, the Truro Historical Society maintains a collection of old firearms and historic artifacts, many from shipwrecks.

If you enjoy golfing by the ocean, the Highland Golf Club, has a magnificent view of the Atlantic over the dunes. Truro has a unique wildness about it that you won't soon forget.

**The
Summer
House**
Pond Road
North Truro, MA
02652
(508)487-2077

Innkeeper:
Diana Worthington

Open June to
September.
5 rooms/1 bath.

Rates: 6/15 to 9/15,
$60 (for two). No
credit cards accepted.

Amenities: No
children. No pets.
Walk to the bay beach.
Additional outside hot
shower. Two-night
minimum stay during
the summer.

Directions: Route 6 to
the Route 6A exit in
North Truro. Turn left
on Pond Road.

The Summer House

"The Summer House is well worth noting as an option to P'town for people who like to be surrounded by peace and art," noted the *Boston Sunday Globe.*

This is a place for people who want to get away to a simpler life amidst the rugged beauty of Truro. The house has Victorian front doors with glass etching. The wide front porch holds large redwood beach furniture for relaxing. Inside, you will find an impressive collection of Cape art and old photographs of Truro and its trapfishermen. Like most old Cape Cod houses, this one has wide floorboards. And its well-used antique furniture, colorful cotton bedspreads, and oval braided rugs create a rustic ambience suitable to the wildness of this beach community.

A continental breakfast consisting of muffins, homemade jams, coffee, and juice is served outdoors on the porch, or inside at the large kitchen table.

The Summer House's
Fresh Lemon and Ginger Muffins

2 T. coarsely chopped, peeled ginger root	2 T. lemon peel
½ C. butter, at room temperature	½ C. granulated sugar
2 large eggs	1 t. baking soda
1 C. plain yogurt or buttermilk	2 C. all-purpose flour

Heat oven to 375°. Grease muffin cups or use foil or paper baking cups. Finely chop the ginger. Finely grate the lemon peel. In a large bowl, beat butter and sugar until pale and fluffy. Beat in eggs, one at a time. Add ginger and lemon peel. Stir baking soda into yogurt or buttermilk; it will start to bubble and rise up. Fold flour into ginger mixture one third at a time, alternating with the yogurt. When well blended, scoop into muffin cups. Bake 18-20 minutes or until lighly browned and springy to the touch. Remove from pan and let cool 3-5 minutes.

B & B on Board

Bunk and Breakfast on Board is for those who enjoy the unusual and want a different adventure.

The New England coast is one of the most delightful places in the country. What better way to enjoy it than to sail its picturesque harbors, sleep onboard in a quiet, protected cove, be served a hearty breakfast on a deserted beach, and then enjoy a full day of sailing, fishing, and swimming? Guests may also "crew" if they wish.

Because space is limited on a the small sloop, parties of two are best accommodated. Your host, guide, captain, and cook has sailed these waters in the Wellfleet to Provincetown area of Cape Cod Bay for thirty years. Day trips are also available.

B & B on Board

Box 201K
Jaffrey, New
Hampshire 03452
(603) 532-8083

Host: Joe Manning

Limited to parties of 2. Operates June through September. Bring sleeping bags.

Rates: $140 for a party of 2, for 24 hours.

Directions: Contact your host.

Bunk & Breakfast on Board's Cheesey Yankee Scrambled Eggs

Ingredients per person:

2 eggs (Rhode Island Red)
2 T. cream (from the
    Connecticut Valley)

¼ C. Vermont cheddar
(the lumpy, bumpy kind)
3 strips of lean bacon (from Maine)

Fry bacon well. Drain. Beat eggs and cream, then cook until just starting to solidify. Add cheese and fold. Keep moist. Serve on an overturned, washed ashore fish box (there is no fish smell) on a sunny Cape Cod Bay sand spit by a Granite State skipper, with hot coffee!

Parker
House

P.O. Box 114
Truro, MA 02666
(508) 349-3358

Innkeeper:
Jane Parker

Open all year.
3 rooms/2 baths.

Rates: In season, $55
(for two). No credit
cards accepted.

Amenities: No
children. No pets. 1 ½
miles to the beach.

Directions: From
Route 6, take the
Pamet exit toward
Truro Center. At
Depot Road, make a
right turn. The Parker
House is just after the
library on your right.

Parker House

The Parker House is a circa 1800 Cape which has been in the Parker family for almost seventy years. Innkeeper Jane Parker has welcomed guests to her comfortable retreat for six years. You enter the kitchen through a wonderful old kitchen complete with old stove and drying herbs. Guest rooms are simply furnished in the style of a beach house in this "least developed town on the Cape."

Parker House's
Maude Duganne's Oatmeal Bread

2 C. boiling water   1 C. lukewarm water
1 C. Quaker Oats   1 t. salt
½ C. molasses   1 yeast cake

6 C. flour

Pour boiling water over oats in a big bowl and let cool. Then add all other ingredients, including yeast dissolved in lukewarm water. Stir with a big spoon until thoroughly mixed. Put the bowl in a reasonably warm place, covered with an old towel. When it has about doubled in bulk (about 2 hours), punch it down and stir until air bubbles are gone. Put into two greased bread pans and let rise again. Heat oven to 400° (if using glass pans, 350°). Bake for 40-60 minutes. Turn out on wire racks, on sides, and let cool.

Wellfleet

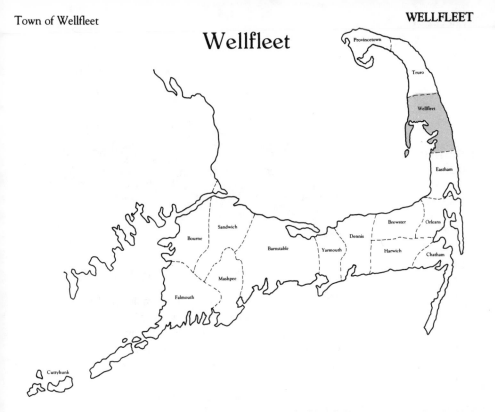

Wellfleet is another one of the few towns on Cape Cod where you can enjoy various activities on the oceanside as well as the bayside. Even at the height of the summer season you can always find a beach to explore alone.

Oysters, whales, and pirates all figure prominently in the story of this lower Cape town.

Wellfleet gained recognition in the early 1900s when Guglielmo Marconi brought to it the excitement of the first wireless station, having made the first two-way wireless communication between America and Europe, from a beach here. The Massachusetts Audubon Society's Wellfleet Bay Wildlife Sanctuary draws people from all over the world for field trips.

The village's main street area offers as many as twenty art galleries and an assortment of activities for many tastes. Wellfleet has the distinction of possessing the only town clock in the world that strikes ship's time.

The Inn at Duck Creeke

E. Main Street
Wellfleet, MA 02667
(508) 349-9333

Innkeepers: Bob Morrill, Anne Fortier, Judy Pihl

Open mid-May to mid-October.
25 rooms (17 with private baths/8 with shared baths).

Rates: 6/18 to 9/6, $55-$75 (for two). No credit cards accepted.

Amenities: Children welcome. No pets. Two full-service restaurants. 15-minute walk to the beach.

Directions: Route 6 to the Wellfleet Center Exit sign at the lights. Turn left. The inn is located on the right about 500 yards after making the turn.

The Inn at Duck Creeke

Several buildings comprise the Inn complex, and one of them, the Sea Captain's House, was built in the early 1800s. The inn is situated on five acres, with a duck, abundant bird life, and views of a tidal creek and salt marsh. The rooms are comfortably furnished and nicely decorated with spool beds, Boston rockers, cane bottom chairs, and painted furniture.

The inn's restaurant, Sweet Seasons, overlooks a rush-bordered pond. Its dark wood floors, greenery, lithographs, soft music, and evening candlelight complement the fine cuisine. Both the inn and the restaurant have been reviewed and recommended by many guide books. The Tavern Room is a popular gathering place. Its intimate atmosphere is enhanced by a cozy fireplace, natural beam ceilings, hanging plants, and a unique bar made from a collection of period doors and local marine charts.

A continental breakfast is included.

Seasons' Shrimp
with Rice a la Inn at Duck Creeke

3 T. butter	½ t. freshly ground black pepper
16 large shrimp, peeled and deveined	1 to 2 oz. Ouzo (100 proof)
	2 large tomatoes, chopped coarsely
1 clove garlic, minced	¾ C. crumbled Feta cheese
1 T. chopped fresh parsley	hot cooked rice

Melt the butter in a sauté pan. Add the shrimp. Cook gently, keeping the pan moving during cooking. Add the garlic, parsley, and black papper. Pour the Ouzo over the shrimp and flame. When the flame subsides, add the tomatoes and crumbled Feta. Cook until the cheese begins to melt. To serve, arrange the shrimp tails up around a mound of rice and pour the sauce over the shrimp. NOTE: Top the rice with leaves of kale and a tomato rose for a lovely presentation. Serves 4.

Yarmouth

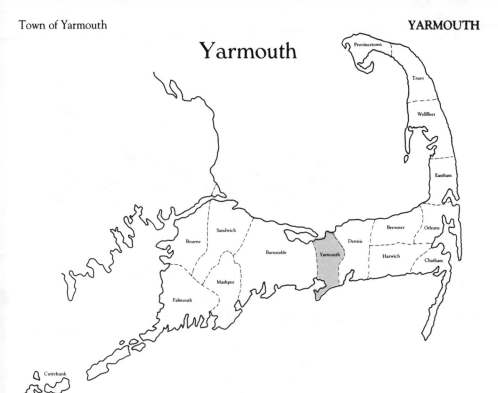

Yarmouth, considered to be one of the foundation towns of the Cape, is composed of the villages of **Bass River, South Yarmouth, West Yarmouth,** and **Yarmouth Port.** The town stretches along Cape Cod Bay on the north and touches the shores of Nantucket Sound to the south. Yarmouth is rich in agricultural, spiritual, and maritime history.

During your stay, try to visit the Farris Mill, the oldest windmill in the nation, which was built in Sandwich in 1633, moved to Bass River in 1750, to South Yarmouth in 1782, and to West Yarmouth in 1894. Stop by the Quaker Cemetery where all the stones are set without epitaphs in straight lines with the same design, signifying their belief in equality. The Nature Trail behind the post office in Yarmouth Port is a popular site, with its "Wheel of Thyme" herb garden. The Bangs-Hallet House and the Winslow Crocker House are two other restorations maintained by the Historical Society. Antique shops and fine restaurants line Route 6A (Main Street) in Yarmouth Port. Many brides come to Cape Cod to get married at the Kelley Chapel. A good part of the town is declared to be historic in nature and thus protected from change. Main Street in Yarmouth Port is listed in the National Register of Historic Places. The whole town celebrated the 350th anniversary of its founding in 1989.

Blue Rock Golf Course, Bass River Golf Course, and the new Bayberry Hills Golf Course are three excellent courses. Swimming may be enjoyed at Bass River Beach, Parkers River Beach, Sea Gull Beach, Seaview Beach, Bass Hole, and Dennis Pond.

The Anchorage Inn

122 So. Shore Drive
Bass River, MA 02664
(508) 398-8265

Innkeeper:
Ruth Masciarotte

Open all year.
3 rooms/ 3 baths.

Rates: 7/1 to 9/15,
$42-$50 (for two). No
credit cards accepted.

Amenities: No
children. No pets.
Cable TV. Just across
the street from the
beach.

Directions: Route 6 to
Exit 7. Left on Willow
Street. Take the first
left on Higgins Crowell
Road. Continue to
Route 28. Turn left on
Route 28 and proceed
aproximately 1 mile to
Sea View Avenue.
Turn right on Sea
View, then left on So.
Shore Drive.

The Anchorage Inn

There is always an ocean breeze at The Anchorage Inn, located across the street from Nantucket Sound. Each large living room-bedroom combination has twin beds, large comfortable chairs, cable television, and a separate entrance.

The patio, where guests gather for a breakfast of homemade muffins and breads is surrounded by lovely flower beds and a meticulously kept lawn.

The Anchorage Inn's Cranberry Muffins

2 C. flour	½ t. ginger
1 C. sugar	½ C. shortening
1½ t. baking powder	¾ C. orange juice
2 t. grated orange peel	1 T. vanilla
1½ t. nutmeg	2 eggs slightly beaten
1 t. cinnamon	1½ C. cranberries, chopped
1½ C. chopped nuts	½ t. baking soda

In a medium bowl mix flour, sugar, baking powder, baking soda, orange peel, nutmeg, cinnamon, and ginger. Cut in shortening with two knives. Stir in juice, vanilla, and eggs. Fold in cranberries and walnuts. Spoon into 18 well-greased or paper muffin cups. Bake in 350° oven for 25 minutes or until golden. Serve hot!

The
Belvedere
Inn
167 Main Street
Bass River, MA 02664
(508) 398-6674

Innkeepers:
Dick & Judy Fenuccio

Open all year.
3 rooms/2 baths. A
carriage house is
available for parties of
four.

Rates: $55-$65 (for
two). No credit cards
accepted.

Amenities: Children
over 12 years welcome.
No pets. Working
fireplace in the parlor.
3-minute drive to the
beach. No smoking in
the house.

Directions: Route 6 to
Exit 8. Turn right on
Union Street, which
becomes Station
Avenue. Cross Route
28 onto Main Street,
to the inn on your left.

The Belvedere Inn

The Belvedere Inn, a restored sea captain's home, is situated on an acre of beautifully landscaped, shaded property. Floors are original wide-pine board. Walls are stenciled and a crystal chandelier illuminates the formal dining room.

The rooms are carefully decorated and provide comfortable guest accommodations, all on the second floor. One has a queen-size bed, an antique dressing table, and a lively colonial floral print wallcovering. Another is a Victorian-style room furnished with four-poster mahogany twin beds. Lace trimmed curtains cover the windows, walls are covered in a pale blue and white floral print. A raspberry velvet chair accents the color scheme.

A "full" continental breakfast is included.

The Belvedere's Poppy Seed Loaf with Apricot Butter

¼ C. butter or margarine, softened	½ t. salt
1 C. sugar	¼ t. ground nutmeg
2 eggs	1 C. milk
1 t. grated orange peel	1/3 C. poppy seeds
2 C. all-purpose flour	½ C. chopped nuts
2½ t. baking powder	½ C. golden raisins (optional)

Beat together butter and sugar until creamy; add eggs, one at a time, beating after each addition. Mix in orange peel. In a separate bowl, stir together flour, baking powder, salt and nutmeg until thoroughly blended. To cream mixture, add flour mixture alternately with milk, stirring until blended; then stir in poppy seeds, nuts, and raisins, if desired. Turn batter into a well-greased and floured 9" x 5" loaf pan. Bake in a preheated 350° oven (325° for glass pan) for 1 hour and 10 minutes. Let bread cool in pan for 10 minutes, then turn onto rack to cool completely. Meanwhile, prepare apricot butter to be used as a spread. Makes 1 loaf.

Apricot Butter

Beat together ½ C. (¼ lb.) softened butter, ¼ C. apricot jam, 1 t. grated lemon peel, and 1 T. lemon juice.

Captain Isaiah's House

**Captain
Isaiah's
House**

33 Pleasant Street
Bass River, MA 02664
(508) 394-1739

Open June to
September.
8 rooms/2 private
baths.

Innkeepers: Marge &
Alden Fallows

Rates: $35-$45 (for
two). No credit cards
accepted.

Amenities: Children
over 5 welcome. No
pets. Four working
fireplaces. 20-minute
walk to the beach.

Directions: Route 6
to Exit 8. Right on
Union Street, which
becomes Station
Avenue. Cross Route
28. Turn left at Akin
Avenue to the corner
of Akin and Pleasant
Streets.

Captain Isaiah Crowell's house is a historical home from the early 1800s Quaker village. It has a long history as a boarding house for summer visitors and the tradition of New England hospitality has been revived by innkeepers Marge and Alden Fallows. Rooms are airy and comfortable and some have fireplaces. All are furnished with quilts and braided rugs, handmade by Marge. Garden flower bouquets adorn the rooms and sitting parlor. Everything is white, bright, and charming.

"We like to send guests off with the feeling that they have been among friends," says Marge. By using first names and by sharing vacation and travel tips with guests as they sit around the large breakfast table, the Fallows really do treat travelers as friends or family members.

Captain Isaiah's House's Blueberry Muffins

½ C. butter or margarine   2 eggs
2 C. flour   ½ C. milk
1 C. sugar   2 t. baking powder
2 C. blueberries   1 t. vanilla

Cream butter and sugar, add eggs one at a time. Blend all ingredients well, adding dry ones to batter, alternating with milk and vanilla. Fold in blueberries. Fill greased muffin tins ½ to ¾ full. Bake in 350° oven until golden. Serve hot.

Old Cape House

"Lovely and friendly, a bit of jolly England," commented one guest of Old Cape House. Innkeeper Linda Arthur, born and bred in London, maintains British tradition by offering strawberries and cream in the summer while the Wimbledon tennis matches are being held.

There are three suites with private baths and televisions in the inn. One suite has its own private entrance, and small kitchen unit. A double room and a single room share one bath. All rooms are comfortably furnished with lacy curtains, white bedspreads, and handmade quilts. A private courtyard and porch, and a barbecue area in the garden are available for use.

A continental breakfast is included.

Old Cape House's Poppy Seed Bread

3 C. flour	½ C. poppy seeds
1 t. baking powder	2 eggs
1 ½ t. baking soda	1 C. sugar
1 t. cinnamon	1 C. milk
1 t. ground ginger	½ C. vegetable oil

Mix together all dry ingredients, add eggs, oil, and milk, and stir until well moistened. Divide the batter between two well greased loaf pans and bake in a preheated oven at 350° for approximately 45 minutes. Best served warm with lots of butter.

Old Cape House
108 Old Main Street
Bass River, MA 02664
(508) 398-1068

Innkeepers: Linda & George Arthur

Open May to October. 5 rooms/4 baths.

Rates: 6/15 to 9/15, $45-$65 (for two). No credit cards accepted.

Amenities: Children over 15 years welcome. No pets. Friendly cat on premises. Televisions. Barbeque facilities. One suite has a fireplace. No smoking at any time. 15-minute walk to the beach.

Directions: Route 6 to Exit 8. Turn right on Station Avenue. Cross Route 28 onto Main Street. The inn is on the right.

Colonial House Inn

277 Main Street
Yarmouth Port, MA
02675
(508) 362-4348

Innkeeper:
Malcolm J. Perna

Open all year.
21 rooms/21 baths.

Rates: Memorial Day
to Columbus Day, $80
(for two, including
dinner).
VISA/MC/AMEX
DIS/DC

Amenities: Children
welcome. No pets.
Full-service, first class
restaurant. Working
fireplaces. 15-minute
walk to the beach.
Rates include dinner.

Directions: Route 6 to
Exit 7. Turn right on
Willow Street to Route
6A. Turn right on
Route 6A, and proceed
for 1.5 miles to the inn
on your right.

Colonial House Inn

The original part of Colonial House Inn was built in the 1730s and houses 11 guest rooms plus a first-class restaurant in three intimate dining rooms. Each of the large guest rooms is furnished with handsome period pieces which innkeeper Malcolm Perna goes to great lengths (and many auctions and yard sales) to find. Beautiful stenciling decorates hallways, guest rooms, and one of the dining rooms. The inn features New England cuisine with a continental flair, and dinner from a limited but delightful menu is included in room rates. There is an extensive wine cellar as well, and a fireplaced lounge.

The newly renovated Carriage House, added on to the inn in 1860, has 10 additional guest rooms with the same charm and comfort as the original house. It includes a jacuzzi, a TV room, a reading area, and a function room for large parties, conferences, and receptions. A light breakfast is included.

Colonial House's Haddock de Journee

2 lbs. haddock, filleted	1 T. lemon juice
4 oz. shrimp, chopped fine	2 T. white wine
4 oz. scallops, chopped fine	1 T. Worcestershire sauce
2 oz. lobster, chopped fine	pinch of thyme
pinch of salt and pepper	½ C. heavy cream

Combine all ingredients except haddock and cream in a stainless steel mixing bowl. Place bowl over ice. Add cream slowly, whipping constantly with a wire whisk until well blended. Butter an oven-proof baking dish. Slit haddock to make a pocket, and stuff with mixture. Place in dish and bake at 350° for 20 minutes or until fish flakes when tested. Top with Hollandaise Sauce before serving.

Hollandaise Sauce

½ C. melted warm butter	4 T. boiling water
1 to 1 ½ T. lemon juice or tarragon vinegar	¼ t. salt
3 egg yolks	pinch of cayenne

Place egg yolks in double-boiler (cook over hot water, NOT boiling water), stirring constantly until they begin to thicken. Add 1 T. boiling water, repeat until all 4 T. of water have been added. Beat in warm lemon juice. Remove from heat. Add warm melted butter very slowly, beating constantly with wire whisk. Add salt and cayenne. Serve at once. HINT: This sauce can be stored in a large mouth thermos until ready to serve.

Crook' Jaw Inn
186 Main Street
Yarmouth Port, MA
02675
(508) 362-6111

Innkeepers: Ed
Shedlock & Don
Spagnolia

Open all year.
5 rooms/5 baths.

Rates: Memorial Day
to October 1, $90 (for
two, including dinner).
AMEX/VISA/MC

Amenities: Children
welcome. No pets.
Working fireplaces in
the common rooms. 3-
minute drive to the
beach.

Directions: Route 6 to
Exit 7. Turn right on
Willow Street to Route
6A. Turn right on
Route 6A for 4/10 of a
mile to the inn on
your left.

Crook' Jaw Inn

The 250-year-old Crook' Jaw Inn was at one time a "way station" for the changing of stagecoach horses between Boston and Provincetown. The hosts continue the tradition of warm hospitality in a comfortable colonial setting. Each room is decorated with period furniture on wide-board floors, and colonial wallpaper, quilts, and curtains. On the second floor, one room has a deck which overlooks the lavish English country garden.

Innkeeper Don Spagnolia is a gourmet cook. It is a treat to sit at his table in the dining room with the fire crackling, while dining on one of the specialties of the house, such as Paupiere of Sole with clam stuffing and sherried white sauce. Breakfast and dinner are also served on the brick patio surrounded by the English garden. Delicious picnic baskets are available continental style or American style to add to a day's outing.

Crook' Jaw Inn's Pork Madeira

1 lb. pork sirloin or tenderloin
2 C. flour
Madeira wine

1 t. pepper
½ lb. mushrooms
2 T. butter

Trim excess fat from pork pieces. Cut each sirloin into 3 or 4 pieces. Place each piece between wax paper sheets and pound thinly. Dredge each pounded piece in the flour and pepper mixture. Shake off excess flour and sauté lightly on each side. Set aside. When each piece has been prepared in this way, place butter in a fry pan and heat. Slice the mushrooms and sauté in butter, adding sufficient Madeira to cover bottom of the pan. Continue to turn each piece until butter and Madeira thicken. Remove pieces from pan and cover with mushrooms and sauce. Serve immediately.

Fifty-Four Thacher Shore

54 Thachershore Road
Yarmouth Port, MA
02675
(508) 362-8053

Innkeeper:
Ginger DeLong

Open all year.
1 room/1 bath.

Rates: Memorial Day
to Columbus Day, $75
(for two). No credit
cards accepted.

Amenities: No
children. No pets.
Working fireplace. 10-
minute walk to the
beach.

Directions: Route 6 to
Exit 7. Turn right on
Willow Street to Route
6A. Turn right on
Route 6A, proceed a
short distance, then
turn left on
Gingerbread Lane
(opposite the Bank of
Boston). Go to the end
of Gingerbread Lane.
Fifty-Four Thacher
Shore is directly ahead
on the marsh.

Fifty-Four Thacher Shore

Fifty-Four Thacher Shore is a former duck hunting lodge, with the rustic, isolated feeling of Cape Cod's famous Outermost House. It sits right on the edge of the marsh and has expansive views of the marsh and the water beyond. Just one room is available, with a private bath close by, so you really have the house to yourself. The room is comfortably furnished with twin beds.

A glass enclosed porch and private backyard are perfect for a quiet afternoon or evening. In cooler weather you might like to sit by the fireplace in the living room. A hearty breakfast is served every day.

Fifty-Four Thacher Shore's Trailway Pancakes

A great breakfast for cool mornings . . .

To your favorite pancake mix, add granola. Then serve pancakes with hot apple slices, and sprinkle with brown sugar and cinnamon. (Apple slices may be canned.) Delicious!

Heather & Roses Inn

Built in 1805, the Heather and Roses Inn has authentic architectural details such as six over six windows, a central chimney, hip roof, and Federal lights outlining the front door. The interior has been charmingly restored and updated. One guest room offers a queen-size bed with a private bath, beautifully decorated in the Cape Cod tradition. Another has a double bed and a single bed and shares a bath with one other room with a double bed.

Innkeeper Margaret McAskill is justifiably proud of the gardens which are a new addition to the property. If you would like a picnic lunch prepared, just let her know. For a reasonable charge she will pack enough to keep you going until dinner time at a restaurant within walking distance.

Afternoon tea is also offered for an additional charge. Breakfast is served in the bright sun room which is in the new addition in the back of the house.

The Heather & Roses Inn's Raisinbread French Toast

2 slices of raisinbread per person (2-3 days old)
1 egg (beaten) per 2 slices of bread
1 drop oil
pinch of cinnamon and nutmeg

Mix egg, oil, and spices together. Dip each slice of bread in the mixture and fry in a hot teflon pan if possible. Serve hot with maple syrup or your favorite syrup.

Heather & Roses Inn

495 Main Street
Yarmouth Port, MA
02675
(508) 362-5403

Innkeeper:
Margaret McAskill

Open all year.
3 rooms/2 baths.

Rates: June to
September, $50-$70
(for two).
No credit cards
accepted.

Amenities: Children
welcome if no special
equipment is needed.
No pets. Working
fireplaces. 10-minute
drive to the beach.

Directions: Route 6 to
Exit 8, Union
St./Station Ave. Turn
left toward Route 6A.
Turn right on Route
6A to the inn on your
right.

Joshua
Sears Manor

4 Summer Street and
Route 6A
Yarmouth Port, MA
02675
(508) 362-5000

Innkeepers:
Chris & Ken Vancisin

Open all year.
12 rooms/12 baths.

Rates: 6/15 to 10/15,
$70-$90 (for two).
VISA/MC/AMEX

Amenities: Children
welcome. No pets.
Working fireplaces.
Five minute walk to a
fresh water pond
beach.

Directions: Route 6 to
Exit 7. Turn right on
Willow Street toward
Yarmouth Port. At the
intersection with
Route 6A, turn right
and proceed ½ mile to
the inn on the corner
of Summer Street.

Joshua Sears Manor

The summer of 1988 was the Vancisin's first season as innkeepers and they really enjoyed it. Chris brought her wonderful blintzes and interior design skills, and Ken brought his managerial skills to the Joshua Sears Manor.

The parlor of the inn is spacious with high ceilings and gracious decoration befitting this classic Greek revival edition of a southern mansion. Guest rooms range from the simple to the more elegant. There are some handsome antiques throughout as well as reproductions. Many rooms have access to private screened porches.

Breakfast is set at separate tables in two dining rooms and usually includes a hot dish.

Joshua Sears Manor's
Blueberry Orange Loaf

2 C. flour	2/3 C. orange juice
½ t. salt	1 egg
1 t. baking powder	1 C. sugar
¼ t. baking soda	1 C. fresh blueberries
2 T. butter	2 T. honey
¼ C. boiling water	4 t. grated orange rind

Sift flour, salt, baking powder, and baking soda together. Melt butter in boiling water and add ½ C. orange juice and 3 t. of orange rind. Beat egg with sugar, alternately mix in dry ingredients and orange juice mixture. Fold in blueberries. Bake in greased loaf pan (9″ x 15″) for 70 min. at 325°. Let cool in pan. Combine remaining orange juice and 1 t. orange rind and 2 T. honey. Prick top of loaf with fork and spoon mixture over top of loaf.

Lane's End Cottage

268 Main Street
Yarmouth Port, MA
02675
(508) 362-5298

Innkeeper:
Valerie Butler

Open all year.
2 rooms/2 baths.

Rates: $65-$75 (for two). No credit cards accepted.

Amenities: Children welcome by special arrangement. Pets rarely. Working fireplaces. Walk to fresh water beach. 6-minute drive to salt water beach.

Directions: Route 6 to Exit 7. Turn right on Willow Street to Route 6A. Turn right on Route 6A and proceed about 1/5 miles to the common in Yarmouth Port. Turn left down the lane next to the Church to mail box #268.

Lane's End Cottage

The Lanes End Cottage is a 300-year-old Cape that was moved by oxen and rollers back from Route 6A to its present wooded location. "I enjoy the stewardship of this wonderful old Cape," says innkeeper Valerie Butler, "and delight in sharing it with guests who are seeking an authentic Cape Cod experience." Guests are welcomed by a friendly golden retriever, an old fashioned garden, and the tantalizing aromas from the old wood cook stove which dominates the kitchen and is still used for cooking.

There is a choice of twin or double-bedded rooms, all authentically furnished, and even an antique trundle bed for a young child. Breakfast is served in the keeping room or out on the large terrace, set right in the middle of the woods.

Lane's End Cottage's Cheese and Chile Quiche

6 strips bacon, cooked and crumbled
½ lb. jack cheese shredded
one 4 oz. can green chilies
one 8″ unbaked pie shell
1¼ C. half 'n half
4 eggs

Sprinkle bacon, cheese, and chilies in the bottom of the pie shell. Mix the eggs and half 'n half well. Pour into pie shell. Bake at 350° for 30 minutes until set.

Liberty Hill Inn

77 Main Street
Yarmouth Port, MA
02675
(508) 362-3976

Innkeepers:
Beth & Jack Flanagan

Open all year.
5 rooms/5 baths.

Rates: Memorial Day
to Columbus Day, $75-
$95 (for two).
VISA/MC

Amenities: Children
over 12 welcome. No
pets. Pick up service
from plane, train, or
bus. Cable TV. One
mile to beach.
Courtesy phone.
Dinner by previous
arrangement.

Directions: Route 6 to
Exit 7. Turn right on
Willow Street for 1.1
miles to "Liberty Hill
Parking" sign on your
right, just before the
intersection with
Route 6A.

Liberty Hill Inn

A glance at the guest book in the front hall of Liberty Hill Inn reveals names of visitors from all over the world with comments like, "There is a gentle civility here." The inn, which is listed on the National Register of Historic Places, has a long, terraced lawn leading to the stately columned portico, windows that reach from floor to ceiling, and a graceful curved stairway. Round garden beds dot the front lawn, leaving space for a lively game of croquet.

Typical of B & B's in Europe, cheese is usually served at breakfast, along with fresh fruit and home-baked breads. Breakfast might also include French toast with black raspberry sauce made from berries which grow on the property. There are separate tables covered with lace in the dining room and a Sheraton table which can be opened to seat 12 for conferences, seminars, or parties. Innkeeper Jack Flanagan will often whip up a batch of cookies for afternoon tea. A refrigerator is available for ice or to chill your favorite beverage. Just about every evening, guests congregate in the common room to socialize and to choose a nearby restaurant from the basket full of menus.

Liberty Hill Inn's Dublin Broil

1 flank steak (2-2 ½ lbs.)   2 T. dry sherry
2 t. unseasoned meat tenderizer   1 T. honey
1 T. sugar   2 T. Worcestershire sauce
                    1 t. salt

Pierce surfaces of flank steak at 1" intervals with sharp fork. Combine remaining ingredients. Pour over steak. Let stand at room temperature 1 hour or more, turning occasionally. Broil, with surface of meat about 3 inches from heat, for 3 minutes on each side. To serve, slice with sharp knife into thin slices, carving at an angle against the grain. Serves 8.

Olde Captain's Inn

Innkeeper Sven Tilly is a professional golfer, so there are many outdoor activities to be found at the Olde Captain's Inn, including a golf driving net on the large landscaped lawn. The inn is quite private, although it is conveniently located right on the Old King's Highway.

In addition to the guest rooms in the inn, there are two secluded suites on the ground floor. Each has an outside entrance, one leading to a private patio. There are many conveniences such as cable television and a waterbed. Guest rooms are cool and quiet and include a continental breakfast in the dining room.

Olde Captain's Inn's
New England Glazed Roast Pork with Plum Sauce

Select a fresh center-cut pork roast of 5-6 lbs. Preheat oven to 350°. Sprinkle all surfaces of the roast with cinnamon and place 18 whole cloves directly into the roast. Allow roast to bake approximately one hour before basting with previously prepared plum sauce. Use half the sauce for basting the roast and the other half as a side dish. Continue to baste roast until fully baked (3-4 hours). Pork should never be served pink and if further baking is necessary, do so.

Plum Sauce

Mix: ½ **stick butter**   3 **T. cornstarch**
2 **T. lemon juice**   1 **t. nutmeg**
2 **T. cinnamon**

Serve as a side dish to complement the roast in addition to using the sauce for basting. Drain juice from a large can of purple plums and put plums in a separate dish until ready to add sauce when serving roast. Heat briefly before serving.

Olde
Captain's
Inn

101 Main Street
Yarmouth Port, MA
02675
(508) 362-4496

Innkeepers:
Betsy O'Connor &
Sven Tilly

Open all year.
3 rooms/shared baths.
2 apartments/suites.

Rates: 6/19 to 9/7,
$50-$85 (for two). No
credit cards accepted.

Amenities: No
children. No pets.
Working fireplaces.
Barbeque equipment.
5-minute walk to a bay
beach. Cable TV.

Directions: Route 6 to
Exit 7. Turn right on
Willow Street toward
Yarmouth Port. At
intersection with
Route 6A, turn right a
few hundred yards to
the inn on your right.

Old Yarmouth Inn

223 Main Street
Yarmouth Port, MA
02675
(508) 362-3130

Innkeeper:
Shane Peros

Open April to
November.
5 rooms/5 baths.

Rates: 7/1 to 10/18,
$75-$85 (for two).
VISA/MC

Amenities: No
children. No pets. Full-
service, first class
restaurant. Fireplaces
in the dining rooms. 6-
minute walk to a fresh-
water beach. All rooms
have air conditioning
and cable TV.

Directions: Route 6 to
Exit 7. Turn right on
Willow Street to Route
6A. Turn right on
Route 6A and proceed
one mile to the inn at
the curve in the road,
right after Summer
Street.

Old Yarmouth Inn

Early entries to the guest book of the Old Yarmouth Inn, built in 1696, are framed behind glass in one of the dining rooms and it's fun to read the names and hometowns while you check in. The guest rooms are made up of twelve of the original rooms. Two are 2-room suites and are furnished with some authentic period pieces. One of the suites has a queen-sized bed with a day bed in the separate sitting area, perfect for a family. Three other rooms have queen-size beds, one with a canopy.

The first floor contains an excellent restaurant with several dining rooms. Seafood is the specialty and there is a great salad bar. Reservations are necessary. A generous continental breakfast is included with your room.

Old Yarmouth Inn's Indian Pudding

Combine and blend well:

4 C. cornmeal	1 T. nutmeg
2 C. brown sugar	1 T. cinnamon
2 T. ground ginger	1 T. baking soda

After blending, add the mixture to the following wet ingredients that have been heated in a large double boiler:

1 ½ gal. milk	6 eggs
3 C. molasses	1 lb. butter

Heat slowly and cook until the mixture is thick and smooth, NOT grainy. Serves a bunch!

One Centre
Street Inn
1 Centre Street
Yarmouth Port, MA
02675
(508) 362-8910

Innkeepers:
Stefanie & Bill Wright

Open all year.
5 rooms/4 baths.

Rates: $65-$75 (for
two).
AMEX/MC/VISA

Amenities: Children
welcome. No pets.
Working fireplaces. 15-
minute walk down
Centre Street to salt
water beach. Ample
parking.

Directions: Route 6 to
Exit 8, Union Street.
Turn left at the end of
the exit ramp, and
proceed until you
reach a stop sign at the
end of Union Street (1
½ miles). Turn left
again onto Route 6A
for .2 mile. Proceed to
the third block on the
right.

One Centre Street Inn

One Centre Street Inn, a vintage colonial inn, has been restored with quiet elegance, and welcomes guests now as it did in times past. Guest rooms are immaculately clean and comfortably furnished with authentic antiques and reproductions. This decor is present throughout the inn, from the handsome front hall, parlor, and fireplaced library/sitting room, to the cozy dining room with its brick hearth where breakfast is served. A chiming wall clock sounds the hours and a hutch holds beautiful old pottery. A scrumptious breakfast is usually served outdoors on the patio on lovely summer mornings.

One Centre Street Inn's
Sour Cream Waffles

3 eggs
¾ C. milk
½ C. melted butter
¾ sour cream

1½ C. flour
2 t. baking powder
½ baking soda
1 T. sugar

Separate eggs, put whites aside. Beat yolks, milk, butter, and sour cream together. Add flour, baking soda, baking powder, and sugar, and mix well.Beat egg whites and fold in gently. Cook in Belgian waffle iron. Top with sweetened whipped cream and fresh blueberry sauce.

One Seventy Six B & B

176 Main Street
Yarmouth Port, MA
02675
(508) 362-8091

Innkeepers:
Barbara & Stephen
Hayes

Open May 1 to
October 31.
2 rooms/1 bath.

Rates: 5/1 to 10/31,
$50 (for two). No
credit cards accepted.

Amenities: Children
welcome. No pets.
Working fireplace. 6-
minute walk to a fresh
water pond. 8-minute
drive to salt water.

Directions: Route 6 to
Exit 7. Turn right on
Willow Street to Route
6A. Turn right on
Route 6A for ¼ mile.
On the right will be a
small store called
Yarmouth Port Liquor
Mart. Directly opposite
is the inn.

One Seventy Six B & B

   Hidden from the traffic of the Olde King's Highway, behind a well trimmed hedge, stands One Seventy Six B & B, a 200-year-old colonial. The hedge is trained over an arch which frames the driveway entrance, giving a formal feeling to the property. A beautiful secluded court yard behind the house invites sitting as does the large yard with many shade trees. Inside, the rooms are informal and spacious.
   Breakfast is served family style.

One Seventy Six B & B
Quick Blintz

   Mix cottage cheese and raisins, drizzle with honey, and spread on bread. Grill in butter, making a hot sandwich.

The Village Inn

Guests enter The Village Inn by way of the wonderful old kitchen, which is the heart of the house. For more than 25 years, innkeepers Esther and Mac Hickey have been accommodating the public in their charming colonial inn. Although the inn was built in 1795, it has been modernized with many conveniences. Lovely old touches remain, however, including a wood paneled bathroom with a fireplace.

A breakfast of home-baked muffins is served at separate tables in the dining room. The inn will serve a full breakfast of eggs, bacon, sausage, and English muffins for a small additional charge. But the best part is being invited to sit at the big old wooden table in the kitchen for some of that down-home hospitality.

The Village Inn's Blueberry Muffins

Combine: **4 C. Bisquick**   **1 C. granulated sugar**
4 T. unsaturated oil   **1 t. almond extract**
1 unbeaten egg   **2 C. blueberries**

Mix all ingredients lightly until blueberries are floured. Add 1¼ C. milk. Mix until moistened. Spoon mixture into muffin tins lined with cupcake liners. Fill half way. Bake in a pre-heated oven at 400° for 18 minutes. Makes 18 muffins.

The Village Inn

92 Main
(Hallet) Street
Yarmouth Port, MA
02675
(508) 362-3182

Innkeepers:
Mac & Esther Hickey

Open all year.
10 rooms/9 baths.

Rates: 6/15 to 10/15, $50-$65 (for two).
MC/VISA

Amenities: Children welcome. Pets by reservation only. 10-minute drive to the beach. Every room has cable TV.

Directions: Route 6 to Exit 7. Turn right on Willow Street to Route 6A. Turn right on Route 6A for a few hundred yards. The inn will be on your left.

Wedgewood Inn

83 Main Street
Yarmouth Port, MA
02675
(508) 362-5157

Innkeepers:
Gerrie & Milt Graham

Open all year.
6 rooms/6 baths.

Rates: 6/15 to 11/1,
$85-$135 (for two).
AMEX/MC/VISA/DC

Amenities: Children
over 10 welcome. No
pets. Four working
fireplaces. Evening tea
tray. 5-minute drive to
the beach.

Directions: Route 6 to
Exit 7. Turn right on
Willow Street to Route
6A. Turn right on
Route 6A for 75 yards
to the inn on your
right.

Wedgewood Inn

Wedgewood Inn is a romantic and sophisticated small inn that has been delightfully restored to early nineteenth century charm and elegance. All rooms are elegantly furnished in the Williamsburg style. Beautifully finished wide-board floors and handcrafted cherry pencil-post beds with finely detailed quilts set the scene for a memorable stay. The front entry hall has a unique built-in cabinet clock. There is also a public telephone in the closet under the stairs — quite private.

Two lovely suites have sitting rooms/screened porches. Some rooms have fireplaces. An evening tea tray is provided to each room. Breakfast is served at separate tables with handcrafted bow back Windsor chairs and flowers at every table.

Wedgewood Inn's Pumpkin Bread

2 C. cooked pumpkin (or squash)
1 C. white sugar
1 C. dark brown sugar
½ C. salad oil
2 eggs
2½ C. flour
½ t. salt
1½ t. ground cinnamon
1 t. ground cloves
½ t. grated nutmeg
2 dashes ground ginger
2 t. baking soda

1 C. chopped nuts (or 1 C. raisins)

Combine pumpkin, sugar, oil, and eggs in a large mixing bowl; beat well. Combine remaining ingredients and add to the pumpkin mixture. Spoon batter into 9″ x 5″ x 3″ loaf pan. Bake at 350° for 1 hour. Do not overbake as the bread should be very moist. Using squash results in a more refined taste and texture than with pumpkin. Freezes well.

Cuttyhunk

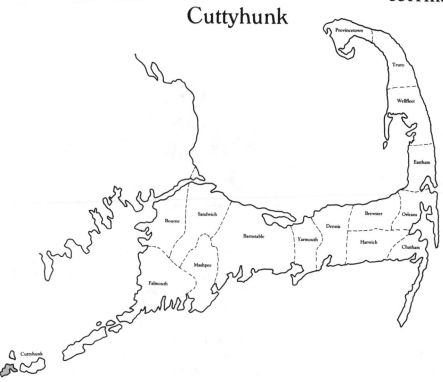

The island of **Cuttyhunk** lies fourteen miles off the Massachusetts coast. Cuttyhunk is pure New England — refined yet rustic, with the long, rich heritage of a coastal island. Only two and a half miles long, three-fourths of a mile wide, and two-thirds completely undeveloped, the island is covered with wild flowers and open meadows. Cuttyhunk Harbor is busy with boats coming and going, and the waters around the island are known to be wonderful sportsfishing grounds. Days can be spent strolling the hills and sandy beaches and coves. This is a great place to just relax and "let the rest of the world go by."

The Allen House

Box 27
Cuttyhunk, MA 02173
(508) 996-9292

Innkeepers:
Nina and Margo Solod

Open from Memorial
Day to October 1.
12 rooms with shared
baths.

Rates: $75-$90 (for
two), in season; $65-
$80 (for two), after
Sept. 1. VISA/MC

Amenities: Children
welcome. No pets.

Directions: Take the
ferry Alert from New
Bedford to come by
boat (508-992-1432),
or fly on the shuttle
flight from New
Bedford (508-
997-4095).

The Allen House

This special inn is cozy yet spacious and the atmosphere relaxing, with comfortable accommodations in the rooms and three cottages. The island of Cuttyhunk is so peaceful (with just two cars on it) that deer often walk up to visitors as they explore or sit on the lawn.

The inn is reknowned for its delicious food! Meals are served in a large glass-enclosed dining room which overlooks the sea and offers a front seat for just sitting back and watching the boats in the harbor.

The Allen House's Famous Carrotcake

2 C. sugar
2 C. flour (cake)
2 t. cinnamon
1½ C. oil
1 C. walnut pieces

1 t. salt
4 beaten eggs
2 t. baking soda
2½ C. fresh grated or shredded carrots
 (approx. 5 carrots)

Combine sugar, oil, and beaten eggs in a large bowl. Sift together flour, salt, soda, and cinnamon. Combine dry ingredients with sugar, oil, and egg mixture, and fold in carrots and walnuts. Do not overmix. Pour into two 9" round cake pans that have been greased and lined with parchment paper. Bake in a 350° oven for 30-35 minutes until cake pulls slightly from sides of pan.

Frosting:
1 lb. confectioner's sugar
9 oz. cream cheese
zest of one lemon

1 t. vanilla
½ C. ground walnuts
2 oz. butter

Cream butter and cream cheese until soft. Add confectioner's sugar and vanilla and blend until creamy. Add ground walnuts and zest of one lemon. Decorate with walnut halves.

Martha's Vineyard

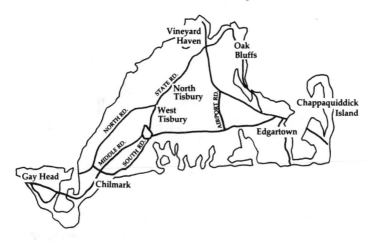

An island for all seasons. **Martha's Vineyard** is located about seven miles from the mainland. Our coverage of the inns on Martha's Vineyard includes those in the villages of Edgartown, Oak Bluffs, West Tisbury and Vineyard Haven.

Edgartown is one of New England's most elegant communities. It has been the county seat since 1642. Main Street is a picturebook scene with its harbor and waterfront. The tall, square-rigged ships that sailed all the world's oceans have passed from the Edgartown scene, but the heritage of those vessels and their captains is alive in the town. For the past hundred years, Edgartown has been one of the world's great yachting centers. The stately white Greek Revival houses built by the whaling captains have been carefully maintained, and they make the town a museum-piece community, a seaport village preserved from the early 19th century.

Oak Bluffs is a mix of the traditional and the unconventional. Circuit Avenue is a vibrant boulevard dotted with boutiques, ice cream parlors, and a variety of restaurants. At the end of Circuit Avenue whirl the Flying Horses, the oldest carousel in the country. Cottage City is a collection of historic gingerbread houses. They encircle the Tabernacle, an early 20-century open air stage, graced in the summer by such talents as Wynton Marsalis, Joan Baez, and the Oak Bluffs Brass Band. The twinkling of countless Chinese lanterns flicker throughout Cottage City during a music filled night in August appropriately titled "The Illumination." This celebration has its origins in the 19th century Methodist Camp Ground Community.

Excellent stores, gift shops, and fine restaurants as well as a beautiful harbor, are some of the qualities which make **Vineyard Haven** special to tourists and residents alike. Attractions in town include the Seaman's Bethel, once a place of rest and refuge for sailors far from home and now a chapel and museum. The chapel has been restored and nautical memorabilia is on display.

West Tisbury has all the characteristics people associate with a typical "New England village" with its white church, general store, post office, old mill, and farms and ponds.

The unspoiled charm of the island's scenic beaches vary from the protected ones on the north and east, to the great stretches of rumbling surf along the southside.

The Arbor

222 Upper Main Street
Edgartown, MA 02539
(508) 627-8137

Innkeeper:
Peggy Hall

Open May 1 to
October 31.
10 rooms/9 baths.

Rates: 6/15 to 9/15,
$75-$95 (for two).
VISA/MC

Amenities: Children
over 12 welcome. No
pets. Working fireplace
in the dining room. 5-
minute walk to the
beach.

Directions: From
Vineyard Haven (the
ferry), take Beach
Road, following signs
to Edgartown. The
Arbor is on the right
just as you approach
the town center.

The Arbor

The outside of The Arbor shows a neatly kept, typical turn-of-the-century shingled house. Inside it is anything but typical. The inn is light and bright with a cathedral ceiling in the modern living room which is painted white, and tall windows that reach to the ceiling. Guest rooms are in a new addition, and are imaginatively decorated with painted furniture and rugs. There is a public phone for your use. There is also a lovely garden with black wrought iron furniture, an amiable place to sit before dinner.

A buffet breakfast is set out in the dining room. Guests are invited to sit at the long table to socialize over the meal.

The Arbor's Irish Bread

4 C. flour
4 t. baking powder
1 C. sugar
2 eggs
½ C. margarine

½ t. salt
1 t. caraway seeds
1 C. raisins
½ C. currants
1 C. milk

Sift flour, baking powder, sugar, and salt. Sprinkle in raisins and currants. Cut in margarine and add beaten eggs and milk. Turn onto floured board. Mould and press into greased spider pan and bake approximately 40-45 minutes at 350°.

Ashley Inn

The distinctive Chinese Chippendale fence at Ashley Inn is admired by visitors and natives alike. It is as unique as the cloverleaf window above the front door. There are two downstairs guest rooms and several on the second and third floors. They are attractive and simply decorated in beach house style.

The dining room is charming, with individual tables and flowers. A continental breakfast is served at the inn.

Ashley Inn's Applesauce Cake

2 ½ C. all-purpose flour*	½ t. ground allspice
2 C. sugar	1½ C. applesauce
1½ t. baking soda	½ C. water
1½ t. salt	½ C. shortening
¼ t. baking powder	2 eggs
¾ t. ground cinnamon	1 C. raisins
½ t. ground cloves	½ C. chopped walnuts

Heat oven to 350°. Grease and flour an oblong pan (13″ x 9″ x 2″). Beat all ingredients in a large bowl, on low for 30 seconds and on high for 3 minutes. Pour into prepared pan and bake for 60-65 minutes in oblong pan, or 50-55 minutes in a layer pan. *DO NOT use self-rising flour.

Ashley Inn
129 Main Street
Edgartown, MA 02539
(508) 627-9655

Innkeeper:
Judy Cortese

Open all year.
10 rooms/9 baths.

Rates: $6/23 to 9/17, $80-$150 (for two). No credit cards accepted.

Amenities: Children over 10 welcome. No pets. 5-minute drive to the beach.

Directions: From the ferry, follow signs to Edgartown. Upon entering town, Cannonball Park will be on your right, and Andrea's Restaurant will be on your left. The inn is next door to the restaurant.

The Chadwick Inn

67 Winter Street
Edgartown, MA 02539
(508) 627-4435

Innkeepers: Peter &
Juarte Antioco

Open all year.
15 rooms/15 baths.

Rates: 6/15 to 9/21,
$125-$225 (for two).
AMEX/MC/VISA

Amenities: Children
over 6 years welcome.
No pets. Working
fireplaces. 6-minute
walk to the beach.

Directions: From
Vineyard Haven,
follow the signs to
Edgartown Center and
turn left onto Pease's
Point Way. Continue
past the flagpole on
Main Street until you
reach the corner of
Winter Street and the
inn.

The Chadwick Inn

The original part of this 1840 house features high ceilings, fireplaces, verandas, and canopy beds. The inn has a wide staircase leading to the second-floor guest rooms. The newer Garden Wing offers a large suite suitable for several people traveling together. Two parlors offer comfortable seating. Innkeeper Peter Antioco is working on a new faux-marble fireplace in the second parlor. Another charming spot to sit is the sunroom, where a flowery theme extends even to the hand-painted twin chandeliers. Breakfast is served here at small tables set with blue cloths, a nice accompaniment to the blue-painted floor. Flowers are on every table.

The Chadwick Inn's Raspberry or Blackberry Crepes

The berries used in this recipe are grown on the Vineyard at a local farm in July and August.
Prepare 24 crepes using a standard recipe.

Filling:

4 oz. cream cheese (at room temp.)	**½ t. freshly squeezed lemon juice**
16 oz. sour cream	**½ t. cinnamon**
pinch of nutmeg	**1 t. vanilla**
	1 C. raspberries or blackberries

1½ t. Grand Marnier (optional)

Place all ingredients except berries in a mixer and beat until smooth. Fill each crepe with 2 T. of the mixture and sprinkle some berries on it. Roll up the crepe. At this point, it can be served with confectioner's sugar and more berries sprinkled on top, or with a warm raspberry or blackberry sauce made as follows:

¼ lb. softened butter
2 C. confectioner's sugar
3 C. raspberries or blackberries

Cream butter and add sugar gradually, beating well. Crush the blackberries or raspberries, adding a little at a time until the sauce is smooth. Heat until warm and pour over the crepes.

The Charlotte Inn

The Charlotte Inn
South Summer Street
Edgartown, MA 02539
(508) 627-4751

Innkeepers: Gery &
Paula Conover

Open all year.
25 rooms/24 baths.

Rates: 6/10 to 10/15,
$115-$325 (for two).
VISA/MC/AMEX

Amenities: Children
over 14 welcome. No
pets. Pay phone in the
main building. TV in
the Garden House
living room. Working
fireplaces. Full service
restaurant (L'Etoile).
Art gallery.

Directions: From
Vineyard Haven (the
ferry), take Beach
Road to Main Street in
Edgartown. Take Main
Street to South
Summer Street. Turn
right on South
Summer to the inn.

First class! Understated elegance in an old English tradition welcomes you as you enter the busy reception room of The Charlotte Inn. Throughout the inn, fine English antiques, plush carpets, lofty ceilings, warm, deep-hued wallpapers and vases of fresh cut flowers add to the atmosphere. There is meticulous attention to detail throughout; an arm chair here, an antique clock there, and no two rooms alike.

The Carriage House located behind the main inn has a quiet, romantic feeling, with its private nooks, generous hearths, and double French doors. It overlooks brick courtyards and gardens reminiscent of England. Equestrian prints and oils carry out the theme of an English squire's country home. The Summer House is reached by a brick path through the lattice entryway and beyond the rose garden. It houses a suite that offers a glimpse of the harbor. Across the street stands the 1705 Garden House, famous for its splendid English garden.

A continental breakfast is complimentary; however, a full breakfast is available at an additional charge.

The Charlotte Inn's Mexican Morning Breakfast

flour tortilla (1 per order)   eggs (2 per order)

Pico de Gallo

1 C. chopped seeded fresh tomatoes   zest and juice of 1 lime
½ bunch fresh cilantro   ¼ C. chopped green peppers
¼ C. chopped red onion   1 jar (12 oz.)
salt and pepper to taste   Salsa Picante Sauce

Combine all Pico de Gallo ingredients and season with salt and pepper to taste. Makes 3 cups. Sauté tortilla in hot oil in large sauté pan. Remove. Keep warm. Scramble eggs seasoned with salt and pepper. Wrap eggs in tortilla and serve with Pico de Gallo.

The Daggett House
c. 1660

59 N. Water Street
Edgartown, MA 02539
(508) 627-4600

Innkeeper:
Sue Cooperstreet

8 rooms open all year.
25 rooms/25 baths.

Rates: Memorial Day
to Columbus Day,
$100-$190 (for two).
VISA/MC

Amenities: Children
welcome. No pets.
Working fireplaces.
Ample off-street
parking. Restaurant is
open for breakfast
only. 2-minute walk to
the beach.

Directions: From the
Vineyard Haven
harbor, take Beach
Road to Main Street in
Edgartown. Follow
Main Street to North
Water Street. Turn
left on North Water to
the inn.

The Daggett House c. 1660

The Daggett House, a shingled colonial, is a landmark for architectural historians. Inside is an interesting collection of antiques and reproductions. The inn has a secret stairway, candlelight doors, and an ancient panelled fireplace in the old breakfast room. Here is where guests are served a continental breakfast while surrounded by Early American memorabilia and a view overlooking the private garden. The breakfast room is open to the public as well.

The long, harbor-front lawn is the setting for the Garden Cottage, a charming 3-room restoration. It proves the inn's claim to being the only bed and breakfast in Edgartown that is on the water. The inn's own private pier juts out into the harbor, providing a perfect spot for picture-taking or a dip in the water.

The Daggett House's
Grapenut Bread

Mix: 2/3 C. Grapenuts   3 T. butter
      1/3 C. wheat germ   ¼ t. salt
           1/3 C. dark brown sugar

Add 1 1/3 C. boiling water. Stir and let cool.

Combine: 1 T. yeast
         1 t. sugar in 2/3 C. warm water. Let stand until bubbly.

Add this to Grapenut mixture and stir. Add 4 C. flour and mix well. Turn dough out on floured surface and knead until soft and smooth. Return to bowl, cover and let rise in warm place until double in size (about 1 hour). Punch down with fists and return to floured surface. Divide into 2 loaves, knead for a few minutes and put into greased pans. Let rise until doubled (about 1 ½ hours). Bake at 360° for 50 minutes.

Governor
Bradford Inn

128 Main Street
Edgartown, MA 02539
(508) 627-9510

Innkeepers: Robin &
Steve Prentiss

Open all year.
16 rooms/16 baths.

Rates: 6/15 to 9/15,
$95-$175 (for two).
Most credit cards
accepted.

Amenities: Children
welcome during the
off-season. No pets.
Working fireplace in
the parlor. 20-minute
walk to the beach.

Directions: From the
Vineyard Haven
harbor (the ferry), take
Beach Road to Main
Street in Edgartown.
Follow Main Street to
the inn on your right.

Governor Bradford Inn

A handsome cherry wood wall and fireplace is the focus of one of the parlors here, at Governor Bradford Inn. Another sitting room called the wicker room has a miniature bar for chilling beverages. All guest bedrooms on the first two floors have a television and king-sized beds. One room is done in Williamsburg style with a beautiful brocade spread.

A continental breakfast is served in the dining room where the blue and white decor is accented by a collection of antique willow ware china.

Governor Bradford Inn's Pear Walnut Coffeecake

½ C. butter, softened
1 C. sugar
1 t. vanilla extract
2 eggs
2 C. flour
   (1 C. white, 1 C. whole wheat)

1 t. baking soda
1 t. baking powder
¼ t. salt
1 C. sour cream
2 large pears,
   peeled and diced

Cream butter and sugar until fluffy. Beat in vanilla and eggs until smooth. Mix dry ingredients. Add to butter mixture alternately with sour cream. Fold in pears. Spread in a greased 13″ x 9″ pan. Sprinkle with nut topping. Bake at 350° for 40-45 minutes.

Nut topping:
1 C. packed brown sugar
4 T. softened butter

1½ t. ground cinnamon
1 C. chopped walnuts

Stir above ingredients until well mixed.

Katama
Guest House

166 Katama Road
Edgartown, MA 02539
(508) 627-5158

Innkeepers: Raymond
& Lorraine St. Pierre

Open all year.
4 rooms/2 baths.

Rates: Memorial Day
to Columbus Day, $60-
$70 (for two). No
credit cards accepted.

Amenities: Children
over 10 years welcome.
No pets. Ample
parking. Working
fireplaces. Bike path to
South Beach is directly
across the street. 10-
minute walk to the
beach.

Directions: From
Vineyard Haven
harbor (the ferry), take
Beach Road to Main
Street in Edgartown.
Follow Main Street to
Katama Road. Turn
right to the Guest
House.

Katama Guest House

A restored 1900 farmhouse, this inn sits on a field of landscaped
lawns with many trees, an adult swing, and a picnic table and chairs
for guests. The harbor view is breathtaking, and if you're a camera
buff, there are many opportunities for taking photographs.

The guest parlor is filled with antiques and is designed for comfort.
Books on island lore and other subjects are available. A small
boutique features handmade island crafts and island photography.
The continental breakfast is served on a crisp white tablecloth
enhanced by antique cloth napkins. This is a true island home that
offers comfortable rooms with a strong dose of hospitality.

Katama Guest House's
Banana Muffins

½ C. margarine   2 C. flour
¾ C. sugar   2 eggs (separated)
½ t. salt   ½ t. baking soda
2 T. milk   1 t. baking powder
                   3 bananas, mashed

Cream butter and sugar, and then add egg yolks. Add mashed bananas
and milk. Add sifted dry ingredients. Fold in beaten egg whites. Bake in
muffin tins for about 25 minutes at 350°.

Point Way
Inn
104 Main Street
Edgartown, MA 02539
(508) 627-8633

Innkeepers:
Ben & Linda Smith

Open all year.
15 rooms/16 baths.

Rates: 7/1 to 9/8,
$115-$190 (for two).
AMEX/VISA/MC

Amenities: Children
welcome. No pets. Ten
working fireplaces. 10-
minute walk to the
beach.

Directions: From the
Vineyard Haven
harbor (the ferry),
follow signs to
Edgartown and then to
"Edgartown Center."
As you approach Main
Street on Pease's Point
Way, watch for the
inn sign on the right
and turn into the
parking lot.

Point Way Inn

Innkeepers Ben and Linda Smith say their goal was to recreate a fine old New England home without the feeling of an antique store. They have achieved that at Point Way Inn. All rooms have full-length mirrors, many have original working fireplaces, and some have canopied four-poster beds. One two-room suite has a private entrance and fireplace. Six rooms have French doors opening onto private balconies. At night, a decanter of sherry is left in each room, and beds are turned down. The living room has a wet bar with a refrigerator. In the library there is an intriguing 500-piece, custom-made wooden jigsaw puzzle that has provided a challenging evening for many guests.

The Smiths are sailors and charts from family cruises and pictures of generations of family boats adorn the walls. Sailing trophies hold fresh flowers in the breakfast room, which is warmed by a Franklin stove. Ben Smith is a champion croquet player and a game is always ready on the lawn. He also enjoys taking guests to a special spot to dig clams, which are later eaten in the garden gazebo.

A continental breakfast is included.

Point Way Inn's
Oatmeal Cookies

1 1/3 C. flour	1 C. butter or margarine
½ t. salt	1 C. packed brown sugar
1 t. baking soda	2 t. vanilla
¼ C. water	½ C. granulated sugar
3 C. oats	1 egg

Combine flour, salt, and soda together. In a separate bowl, combine margarine and sugars. Add egg and vanilla. Mix until light and fluffy. Add dry ingredients alternately with water. Stir in oats. Drop by rounded teaspoonfuls on greased cookie sheet. Bake at 350° for 9 minutes.

The Shiverick Inn

The Shiverick Inn

Pease's Point Way
Edgartown, MA 02539
(508) 627-3797

Innkeepers: Claire & Juan del Real

Open all year.
10 rooms/11 baths.

Rates: June to October, $150-$200 (for two).
AMEX/VISA/MC

Amenities: Children over 12 years welcome. No pets. Four working fireplaces. Two wood stoves. Staff will light fires. 10-minutes walk to the beach.

Directions: From the Vineyard Haven harbor (the ferry), follow signs to Edgartown. Take Cook Street and follow to Pease's Point Way. Turn left on Pease's Point Way. The inn is on the right, just before the flagpole.

Great care has been taken in the restoration of this 1840's mansion built for Dr. Clement Francis Shiverick. The del Reals have preserved the original architectural details and revived the gracious ambience for which the house was known. Interior decoration has been tastefully chosen, true to the spirit of its day. An antique spool cabinet stands in the front hall, and pictures of the innkeepers' ancestors hang in some guest rooms.

One room has mulberry colored wallpaper, and a candy striped canopy bed and dust ruffle. An antique trunk sits at the foot of the bed. A second floor library provides a private spot for relaxing with a book or television. There is a spacious deck just outside the library. A two-room suite is beautifully decorated in blues and pinks with wing chairs covered in crewel work fabric. The sitting room has a sofa which opens to a bed.

The Shiverick Inn's Blueberry Muffins

½ C. sunflower oil
¾ C. sugar
2 eggs

2 t. baking powder
½ C. non-fat milk
2 C. fresh blueberries

2 C. unbleached white flour

Grease 12 muffin tins. Beat oil, sugar, and eggs until fluffy. Add dry ingredients with milk, alternating dry ingredients and milk (start and end with dry ingredients). Gently fold in blueberries and fill muffin tins almost to the top with batter. (Optional: sprinkle sugar lightly over top of muffins before baking.) Bake at 375° for 25 minutes or until golden brown on top.

The Victorian Inn

This is an attractive inn with the casual elegance of a restored whaling captain's home, definitely Victorian yet light in style. There are canopy beds in lovely large rooms, some with balconies affording magnificent views of the harbor. All rooms offer fresh flowers and cream sherry. Cherished antiques are mixed in with family furniture, achieving a pleasing eclectic arrangement. The inn is listed in the National Register of Historic Places.

A gourmet breakfast is served in the breakfast room with its glass-topped tables, or, weather permitting, in the English garden.

The Victorian Inn's Granola

1½ C. rolled oats	¼ C. bran
¼ C. sesame seeds	½ C. almonds
½ C. sunflower seeds	¼ C. oil
½ C. shredded coconut	½ C. wheat germ
¼ C. honey	½ t. almond extract
½ t. vanilla extract	

½ C. raisins

Preheat oven to 300°. Mix together all dry ingredients in a large mixing bowl. Heat oil and honey in saucepan until thin. Stir in vanilla and almond extract. Pour over dry ingredients and stir. Bake in oven at 300° on sheet pan, until brown. Stir from time to time.

The Victorian Inn
24 South Water Street
Edgartown, MA 02539
(508) 627-4784

Innkeepers: Arlene & Lew Kiesler

Open all year.
14 rooms/14 baths.

Rates: 6/1 to 10/18, $87-$177 (for two).
VISA/MC

Amenities: Children welcome. Pets allowed. Working fireplaces in the public rooms. Parking on premises. 5-minute walk to the beach.

Directions: Take Beach Road from Vineyard Haven to Main Street in Edgartown. Turn right on So. Water Street; the inn is 100 yards ahead on the right.

The Admiral Benbow Inn

520 New York Avenue
Oak Bluffs, MA 02557
(508) 693-6825

Innkeepers:
Black Dog Tavern Co.

Open all year.
7 rooms/7 baths.

Rates: 6/15 to 9/15,
$75-$120 (for two).
VISA/MC/AMEX

Amenities: Children
welcome. No pets. The
Black Dog Tavern
restaurant is 2 miles
away. Ample parking.
One working fireplace.
15-minute walk to the
beach.

Directions: From the
Oak Bluffs harbor,
head towards Vineyard
Haven. Turn on New
York Avenue to the
inn.

The Admiral Benbow Inn

The Admiral Benbow Inn offers comfortable rooms decorated in turn-of-the-century style with period furnishings and bow-tied curtains. An imposing carved wood mantel over the fireplace graces one wall of the parlor which otherwise invites relaxed lounging. Guest rooms are simple.

A family with young children runs the inn. They are happy to direct you to features of Oak Bluffs and beyond. A cold buffet breakfast is set out in the dining room where you are invited to gather around the table and socialize with other travelers. A nice touch is the complimentary gift certificate redeemable towards any meal at The Black Dog Tavern or any purchase at the Black Dog Bakery, provided to each room daily.

The Black Dog-Admiral Benbow's Honey Bran Muffins

Moisten 4 C. of bran in a bowl, pouring off excell water. Cream together:

2 C. butter
¾ C. honey

Add 3 eggs to butter and honey mixture, beat in. Add: **1 T. baking soda**

1 T. baking powder
1½ T. cinnamon

Stir in above ingredients thoroughly. Add:

2 C. chopped walnuts	**4 C. whole wheat flour**
3 C. milk	**2 C. raisins**

Stir in the above ingredients thoroughly. Add the 4 C. of moistened bran and stir in until well mixed. Put muffin mixture in paper-lined tins. Bake at 300° in oven, until tester comes out clean, about 25 minutes. Makes about 16 muffins.

The Oak Bluffs Inn

The Oak Bluffs Inn

Corner of Circuit Ave.
and Pequot Ave.
Oak Bluffs, MA 02557
(508) 693-7171

Innkeepers: Will
Elliott & Chris Holley

Open all year.
9 rooms/9 baths, plus 1
apartment.

Rates: 6/16 to 9/18,
$95-$122 (for two).
AMEX/VISA/MC

Amenities: "Well
behaved" children
welcome. No pets.
Working fireplace.
Parking on premises. 3-
minute walk to the
beach. 15-minute drive
to surf.

Directions: From the
Oak Bluffs dock,
proceed 100 yards and
take a left on Circuit
Avenue. Continue 1
block past the shops
and the inn is on your
left.

While the whimsical Victorian style of The Oak Bluffs Inn is recognizable, the interior of this century-old gem is original. The colorful rose exterior, resplendent with gingerbread detail and multi-colored trim, exemplifies the best in colorful Victorian charm. The rich, eclectic interior reflects the romance of the past, yet is fresh, not stuffy or pretentious. Newly restored, the inn is accented with bright colors, as in the peacock blue wallpaper and painted cottage pine headboards. Several stained glass armoires are handsome additions to guest rooms. The inn's tower has a cupola that allows a panoramic view of the town.

A hearty continental breakfast is served in the dining room or on the porch adjacent to the carriage house garden. The fruited coffee cake is luscious and filling.

The Oak Bluffs Inn's Coffee Cake

2 C. unbleached flour
2 t. baking powder
½ t. salt
2 unbeaten eggs

¾ C. brown sugar
¼ C. butter
¾ C. milk

Sift flour, baking powder, and salt together, and then blend in sugar. Cut in butter and add milk, beating 300 times. Add eggs and beat 200 strokes.

Topping:
4 T. melted butter
2/3 C. brown sugar
3 T. flour
1 t. cinnamon
½ C. sliced almonds
¾ C. shredded coconut

2 slices apples
  (2 sm. or 1 large peeled or unpeeled)
1 C. walnuts or ½ C. chopped dates
1 can pineapple chunks, drained well
  (press out excess juice)

Combine butter, sugar, flour, and cinnamon with nuts and fruit. If making the pineapple coffee cake, save a small portion of the coconut to sprinkle on the top.

Grease the bottom of a 10″ casserole dish or a tube pan. Spread ½ of the batter in the pan. Spoon ½ the topping on the batter and swirl lightly into the batter. Repeat with the rest of the batter and topping. Bake for 30-35 minutes at 350°.

Captain Dexter House

Captain Dexter House

100 Main Street
Vineyard Haven, MA
02568
(508) 693-6564

Innkeepers: Roberta Pieczenik and Julia Ross

Open all year.
8 rooms/8 baths.

Rates: 6/15 to 9/15, $95-$140 (for two). No credit cards accepted.

Amenities: Children over 12 welcome. No pets. Working fireplaces. 1½ blocks to the beach. Parking on premises.

Directions: The inn is one block from the ferry on Main Street.

Original wide floorboards, unusual moldings, Count Rumford fireplaces, and colonial colored woodwork reflect the charm and elegance of this 1843 restoration. Guest rooms are tastefully decorated with an eye for comfort. There are fine antiques, hand-sewn quilts, Oriental rugs on wide plank floors, and period reproduction wallpapers. Several rooms have working fireplaces and four-poster beds with lace canopies. There is a real New England colonial ambience in Captain Dexter House.

The nicest aspect is the friendly helpfulness of the innkeepers. There is a courtesy phone for local calls and a public phone for off-island calls. A refrigerator is hidden in the dining room closet. Lemonade is provided in the afternoon and sherry in the early evening. A locked garage protects your bicycles.

Captain Dexter House's Sour Cream Coffee Cake

¾ C. butter
1½ C. sugar
3 eggs
1½ t. vanilla

1½ t. baking soda
1½ t. baking powder
1¼ t. salt
1½ C. sour cream

3 C. flour

Heat oven to 350°. Grease pans (loaf) 9" x 5" x 3". Combine sugar, butter, eggs, and vanilla in large bowl. Beat vigorously for 300 strokes by hand. Mix in flour, baking powder, soda, and salt alternately with sour cream. Spread ¼ of the batter (about 1 ½ C.) in each pan. Sprinkle with ¼ of the filling (about 5 T.). Repeat for each.

Filling:
Mix together: ½ C. brown sugar (packed)
½ C. finely chopped nuts
1½ t. cinnamon
Bake at 350° for 1 hour. Cool slightly in pans before removing.

The Crocker House Inn

4 Crocker Avenue
Vineyard Haven, MA
02568
(508) 693-1151

Innkeepers: Michael
& April Levandowski

Open April to
December.
8 rooms/8 baths.

Rates: 6/14 to 9/11,
$80-$130 (for two). No
credit cards accepted.

Amenities: Children
over 12 years welcome.
No pets. Working
fireplaces. 5-minute
walk to the beach.

Directions: The inn is
located right next to
the harbor so it is just
a short walk from the
ferry. Walk straight
from the ferry until
Main Street, bear
right, and take
Crocker Avenue, the
second street on the
right.

The Crocker House Inn

Like most houses on the Vineyard, Crocker House Inn is a turn-of-the-century Victorian, but the similarity ends there. Every room has been recently renovated by the innkeepers and each one is decorated around a unique theme. The Lace Room is charming with its octagonal shape, fireplace, and abundance of white linens and lace. Another room has a double bed, a pine armoire, and a solid red wall. Another room has a king size bed under a high round window and a cathedral ceiling. There is also a suite with a double bed and a sitting area. Striking blue and green wallpaper provides the backdrop for white wicker chairs and lace curtains. Several rooms have private entrances, balconies, harbor views, and fireplaces.

April and Michael Levandowski's warm hospitality can be seen in all the little touches throughout the inn. Continental breakfast is served at separate scrubbed pine round tables in the dining room. The bran muffins, warm from the oven, are a real treat.

The Crocker House Inn's Bran Muffins

Stir in a bowl: **2 C. bran flakes, 2 C. boiling water.** Let stand until cool.

Mix in a large bowl: **⅞ C.oil**
3 C. sugar (2 white, 1 brown)
Add bran and water mixture to sugar and oil.

Beat in: **4 beaten eggs**
½ qt. light cream
½ qt. milk

Sift together and add to mixture:

5 C. flour	2 t. salt
4 C. bran cereal	1 t. ginger
2 t. cinnamon	1 C. raisins
5 t. baking soda	1 C. dates

Bake at 400° for 15-20 minutes. This recipe makes 1½ gallons of batter, and it lasts up to 6 weeks in the refrigerator.

Hanover House

10 Edgartown Road
Vineyard Haven, MA
02568
(508) 693-1066

Innkeeper: Marc
Hanover

Open all year.
16 rooms/16 baths.

Rates: 6/13 to 9/25,
$93-$130 (for two).
VISA/MC/AMEX

Amenities: Children
welcome. No pets, but
will arrange boarding
nearby. Color cable
TV in each room. 10-
minute walk to the
beach. Outdoor grills,
picnic tables, and free
bicycles. Parking on
premises.

Directions: Take a left
from the ferry. Take
the next right onto
Beach Street. Bear left
at the blinking light
onto State Road. Take
the third left onto
Edgartown Road to the
house on the left.

Hanover House

Hanover House is a large old inn that has been renovated to give you the conveniences of a modern hotel, while still retaining the personalized hospitality of the old days. It is immaculate, quaint and furnished in country style with maple furniture. The white wicker porch has upholstery done in strong pinks and blues.

All rooms have a queen-size bed or two double beds. Many rooms have air conditioning. The newly refurbished rooms have private entrances that open onto spacious sundecks. There are also housekeeping units with fully equipped kitchens. A continental breakfast is served daily.

Hanover House's
Very Special Banana Bread

2 C. flour	½ C. vegetable oil
1 C. sugar	2 or 3 bananas, mashed
2 eggs	½ C. chopped walnuts

1 t. baking soda

Mix the flour, sugar, eggs, baking soda, and oil in a bowl. Beat until fairly smooth, then add mashed bananas and walnuts. Put into a greased loaf pan. Bake at 325° for one hour. Cool before cutting.

High Haven House

A charming colonial, High Haven House is located in a quiet residential area away from the noise of town. There is a common gathering room with a television, located next to the pool and patio.

Complimentary wine and cheese are served on weekends by the pool. Guests have commented on the friendly atmosphere and wonderful hospitality here.

A continental breakfast is included.

High Haven House's Banana Bread

½ stick butter
½ C. sugar
½ C. honey
2 eggs

1½ C. mashed ripe bananas
1½ C. flour
½ t. baking soda
½ t. salt

½ C. walnuts, chopped

Cream butter. Add sugar and honey. Beat until creamy. Add eggs. When thoroughly mixed, add banana. Add all dry ingredients and then nuts. Pour into a greased loaf pan. Bake at 350° for 1 hour.

High Haven House

69 Summer Street
Vineyard Haven, MA
02568
(508) 693-9204

Innkeepers: Kathleen & Joseph Schreck

Open all year.
11 rooms/5 baths.

Rates: 6/15 to 9/14, $55-$85 (for two).
VISA/MC/AMEX

Amenities: Children welcome. No pets. Swimming pool. Two working fireplaces. 10-minute walk to the beach.

Directions: From the Vineyard Haven harbor, drive up Union Street, and turn left on Water Street into town. Turn right on Main Street, left on Center Street, and right on Pine Street to Summer Street. Turn left on Summer Street; the house is on your right.

Lothrop Merry House

**Lothrop
Merry
House**

Owen Park
Vineyard Haven, MA
02568
(508) 693-1646

Innkeepers:
John & Mary Clarke

Open all year.
7 rooms/5 baths.

Rates: 6/20 to 10/19,
$92-$135 (for two).
VISA/MC

Amenities: Children
welcome. No pets.
Working fireplaces.
Private beach right in
front of the house.
Parking available.

Directions: Walk one
block from the
Vineyard Haven dock
to Owen Park and the
inn.

This is a delightful 18th century guest house, tastefully restored. The whole house is for guests. Most rooms have a beautiful harbor view; some have their own fireplaces and private baths. Many rooms are on the first floor. The common room is charming and comfortable, furnished with nice period pieces. A continental breakfast is served here or, in nice weather, outside on the flower-bordered terrace.

If you would enjoy a sail (in season), your hosts' 54′ Alden Ketch, the "Laissez Faire," takes up to six passengers for day, evening, or overnight cruises among the many coves and harbors of the Vineyard and the Elizabeth Islands. In addition, there is a canoe and a sunfish which guests may use. The gently sloping lawn in front of the guest house takes you to a private beach.

Lothrop Merry House's
Pear Bread

½ C. butter or margarine
1 C. sugar
2 eggs slightly beaten
1 C. grated pears
1 C. white flour

½ t. salt
1 t. baking soda
1 C. whole wheat flour
1/3 C. hot water
½ C. sunflower seeds

This can also be made with bananas or zucchini, but pears are best. Melt butter, add sugar, then eggs and pears. Mix white flour with salt, soda, and whole wheat flour. Add dry ingredients alternately with hot water. Stir in sunflower seeds. Turn into greased 9″ x 5″ loaf pan. Bake at 325° for 1 hour and 10 minutes. Crunchy and delicious!

Thorncroft Inn

The Thorncroft Inn's main house was built as the guest house of a large Island estate; therefore, it is an ideal bed and breakfast. Innkeepers Karl and Lynn Buder have searched New England for the perfect blend of antiques for each room and their collection has been carefully restored by Island craftsmen. A special suite has been created for the 1989 season: there is a fireplace in the sitting room and a two-person jacuzzi.

A hearty breakfast is served in the dining room where high back chairs have been stripped to a light oak color and exquisite lace curtains hang in the windows.

The Thorncroft Inn's Cheese Strata

8 slices of white bread, cubed	½ stick butter, melted
2 C. sharp cheddar cheese, grated	2 C. milk
8 large eggs	½ t. dry mustard

Grease souffle dish, then layer bread and cheese, ending with cheese. Combine other ingredients in blender. Pour mixture over bread and cheese. Cover and store overnight. Bake at 350° for 1 hour.

Thorncroft Inn
278 Main Street
Vineyard Haven, MA
02568
(508) 693-3333

Innkeepers:
Karl & Lynn Buder

Open all year. 18 rooms/18 baths.

Rates: 6/16 to 9/4, $95-$195 (for two). VISA/MC/AMEX

Amenities: Children over 12 welcome. No pets. Additional 5.3% gratuity charged. Non-smoking rooms available. All common areas are non-smoking. Bicycle storage available. Centrally air conditioned. Seven fireplaces.

Directions: From the Vineyard Haven ferry dock, traffic is directed to the left. Proceed to the stop sign and turn right. Take the next right onto Main Street. The inn is one mile up on your left.

Lambert's Cove Country Inn

off Lambert's
Cove Road
West Tisbury, MA
02575
(508) 693-2298

Innkeeper:
Marie Burnett

Open February to
January.
15 rooms/15 baths.

Rates: 5/26 to 10/16,
$95-$125 (for two).
VISA/MC/AMEX/DC

Amenities: No
children. No pets.
Tennis court on
premises. 4-Star
restaurant on premises.
Dinner by reservation
only. Working
fireplaces. 15-minute
walk to the beach.

Directions: From
Vineyard Haven
harbor take State Road
to Lambert's Cove
Road. Turn right on
Lambert's Cove Road
and follow signs to the
inn.

Lambert's Cove Country Inn

As you bump along the private road for a mile and a half, you begin to wonder if you will ever get to Lambert's Cove Country Inn. Then you see the rock wall of the lovely old country estate and you know it was worth the ride. The inn is located in a beautiful country setting of lawn, meadows, gardens, and woodlands with an orchard and private tennis court. Inside, handsome period furnishings are thoughtfully arranged for comfort and to take advantage of outdoor views. The second floor has a sitting room and balcony. Each room has its own individual charm; some open onto decks or terraces and one has its own greenhouse.

A continental breakfast is served in the breakfast room. First-rate croissants and homemade nut muffins brought warm to the table are typical fare. They may be accompanied by a beach plum conserve made at the inn. The dining room, like the rest of the house, is comfortable and has a welcoming fire in the grate. Like all the towns on the island, except for Edgartown and Oak Bluffs, West Tisbury is a "dry" town, but the staff is happy to chill, open, and serve any beverage guests bring with them. The inn also makes an ideal conference center.

Lambert's Cove Country Inn's
Bay Scallop Stew

2 T. finely chopped shallots	3 T. snipped fresh chives
2 T. unsalted butter	2 C. milk
1 C. heavy cream	1 lb. bay scallops
1 C. dry white wine	1 t. white pepper

In a large heavy saucepan, cook the shallots in the butter over moderately low heat, stirring occasionally, until softened. Then add the wine, bringing the liquid to a boil. In a saucepan, scald the cream and the milk with the chives. Add the scallops to the wine mixture, bring the mixture to a simmer, stirring occasionally, and stir in the cream mixture, the white pepper, and salt to taste (the stew will separate slightly). Makes about 6 cups, and serves 4.

Sea Horse Guests

This guest house is in a country atmosphere nestled among lovely pine and maple trees. It is a peaceful haven where you can retreat from the world in simple surroundings. The typical Cape Cod house is decorated in a whimsical style.

Another nice part of this location is the five-minute walk to one of the most beautiful beaches on Martha's Vineyard. The beach is restricted to town residents and their guests so it is private and uncrowded, even at the height of the season.

A continental breakfast is included.

Sea Horse Guests' Corned Beef Ball

Mix: two 8 oz. pkgs. cream cheese, softened
1 T. mayonnaise
½ t. lemon juice
few dashes of garlic salt or powder

To the above mixture add: ½ to 1 bunch scallions, chopped fine
2 pkgs. Carl Buddig corned beef,
finely cut up

Form into a ball and refrigerate. Occasionally this innkeeper invites guests to join her for light refreshments, and she always has to share this recipe when it is served.

Sea Horse Guests
Lambert's Cove Road
West Tisbury, MA
02575
(508) 693-0594

Innkeeper:
Muriel Fisher

Open June to October.
4 rooms/shared baths.

Rates: 6/13 to 9/15, $40-$50 (for two). No credit cards accepted.

Amenities: No children. No pets. 5-minute walk to the beach. Parking on premises.

Directions: The inn is about 3.5 miles from the boat landing in Vineyard Haven. Take State Road to Lambert's Cove Road. Turn right, to Sea Horse Guests.

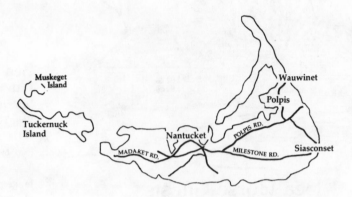

Nantucket

Nantucket, whose Indian name means "far away land," is located thirty miles off the coast of Massachusetts. The town's villages and its historic harbor have retained their simple beauty and serenity. The island includes the town center of Nantucket and the villages of **Siasconset** and **Wauwinet**.

Nantucket offers visitors the best of both the old and the new. Cobblestone streets lead to magnificently preserved buildings, antique shops, museums, art galleries, theaters, fine restaurants, and fifty miles of beautiful beaches.

There is little auto traffic on the island and visitors are encouraged to leave their cars behind with their hectic lifestyles, and relax by bicycling, boating, swimming, surfing, windsurfing, fishing, and playing tennis and golf. A favorite activity is to try the various gourmet restaurants that are famous on the island, and then take a stroll back to a quaint village inn.

Beachway Guests

Comfortably furnished in family style, Beachway Guests is a very pleasant small guest house. The location, between Brant Point and Nantucket town, is super! The rates are reasonable, and offer a great buy on Nantucket. For more than 20 years, tourists have enjoyed bed and breakfast hospitality here.

A continental breakfast is served on a charming sun porch every morning.

This inn welcomes children and the innkeepers will provide a cot or a crib at a nominal fee.

Beachway Guests' Nantucket Cookies

2 C. flour
2 C. ground peanuts, pecans, or almonds
1 C. butter or margarine
¼ t. salt
1 T. vanilla or almond extract
2 C. powdered sugar

In a large bowl, mix all ingredients with mixer. Divide dough into 36 balls, forming them into half moons (crescents). Place them on an ungreased cookie sheet and set oven to 375°. Bake for 12 to 15 minutes. Cool cookies and sift powdered sugar over them. Enjoy!

Beachway Guests
3 North Beach Street
Nantucket, MA 02554
(508) 228-1324

Innkeepers: Joann & George Ponte

Open all year.
7 rooms/5 baths.

Rates: 5/30 to 9/15, $58-$100 (for two). MC/VISA

Amenities: Children welcome. No pets. Fireplace. Cable television. 5-minute walk to beach, also to all town activities.

Directions: From Steamboat Wharf, walk up Broad Street to South Beach Street. Turn right on South Beach Street to Easton Street. The guest house is across the street on the corner of North Beach Street and Easton Street.

Brass Lantern Inn

**Brass
Lantern Inn**

11 North Water Street

Nantucket, MA 02554

(508) 228-4064

Innkeeper: Cindy
Garrison

Open 5/30 to 10/30.
18 rooms/14 baths.

Rates: 5/30 to 9/15,
$70-$140 (for two).
VISA/MC

Amenities: Children
welcome. No pets.
Working fireplaces. 3-
minute walk to
Children's Beach.

Directions: From
Steamship Wharf,
proceed up Broad
Street to North Water
Street. Turn right on
N. Water to the inn.

When you step inside Brass Lantern Inn, you enter a world of charming contradictions. The inn was rebuilt in 1846 as a family home after the great fire of 1845 on Nantucket. It has been artfully renovated with an eclectic blend of old and new. In addition to various single and double rooms in the original part of the inn, there is a large four bedroom suite on the third floor. The suite features nice period pieces, a beamed ceiling, and a central sitting area, and is nice for a group traveling together.

The contradiction is apparent in the wing added in 1983. There are eight large rooms, each with a queen-size bed and private bath. Some rooms have a harbor view. Dramatic angled ceilings and recessed lighting add to the subtly modern decor. There is a lovely outdoor patio, as well as ample space for bicycles.

A continental breakfast is served in guest rooms between 8:30 and 9:00 a.m.

Brass Lantern Inn's
Stuffed French Toast

one 8 oz. pkg. cream cheese, softened	1 C. whipping cream
1 t. vanilla	½ t. vanilla
½ C. chopped walnuts	½ t. ground nutmeg
one 16 oz. loaf French bread	one 12 oz. jar of apricot
½ C. orange juice	preserves

4 eggs

Beat together the cream cheese and 1 t. vanilla until fluffy. Stir in nuts, then set aside. Cut bread into twelve 1½" slices; cut a pocket in the top of each. Fill each with 1½ T. of the cheese mixture.

Beat together eggs, whipping cream, the remaining ½ t. vanilla and nutmeg. Using tongs, dip the filled slices in egg mixture, being careful not to squeeze out the filling. Cook on a lightly greased griddle until both sides are golden brown. To keep slices hot for serving, place them on a baking sheet in a warm oven. Meanwhile, heat together the preserves and juice. To serve, drizzle the apricot mixture over the hot French toast. Makes 10-12 stuffed slices.

The Carlisle House Inn

The Carlisle House Inn has been a first-rate inn for more than 100 years. It has been carefully restored, with modern conveniences added, but still maintains the warmth and charm of antiquity. Innkeeper Peter Conway claims that all the work is a labor of love, and it shows. There are new custom dust ruffles and matching canopies in two rooms. These rooms feature working fireplaces, pine floors, antique furnishings, and wing chairs to curl up in, just the kind of place you want to be on cool evenings when the wind in blowing outside. In one room, the fireplace wall is covered completely in dark pine paneling. The glow from the fire along with the rich red Oriental carpet, sets the coziest of moods. Rooms range from elegant to unbelievably beautiful.

Another favorite part of the inn is the kitchen, with its huge six-foot wide fireplace with baking ovens on either side. The main focal point is the large pine table that will seat sixteen in front of the fireplace. Manager Christie White and her staff almost weekly put on a cookout that guests get involved in and share the expense of. That is when the table really comes in handy, and it is a good evening of inexpensive dining and conversation.

Carlisle House Inn's Wicket's Wedgies

(Wicket is the resident springer spaniel.)

1 C. chopped ripe olives	½ C. mayonnaise
½ C. thinly sliced onions	½ t. salt
1½ C. shredded sharp cheddar cheese	½ t. curry powder
8 English muffins	

Combine the ingredients and spread on a toasted English muffin. Broil until cheese melts, then cut into wedges. This is loved by the guests as well as the dog.

The Carlisle House Inn
26 North Water Street
Nantucket, MA 02554
(508) 228-0720

Innkeeper:
Peter Conway
Manager:
Christie White

Open 4/15 to 1/5.
14 rooms/12 baths.

Rates: Late June to 9/30, $65-$120 (for two). AMEX

Amenities: Children over 10 welcome. No pets. Friendly springer spaniel in residence. 8 working fireplaces. 5-minute walk to the beach.

Directions: From Steamboat Wharf, proceed up Broad Street to North Water Street. Turn right on North Water Street to the inn.

The Carriage House

5 Ray's Court
Nantucket, MA 02554
(508) 228-0326

Innkeeper:
Jeanne McHugh

Open all year.
7 rooms/7 baths.

Rates: 6/15 to 9/30,
$75-$100. (for two)
No credit cards
accepted.

Amenities: Children
over 5 years welcome.
No pets. 10-minute
walk to the beach.

Directions: From
Steamboat Wharf,
walk 3 blocks to
Center Street. Turn
left and walk to Main
Street. Cross Main
Street, turn right then
left on Fair Street.
Proceed 1 block to
Ray's Court; turn
right to the inn on
your right.

The Carriage House

This inn, a Victorian carriage house, is located very close to town but has a sense of privacy because it is located on a quiet country lane. Rooms are an eclectic blend of comfortable furnishings which are attractive, and have convenient lighting by the bed and showers in every bathroom.

A slate floored patio provides a place to have continental breakfast or a shelter for relaxing at the end of the day. The common room has a color cable television, games, and a variety of books on Nantucket.

The Carriage House's Carrot Muffins

Mix:
2 ½ C. sugar   4 C. flour
4 t. cinnamon   4 t. baking soda
                1 t. salt

Add to the above mixture:
1 C. pecans, chopped   1 C. raisins
1 C. coconut, shredded   4 C. carrots, shredded
                2 apples, shredded

Add these remaining ingredients and mix well, but do not over beat!
                6 eggs, beaten
                2 C. vegetable oil
                1 t. vanilla

Put mixture in muffin tins. Bake in a preheated oven at 375° for 20 minutes. Great with cream cheese or honey!

Centerboard Guest House

The Centerboard Guest House is Victorian and romantic. Restored in 1986, accomodations are beautifully appointed with period pieces and thoughtful touches for luxury and comfort. Each spacious room has a queen-size bed or two double beds. The two-room suite is unique. The sitting room is reminiscent of an old English manor house. The white-on-white bedroom includes an oversized four-poster canopy bed. The green marble bathroom has a shower and jacuzzi-bath.

Innkeeper Marcia Wasserman provides white wine, iced tea, and cheese in the dining room in the afternoons. Country breakfasts of homemade breads, cereal, and fresh fruit are a delicious way to start the day.

Centerboard Guest House's
1-2-3-4 Cake

½ C. butter
½ C. shortening
2 C. sugar
4 eggs, added gradually

½ t. vanilla
½ t. almond flavoring
3 C. cake flour
1 t. baking powder

1 C. milk

Mix all ingredients together and pour into a greased cake pan. Bake at 325° for 1 hour or until done.

**Centerboard
Guest House**

8 Chester Street
Nantucket, MA 02554
(508) 228-9696

Innkeeper:
Marcia Wasserman

Open all year.
7 rooms/7 baths.

Rates: 7/1 to 10/15, $125-$195 (for two). No credit cards accepted.

Amenities: Children over 12 welcome. No pets. Working fireplace. Telephone, refrigerator, and color TV in each room. 10-minute walk to the beach.

Directions: From Steamboat Wharf, walk up Broad Street to North Water Street. Turn right on North Water Street to the fork in the road at North Avenue and Cliff Road. Take the left fork, Cliff Road to Chester Street. Turn left to the inn.

The Century House

10 Cliff Road
Nantucket, MA 02554
(508) 228-0530

Innkeepers:
Jean Heron & Gerry
Connick

Open all year.
10 rooms/9 baths, plus
2 cottages.

Rates: 6/15 to 9/15,
$75-$130 (for two). No
credit cards accepted.

Amenities: No
children. No pets. Six
antique working
fireplaces. 5-minute
walk to the ocean.

Directions: From
Steamboat Wharf take
the first right onto
South Beach, then the
first left onto Easton
Street. Take the first
right onto Cliff Road,
to the inn on the left.

The Century House

Innkeepers Jean Heron and Gerry Connick are reformed city dwellers exhilarated by the fresh sea breezes of this historic island. They have restored this 1833 sea captain's mansion and made it informal and comfortable. Set on a hilltop offering glimpses of the harbor below, the inn typifies the late-Federal period of island architecture. Outings are limited only by the imagination, and may range from a snowy day picnic on the rolling dunes, to a pre-dawn excursion to the island's planetarium.

The rooms are decorated with English country antiques and fabrics. Shades of cranberry are used throughout. Guest rooms have canopied queen-size beds. Six guest rooms have non-working fireplaces, and the nineteenth century parlor has a working hearth. The innkeepers host late afternoon get-togethers, with sherry served at fireside or on the wide veranda.

A continental breakfast is included.

The Century House's Nantucket Bluefish Paté

1 to 1 ½ lbs. smoked or poached bluefish. The smoke provides a strong flavor; the poached, a lighter consistency and taste.

¾ **C. medium cream**	¾ **C. butter**
1 egg	**½ med. onion, grated**

white pepper to taste

Debone and remove skin from fish. Cut into small pieces and set aside. Melt butter in a double boiler; set aside. Beat egg and cream together and gradually add this mixture to melted butter, gently stirring until mixture thickens enough to coat spoon. Set aside. Place fish and onion in a food processor with a cutting blade and purée. Gradually add cream mixture until it is a smooth consistency. With a rubber spatula remove mixture from cutting bowl and place in a large, buttered tureen, or several small tureens. Chill 3-6 hours, until serving time. Garnish with fresh dill. Serve with toast points or spread on crackers.

*The secret to preparing this recipe is to accept the fact that the bluefish can be a thickening agent, causing the mixture to become stiff. Therefore, you need to "play" with the ingredient amounts to reach the consistency and taste desired.

The Cliff Lodge

The Cliff Lodge is a 1771 whaling master's home and features lovely antique furnishings. Many rooms have king-size beds and fireplaces. Guests are invited to enjoy cocktails from the self-serve pantry and entertain friends in one of several sitting rooms furnished with period pieces.

A continental breakfast featuring home baking is served in the patio garden, a charming spot. There is also a widow's walk for sitting, reading, or enjoying the view of the town and harbor. Innkeeper Mary Coughlin also manages waterfront apartments which have a magnificent view of the harbor.

Cliff Lodge's
Sour Cream Coffee Cake

Cream together: **¾ C. softened butter**
       1½ C. sugar

Add to the above mixture and mix well: **4 eggs**
       12 oz. sour cream
       1 t. vanilla

Sift the following together and add to wet mixture:
       3 C. flour
       1½ t. baking soda
       1½ t. baking powder

Grease an angel tube pan. Add ½ of the batter and sprinkle a topping of sugar, pecans, cinnamon, and nutmeg. Add remaining batter and top again with nut mixture. Bake in a preheated oven at 350° for 1 hour.

Filling and topping: **sugar, pecans, cinnamon, and nutmeg.**

Cliff Lodge
9 Cliff Road
Nantucket, MA 02554
(508) 228-9480

Innkeeper:
Mary Coughlin

Open all year.
12 rooms/12 baths.

Rates: 6/15 to 9/15,
$85-$120 (for two). No
credit cards accepted.

Amenities: Children
over 5 years old
welcome. No pets.
Working fireplaces. All
rooms have telephones
and televisions. 5-
minute walk to the
beach.

Directions: From
Steamboat Wharf,
walk up Broad Street
to North Water Street.
Turn right on North
Water Street, which
becomes Cliff Road
when it crosses Easton
Street. The Guest
House is on your right.

The Corner House

49 Centre Street, Box 1828
Nantucket, MA 02554
(508) 228-1530

Innkeepers: Sandy & John Knox-Johnston

Open all year.
14 rooms/14 baths.

Rates: 5/26 to 10/24, $75-$120 (for two). No credit cards accepted.

Amenities: Children over 8 welcome. No pets. Working fireplace in sitting rooms. 5 minute walk to ocean beach.

Directions: The inn is in the heart of the old historic district, a 3-minute walk from Steamboat Wharf, on Centre Street.

The Corner House

Country charm is visible everywhere in the original details of The Corner House, including wide-board pine floors, paneling, and fireplaces. Each room is furnished with English and American antiques which create the romantic mood of an early Nantucket seaport house. Canopy beds are available in many queen-size and double-bedded rooms; several master rooms also have private television. Every room has soft towels, pretty sheets, down comforters and plenty of pillows piled on an antique bed.

Several guest sitting rooms have cable TV and a fire glows in the hearth on chilly days. A screened-in porch furnished with wicker and flowers overlooks the private garden patio and offers a wonderful place for relaxing. A delicious continental breakfast of homebaked muffins and coffee cakes is served on the sideboard in the keeping room. It can be enjoyed there by the fire on cool mornings, or taken to the porch or garden on lovely days. Afternoon tea is available every day, served with homemade fruit breads and cookies.

The Corner House's Muffins

2 C. bran flakes cereal	1 t. salt
1½ C. milk	1 T. cinnamon
2 large eggs, beaten lightly	½ C. chopped dried apricots
½ C. corn oil	1 Granny Smith apple,
½ C. sugar	peeled, cored, and chopped
2 T. double-acting baking powder	1/3 C. raisins
2 C. all-purpose unbleached flour	½ C. chopped, dried apples

In a large bowl, let the bran flakes soak in milk for 5 minutes. Add the eggs and the oil and whisk the mixture until it is combined well. In another bowl, sift together the flour, sugar, baking powder, salt, and cinnamon. Stir the mixture into the bran mixture until just combined. Then stir in the apple, the apricots and the raisins. Divide the batter among 18 well buttered 1/3 cup muffin tins. Bake in the middle of a preheated 375° oven for 18-20 minutes or until a tester comes out clean, and turn out onto racks. Makes 18 muffins.

Easton House

Easton House
17 North Water Street
Nantucket, MA 02554
(508) 228-2759

The Easton House has been a family-run business for over fifty years, and the innkeepers are known for their gracious hospitality. The inn is a lovely 1812 colonial home decorated with Oriental rugs and antique furnishings. The atmosphere is formal, but comfortable as well. The warmth of the original wide-board floors and wood paneling create an antique ambience. All rooms are attractively furnished for comfort with chairs for reading and a choice of single, double, twin, or queen-size beds, some with canopies.

The English country garden is special and a nice place to sit, as is the private back yard. There is a fireplace in the sitting room, as well as cable television. Bicycle racks are provided for parking bicycles or mopeds. A continental breakfast is served every morning.

Innkeepers:
Judith & Cyril Ross

Open all year.
11 rooms/9 baths.

Rates: 6/15 to 9/30,
$80-$120 (for two).
AMEX.

Amenities: Well-behaved children over 3 years welcome. No pets. Fireplace in the sitting room. 10- to 15-minute walk to the beach.

Directions: From Steamboat Wharf, walk straight up Broad Street and take the second right on North Water Street. The inn is on the third block on the right.

Easton House's Bran Muffins

15 oz. box of Raisin Bran cereal	4 eggs, well beaten
3 C. sugar	2 t. salt
5 C. flour	1 quart buttermilk
5 t. baking soda	1 C. corn oil

Combine cereal, sugar, flour sifted with baking soda, and salt in a large bowl. Add mixture of eggs, buttermilk, and oil. Mix well. Use or refrigerate, covered. Batter will keep for six weeks. When ready to use, fill muffin cups 2/3 full. Bake at 400° for 15 minutes.

Eighteen Gardner Street Inn

18 Gardner Street
Nantucket, MA 02554
(508) 228-1155

Innkeepers: John,
Mary, & Elizabeth
Kennan

Open all year.
10 rooms/10 baths/2
bedroom apartment.

Rates: 6/1 to 9/30,
$90-$130 (for two).
VISA/MC/AMEX

Amenities: Children
welcome. No pets.
Decorative fireplaces.
10-minute walk to the
beach.

Directions: From
Steamboat Wharf,
walk up Broad Street.
Turn left onto South
Water Street to Main
Street. Turn right on
Main Street to
Gardner Street. Turn
right on Gardner
Street to the inn on
your left.

Eighteen Gardner Street Inn

This is a large colonial residence built in 1835, but it is new as an inn and has been beautifully restored. The widow's walk and charming furnishings have an authentic Nantucket flavor. Guest rooms are furnished with antiques and reproductions. Some rooms have canopy beds and decorative fireplaces. A two-bedroom apartment with a full kitchen is available for families.

The Kennans specialize in attentive service. They provide a guest refrigerator, set-ups in the luxuriant garden room, and sherry to sip in front of a crackling fire. Homemade muffins and English teas are breakfast highlights.

Eighteen Gardner Street's Raspberry Muffins

2 C. flour
1 T. baking powder
½ t. salt
2/3 C. sugar
1 C. raspberries, fresh or frozen

1 egg, beaten
½ C. melted butter or margarine
½ C. milk
½ C. sour cream
1 t. vanilla

Preheat oven to 375°. Sift together dry ingredients and stir in egg, milk, sour cream, and vanilla. Fold in raspberries. Fill greased muffin tins almost full. Bake for approximately 15 minutes. Makes 12 muffins.

Fair Gardens

The ambience of Fair Gardens is much more than that of gracious and charming rooms. The inn has a friendly, informal atmosphere. Innkeepers Lee and Stuart Gaw provide quiet luxury in their restored historic colonial. Furnishings are a mix of maple and oak antiques and colonial reproductions. Double and triple rooms are available.

A light breakfast is served each morning in the English country garden, a tranquil and intimate spot. The inn is located just off Main Street, convenient to shops, and is surrounded by other stately, historic homes.

Fair Gardens' Robyn's Banana Bread

5-7 ripe bananas, mashed	6 oz. butter, melted
1 t. vanilla	3 eggs, beaten
½ C. milk, boiled (dissolve 2 flat t. baking soda in it)	
Blend: 1 ½ C. sugar	2¼ C. wholemeal flour
2 heaping t. baking powder	

Add mashed bananas to dry ingredients. Pour in wet ingredients. Add soda dissolved in milk at last minute and blend until just mixed. Bake at 400° for about an hour. Use a ring tin for baking and slice into 16 pieces. Delicious with natural vanilla yogurt.

Fair Gardens
27 Fair Street
Nantucket, MA 02554
(508) 228-4258

Innkeepers: Lee & Stuart Gaw

Open April to December.
8 rooms/8 baths.

Rates: Memorial Day to Columbus Day, $95-$125 (for two). No credit cards accepted.

Amenities: Children welcome. No pets. Fireplaces. 5-minute drive to the beach.

Directions: From Straight Wharf, walk up Main Street to Fair Street. Turn left on Fair Street, to the inn on your right.

The Four Chimneys

38 Orange Street
Nantucket, MA 02554
(508) 228-1912

Innkeeper:
Betty York

Open late April to
early December.
10 rooms/10 baths.

Rates: In season, $98-
$155 (for two).
VISA/MC/AMEX

Amenities: No
children. No pets.
Fireplace in the living
room. Guest phone
available. 15-minute
walk to one of many
island beaches.

Directions: From
Straight Wharf, walk
up Main Street to
Orange Street. Turn
left on Orange Street,
and proceed 4 blocks
to the inn on your left.

The Four Chimneys

Furnishings are luxurious in this captain's mansion, restored in the gracious style of Nantucket's Golden Era. Five original "Master Rooms" have been authentically restored and furnished with period antiques, canopy beds, and Oriental rugs. Each of these traditional four-square rooms has its original fireplace and one has its own porch. Fire laws prohibit the use of fireplaces in the bed chambers, however, so the innkeeper lights the one in the drawing room. A suite on the third floor furnished in pine and country pieces has a sitting room with a harbor view.

The "Publick Room" is a double parlor with twin fireplaces, cable television, and a piano. The antique Chinese rugs and porcelains are subtle reminders that the house was built in the heyday of the whalers and the China Clippers. There is a hospitality hour at 5 p.m. when appetizers are served and the innkeeper provides ice and glasses for your spirits. A continental breakfast is served in the Publick Room on the first floor porch furnished with antique white wicker, or in guest rooms. There is a lovely secluded garden, too, and porches across three levels of the house.

The Four Chimneys'
Parmesan Cheese Leaves

1 C. flour	¼ t. salt
½ C. butter	pepper, cayenne
1 C. grated cheese	1 egg, slightly beaten

paprika

Blend flour and butter. With a fork, stir in cheese, salt, pepper, and cayenne. Sprinkle with 2 T. cold water, toss, and form into a ball. Flatten slightly. Between wax paper sheets on a damp surface, roll to ½" thickness. Cut out with leaf-shaped cookie cutter. Cover and freeze. Preheat oven to 400°. Place leaves on a baking sheet. Brush the tops with egg yolk and sprinkle with paprika. Bake for 10 minutes, then cool. Delicious served warm.

Great Harbor Inn

An old seafarer's house, Great Harbor Inn is a pretty colonial and a beautifully restored example of an 18th century home. Each of the rooms is large and airy, and is decorated with handmade quilts and 19th century American antiques. All rooms have modern private baths, and canopy or four-poster beds.

Breakfast is ample and delicious, and may be served in rooms, in the living room, or on the outdoor patio. In season, June 20 to September 15, a minimum three night stay is required. However, if there is an opening in between reservations, the innkeepers are happy to accommodate visitors.

Great Harbor's Blueberry and Raspberry Muffins

Blend:

4 t. cinnamon	**1¼ C. sugar**
3 C. flour	**½ t. salt**
1 T. baking powder	**¼ t. baking soda**

Blend into dry ingredients: **9 oz. pkg. frozen blueberries (do not thaw)**
9 oz. pkg. frozen raspberries (do not thaw)

Mix: **3 eggs**
1 C. melted butter or margarine
1 C. milk

Add wet ingredients to dry ones. Mix gently until just blended. Fill muffin tins full and bake at 400° for 20-30 minutes. Yield: 1½ to 2 dozen.

Great Harbor Inn
31 India Street
Nantucket, MA 02554
(508) 228-6609

Innkeepers:
Lee & Stuart Gaw

Open all year.
6 rooms/6 baths.

Rates: Memorial Day to Columbus Day, $95-$125 (for two).
VISA/MC

Amenities: Children welcome. No pets. Each room has color cable TV. Working fireplace. 5-minute drive to the beach.

Directions: From Straight Wharf, walk up Main Street to Center Street. Turn right on Center Street to India Street on your left. Turn left to the inn.

Grieder Guest House

**Grieder
Guest House**

43 Orange Street
Nantucket, MA 02554
(508) 228-1399

Innkeepers:
Ruth & Bill Grieder

Open 5/15 to 10/15.
2 rooms/1 bath.

Rates: 6/15 to 9/15,
$60-$80 (for two). No
credit cards accepted.

Amenities: Children
welcome. No pets.
Parking available. 20-
minute walk to the
beach.

Directions: From
Straight Wharf, walk
up Main Street to
Orange Street. Turn
left on Orange Street
to the inn on your
right.

Grieder Guest House has just two rooms, so there is an intimate, homey feeling. Visitors are the innkeepers personal guests at the beach, and invited to use the picnic table and benches in the large backyard, as well as the bicycle racks. Just ask for the parking permit for the beach. There is a refrigerator, too.

The house is full of country charm. It was built in the early 1700s and the Grieders have furnished it comfortably with twin four-poster beds and braided rugs. The bedrooms share an oversized modern bath.

A continental breakfast is included.

Grieder Guest House's
Scallop Casserole

1 lb. bay scallops	**¼ C. butter or margarine**
18 Saltine crackers, crumbled	**1 C. cream or half 'n half**

Melt butter and add crumbs. Layer scallops and crumbs in baking dish, then pour cream or half 'n half over all. Bake uncovered for 30 minutes at 350°. Serves four.

House of the Seven Gables

Built in the 1880s, the inn was originally the annex for the Sea Cliff Inn, one of Nantucket's oldest hotels, before its destruction in 1972. The annex was constructed during the Victorian era and is one of the few and finest examples of architecture of that period. It is a quiet, informal guest house. The rooms are nicely furnished with an eclectic blend of pieces, including period antiques. Cable television and a fireplace enhance the Victorian parlor. The house faces north across Nantucket Sound towards Hyannis Port, and has a lovely view of the harbor.

In July and August, a continental breakfast is served in guest rooms by the chambermaid. The tray is set with fresh flowers and there is a choice of home-baked coffee cakes, croissants, muffins, or Portuguese rolls. In the off-season, breakfast is served in the parlor.

House of the Seven Gables' Whispering Coffee Cake

¾ C. softened butter
1 C. sugar
2 eggs
1 C. sour cream
2 C. all-purpose flour
1 t. ground cinnamon

1 t. baking powder
1 t. baking soda
½ t. salt
1 t. ground nutmeg
¾ C. firmly packed brown sugar
½ C. chopped walnuts

Butter a 13" x 9" x 2" baking pan and lightly dust with flour. Cream butter and sugar until light and fluffy. Add eggs and sour cream and mix well. Combine flour, baking powder, baking soda, salt, and nutmeg. Add to batter and mix well. Pour into baking pan. In a separate bowl, combine brown sugar, nuts, and cinnamon. Mix well and sprinkle evenly over batter. Cover and chill overnight. In the morning, uncover and bake at 350° for 35-45 minutes or until done. Serves 15.

House of the Seven Gables

32 Cliff Road
Nantucket, MA 02554
(508) 228-4706

Innkeepers:
Sue & Ed Walton

Open all year.
10 rooms/9 baths.

Rates: 6/24 to 9/19, $75-120 (for two). Credit cards accepted. Personal checks or cash preferred.

Amenities: Children over age 16 welcome. No pets. Fireplace in the parlor. 10-minute walk to the beach.

Directions: From Steamboat Wharf, walk up Broad Street two blocks to North Water Street on your right. Turn onto North Water Street to Easton Street. Cross Easton Street and continue on Cliff Road to the house on your left.

**Lynda Watts
Bed &
Breakfast**

10 Upper Vestal Street
Nantucket, MA 02554
(508) 228-3828

Innkeeper:
Lynda Watts

Open all year.
2 rooms/1 bath.

Rates: $60 (for two).
No credit cards
accepted.

Amenities: Children
welcome. No pets.
Television and
refrigerator in each
room. 5-minute drive
to the beach.

Directions: From
Straight Wharf, follow
Main Street to Bloom
Street. Turn left on
Bloom Street to Vestal
Street. Turn right on
Vestal Street to Upper
Vestal, to the bed and
breakfast.

Lynda Watts Bed & Breakfast

This casual bed and breakfast is located on a quiet street in a residential neighborhood. The saltbox house is only thirteen years old and furnished in a simple beach house style. Both guest rooms have a television and a refrigerator. Parking space is provided, a premium on Nantucket.

Weather permitting, a continental breakfast is served on the patio. A two-night minimum stay is required.

Lynda Watts Bed and Breakfast's Nut Bread

1 egg	½ t. salt
1 C. sugar	4 flat t. baking powder
4 T. butter	1 C. milk
2 C. sifted flour	1 C. chopped pecans

½ C. currants

Cream shortening, sugar, and egg together. Add sifted flour, salt, baking powder, and milk, and then the currants and nuts. Pour into a greased and floured loafpan and bake in a 350° over for 45 minutes. Good for breakfast or tea time!

The Periwinkle Guest House

Two adjacent nineteenth century homes in the heart of Nantucket town comprise the Periwinkle. Several top-floor rooms command a harbor view. For families there is a suite with a private bath or a private floor (three rooms with one bath). All are decorated in country style with antiques, some reproductions, and authentic old quilts or lace covers on the bed.

The advantage of two houses is a private double backyard where guests are invited to use the picnic table and chairs. Public phones are available on the first floor. Ample space is provided for parking bicycles.

A continental breakfast is served every morning.

The Periwinkle Guest House's Golden Harvest Cupcakes

Mix:

½ C. butter	1 t. baking soda
¾ C. sugar	1 t. baking powder
1 egg	¼ t. salt
¼ C. molasses	1 C. cooked squash
1¾ C. flour	½ C. raisins

Spoon into muffin tins and bake at 375° for 30 minutes.

The Periwinkle Guest House
7 & 9 North Water Street
Nantucket, MA 02554
(508) 228-9267

Innkeeper: Sara Shlosser-O'Reilly

Open all year.
18 rooms/8 with private bath.

Rates: 6/23 to 9/4, $65-$120 (for two). VISA/MC/AMEX

Amenities: Children welcome. No pets. 2-to 3-minute walk to the beach. Public phone. Bicycle rack.

Directions: From Steamboat Wharf, walk up Broad Street to North Water Street. Turn right to the inn on your right.

Phillips House

54 Fair Street
Nantucket, MA 02554
(508) 228-9217

Innkeeper:
Mary Phillips

Open all year.
4 rooms/1 with private
bath.

Rates: In season, $50-
$75 (for two). No
credit cards accepted.

Amenities: Children
welcome. No pets.
Fireplace. 15-minute
bike ride to the beach.

Directions: From
Straight Wharf,
proceed up Main
Street to Fair Street.

Phillips House

This house is about 204 years old, a former whaler's home. The atmosphere is casual country. The first floor guest room has a fireplace, a patchwork quilt on the bed, and a private bath. Upstairs are three rooms with two shared baths. If your hostess has gone fishing, you'll find a note taped to the stairway post telling you which room is yours. A tiny front yard is for lounging and has a bicycle rack.

Breakfast with homemade muffins is served in the kitchen, which looks out on a tiny tucked-away garden. To the right of the kitchen fireplace hangs a handmade quilt of the house, made by a guest.

Phillips House's Cranberry Muffins

1¼ C. sifted flour	1 T. lemon rind, grated
1½ C. granulated sugar	2 eggs
1 t. salt	2 C. buttermilk
4 t. baking powder	½ C. oil
1 t. baking soda	2 C. cranberries, cut in half

Whisk liquids, then add dry ingredients. Gently fold in berries. Grease muffin pan and fill to the brim with batter. Makes 18 muffins. (Whole cranberry sauce can be substituted; use 1 C. milk instead of 2.) Bake at 375° for 20 minutes.

Safe Harbor Guest House

Safe Harbor Guest House

2 Harborview Way
Nantucket, MA 02554
(508) 228-3222

Innkeepers: Sylvia &
Larry Griggs

Open all year.
5 rooms/5 baths.

Rates: June to
October, $90-$130 (for
two). No credit cards
accepted.

Amenities: No
children. No pets.
Fireplace in the living
room. 5-minute walk
to the beach.

Directions: From
Steamboat Wharf, 2½
blocks to the right on
So. Beach Street, to
the inn on Harborview
Way.

This guest house is on the harbor at Children's Beach, a lovely site. The house was built in the 1920s as a private residence and is set on wide lawns in the heart of the historic district. All the rooms have a harbor view. Some have private decks and private entrances. The house is furnished casually with antiques and reproductions.

Breakfast is continental and served buffet style. Fresh flowers from the garden grace the house.

Safe Harbor's Cheese Puff

¼ C. butter
1 C. milk
1 C. flour
¼ t. salt

4 eggs
¾ to 1 C. cheese, grated plus ¼ to ½
C. extra for topping

In a pan, melt butter in milk. Add flour and salt all at once. Stir until mixture forms a ball and leaves the side of the pan. Add eggs one at a time, beating well after each. Stir in ¾ to 1 C. cheese. Place spoonfuls in a ring on a well greased cookie sheet. Top with ¼ to ½ C. grated cheese. Bake at 400° until brown and puffy, about 25 minutes.

Seven Sea Street

7 Sea Street
Nantucket, MA 02554
(508) 228-3577

Innkeeper: Matthew
Steven Parker

Open all year.
8 rooms/8 baths.

Rates: 4/21 to 10/15,
$95-$160 (for two.
VISA/MC/AMEX

Amenities: Children
welcome. No pets.
Working fireplace in
the common room.
One guest room has a
wood stove. Cable TV
and refrigerator in
each room. 2-minute
walk to the beach.

Directions: From
Steamboat Wharf,
walk up Broad Street
to So. Beach Street.
Turn right on So.
Beach Street, then left
on Sea Street to the
inn on your left.

Seven Sea Street

Seven Sea Street is a newly constructed red oak post and beam guest house. Nevertheless, it has the ambience of a small country inn offering comfortable accommodations. Colonial furnishings are found throughout the house, combined with modern conveniences. All guest rooms come with a queen-size canopy bed, a cable television, and a small refrigerator.

A real treat is in the full-size heated jacuzzi whirlpool bath. The widow's walk deck on the roof is ample and affords a spectacular view of Nantucket Harbor. A continental breakfast is served downstairs, or in rooms if requested.

Seven Sea Street's Juicy Peach Muffins

2 C. flour
1 T. baking powder
½ t. salt
½ C. sugar
1½ C. chopped peaches, peeled and stoned

1 egg, beaten
½ C. sour cream
1/3 C. butter, melted
1 t. vanilla
½ C. milk

Preheat oven to 400°. Sift together dry ingredients. Mix in the egg, milk, sour cream, butter, and vanilla, just until all are moistened. Fold in peaches. Bake for 20 minutes. You will love them!

76 Main Street

76 Main Street

76 Main Street
Nantucket, MA 02554
(508) 228-2533

Innkeeper:
Shirley Peters

Open all year.
18 rooms/18 baths.

Rates: 6/15 to 10/15,
$100-$130 (for two).
AMEX/VISA/MC

Amenities: Children
welcome. No pets. A
wood stove is in the
main parlor. 10-minute
walk to Children's
Beach.

Directions: From
Steamboat Wharf,
walk up Main Street to
the third house on the
left in the residential
section of Main Street.

Innkeeper Shirley Peters enjoys the life of Nantucket and that enthusiasm is passed on to you. Mitch Blake manages the inn, a restored 1883 sea captain's mansion. Decoration is simple Ethan Allen. In the twelve rooms of the main house there are no televisions or telephones, and no smoking is allowed.

Children and families are comfortably accommodated in six units which surround the patio in the rear of the inn. Three of the units have one double bed and one single bed. One unit has a double bed and two single beds, and another has a double bed and three single beds. These units all have a refrigerator and cable television.

The continental-plus buffet breakfast is served on two round tables in the breakfast room, or in good weather, on the delightful, secluded patio.

Fourth of July Coffee Cake

Prepare the topping first:

1 stick sweet butter	**1 C. brown sugar**
1 C. shredded coconut	**1 C. sliced almonds**
1 C. Grapenuts	**1 t. almond extract**

Heat all of above in saucepan over low heat.

Pre-heat oven to 350°. Sift together:

4 C. flour	**½ C. sugar**
2 T. baking powder	**¼ t. salt**

Mix thoroughly:

1½ C. milk	**1 t. vanilla**
½ C. oil	**2 eggs**

½ C. lemonade concentrate

Combine liquid and dry ingredients and divide equally into three bowls. Add 1 C. blueberries to first bowl. Add 1 C. cranberries to second bowl. Add 1 C. sliced almonds to third bowl. Spread blueberry mixture evenly on bottom of greased 14" x 9" x 2" baking pan, then spread almond mixture and finally the cranberry mixture. Spread on topping and bake for 25-30 minutes or until done. Sprinkle top with silver cake ornaments and a few American flags on toothpicks. Serve when cool.

Ships Inn

Fair Street
Nantucket, MA 02554
(508) 228-0040

Innkeepers: Joyce
Berruet & John Krebs

Open March to
mid-December.
12 rooms/11 baths.

Rates: 6/15 to 11/1,
$90 (for two).
AMEX/MC/VISA

Amenities: Children
over 2 years welcome.
No pets. Full service
restaurant. Working
fireplaces in the living
room and dining room.
10-minute drive to the
beach.

Directions: From
Straight Wharf, walk
up Main Street to Fair
Street. Turn left to the
inn.

Ships Inn

A fine full-service restaurant is on the premises here. The innkeepers offer a selection of veal, poultry, lamb, beef, and seafood dishes with some interesting wines to accompany them. The inn was built in 1812 by Captain Obed Starbuck, and many of the rooms are named for ships that he commanded. Rooms are furnished with colonial furniture, some dating back to the time of the Captain himself, so it is quite authentic. The home is also the birthsite of Lucretia Mott, America's first woman abolitionist and advocate of women's suffrage.

The cheery fireplace in the living room adds warmth on chilly evenings. Guests can relax with cocktails by the unusual bar made from an old dory.

The Ship's Inn's Creamed Mussels

1 lb. mussels, scrubbed and washed
   thoroughly
large handful of chopped fresh parsley
1 C. dry white wine
1-2 onions, chopped
1-2 t. curry powder
¼ t. sea salt
1 C. heavy cream

chopped fresh parsley to garnish

Put all ingredients in a large saucepan and cook over a brisk heat, turning frequently, until all the mussels are open, about 5-6 minutes. Take the mussels out of the pan with a perforated spoon. Leave the sauce on a low heat to reduce to a thick creamy consistency. Discard half the empty shells and arrange the mussels in half shells on a serving dish. Pour the hot sauce over and sprinkle with chopped parsley. Serve immediately with toast. Serves 2.

Stumble Inne

All guest rooms at Stumble Inn are furnished with fine antiques and reproductions. There are really two houses on the property. Six of the guest rooms are located in the Starbuck House, an early nineteenth century "half-house" which is across the street from the Stumble Inne. Each room has a private bath, antique bed with handstitched quilt, and wide pine floors. The rooms are large, accommodating up to four people. Cable television and bar refrigerators are available in some rooms.

A continental breakfast is served around a long table with shield back chairs.

Stumble Inne's Cranberry Muffins

2 C. flour	1½ t. nutmeg
¾ C. orange juice	1 C. sugar
1 t. cinnamon	1 T. vanilla
1½ t. baking powder	½ t. ginger
2 eggs, slightly beaten	½ t. baking soda
6 T. shortening	2 t. grated orange peel

1½ C. each cranberries and pecans

Mix all the dry ingredients in a medium bowl. Cut in shortening with a pastry blender. Stir in juice, vanilla, and eggs. Fold in chopped cranberries and chopped nuts. Spoon into eighteen 2½" muffin cups. Bake at 350° for 20-25 minutes or until golden. Serve hot! These freeze well.

Stumble Inne

109 Orange Street
Nantucket, MA 02554
(508) 228-4482

Innkeepers: The Condon Family

Open all year.
13 rooms/12 baths.

Rates: 6/24 to 9/17, $65-$115 (for two).
VISA/MC/AMEX

Amenities: Children welcome. No pets. Cable TV and refrigerators in some rooms. Decorative fireplaces. 5-minute drive to a surf beach.

Directions: From Straight Wharf, walk up Main Street to Orange Street. Turn left to the inn on your right.

Ten Lyon Street

10 Lyon Street
Nantucket, MA 02554
(508) 228-5040

Innkeepers: Ann
Marie & Barry Foster

Open mid-April to
mid-December.
7 rooms/7 baths.

Rates: Mid-June to
mid-September, $95-
$140 (for two).
VISA/MC/AMEX

Amenities: Children
over 16 welcome. No
pets. 20-to 25-minute
walk to the beach.

Directions: From
Straight Wharf,
proceed up Main
Street to Fair Street.
Turn left on Fair
Street to Lyon Street.
Turn right to the inn.

Ten Lyon Street

Ten Lyon Street is an elegant inn with spacious guest rooms. Many rooms have handsome quilts, fine linens, country antiques, and even a wonderful old bathtub on legs. The upstairs sitting room is unique with its white walls and oil-pine floors and framings. There are plants and flowers throughout the inn.

The house sits sideways on the lot, so the front of the inn faces the luxuriant garden. The inn was restored in 1985.

A continental breakfast is served in the first floor breakfast room. The inn is truly a romantic, elegant island retreat in Nantucket's historic district.

Ten Lyon Street Inn's Blueberry Muffins

Group A: **2 C. flour**
            1 T. baking powder
            ¼ C. sugar

Mix all of above and add 1 C. frozen blueberries (or fresh, if available).

Group B: **¾ C. orange juice**
            1 large egg
            1 t. vanilla
            2 T. butter (grease a 12-muffin tin with brush, then add the
rest of the butter to liquid ingredients)

Mix Group A and Group B together lightly, fill tins, and bake at 350° until golden, about 20 minutes.

Tuckernuck Inn

60 Union Street
Nantucket, MA 02554
(508) 228-4886 or
800-228-4886

Innkeepers: Phyllis &
Ken Parker

Open all year.
16 rooms/16 baths.

Rates: 6/29 to 9/16,
$110 (for two).
VISA/MC/AMEX

Amenities: Children
over 12 welcome. No
pets. Laundry facilities.
2-minute walk to a
harbor beach. 5-
minute drive to the
nearest surf beach.

Directions: From
Straight Wharf, walk
up Main Street to
Washington Street.
Turn left on
Washington Street to
Francis. Turn right on
Francis to Union
Street. Turn left on
Union Street to the
inn on your left.

Tuckernuck Inn

Tuckernuck Inn was once a run down single family home with a small cottage in even worse condition. Innkeepers Phyllis and Ken Parker bought the home and renovated it to the modern, yet colonial inn it is today. Guest rooms have all new beds, queen-size or twins, with firm mattresses.

The "new" widow's walk (roof deck) with its panoramic view of Nantucket Harbor is a special place to view the stars. The innkeepers have also landscaped the back yard into a pleasant outdoor relaxation area, complete with manicured lawn, rose bushes, and lawn furniture with sun umbrellas. Croquet and badminton equipment are set up for the use of guests. And last but not least, the ulimate convenience — laundry facilities for those planning to stay awhile.

A continental breakfast is served.

Tuckernuck Inn's Scallop Delight

1 C. bay scallops, halved
  (or ¾ C. sea scallops, quartered)
¼ C. melted butter
salt and pepper

1 C. crushed cracker crumbs,
  your choice
1 C. whole milk
parsley garnish

Bring all ingredients except scallops, cracker crumbs, and parsley to boiling point. Then add scallops and crumbs, stir well, and then transfer to casserole dish in a 350° oven for 40-45 minutes or until golden brown. Serve with tossed green salad, sweet corn, and enjoy!

The Woodbox Inn

29 Fair Street
Nantucket, MA 02554
(508) 228-0587

Innkeepers:
The Dexter Tuteins

Open June to
mid-October.
9 units/9 baths.

Rates: $100-$170 (for
two). No credit cards
accepted.

Amenities: Children
welcome. No pets.
Excellent restaurant
on the premises.
Fireplaces in suites. 10-
minute walk to the
beach.

Directions: From
Straight Wharf, walk
up Main Street to Fair
Street. Turn left to the
inn.

The Woodbox Inn

The innkeepers at The Woodbox Inn are justifiably proud to be able to call their establishment the oldest inn on Nantucket. Built in 1709, the inn is an old colonial ship captain's house decorated with charm using fine Early American antiques. The pine paneled walls, low beamed ceiling, and brass candlesticks in the dining rooms make for a warm feeling of hospitality. Of the nine units, six are suites with one or two bedrooms and working fireplaces.

The restaurant at the inn is noted for its gourmet dining at both breakfast and dinner, with such items as Beef Wellington, Duck Orange, Lamb Noisettes, and Veal Medallions with Sauce de Chef. There is a charge for breakfast.

The Woodbox Inn's Famous Popovers

4 C. flour   12 large eggs
4 C. milk   ½ t. salt
                        vegetable oil

Mix all ingredients in a large bowl. Preheat oven to 400°. Cover each cup in a 12-muffin pan with ⅛ or ¼ inch vegetable oil. Then fill cups ⅞ full with popover mix. Bake approximately 45 minutes or until crisp.

Reservation Services

Bed & Breakfast Cape Cod, Box 341, West Hyannis Port, MA 02672
(508) 775-2772

Cape Cod Inns, P.O. Box 112, Yarmouth Pcrt, MA 02675
(508) 362-4319

Dukes County Reservations Service (Martha's Vineyard) Box 1522, Oak Bluffs, MA 02557
(508) 693-6505

House Guests Cape Cod, Box 1881, Orleans, MA 02653
(800) 666-HOST or (508) 896-7053

Orleans B & B Association, Box 1312, Orleans, MA 02653
(508) 255-3824

Martha's Vineyard Reservations, Box 1322, Vineyard Haven, MA 02568
(508) 693-7200

Index to Inns

(with recipes cross-referenced)

Recipe Index

(with inns cross referenced)

INDEX